Adele Ferguson is a multi-award-winning senior business writer and columnist for *The Age*, the *Sydney Morning Herald* and the *Australian Financial Review*. She is a regular guest reporter on ABC's *Four Corners* and *7.30*, and is the author of the bestselling unauthorised biography *Gina Rinehart: The untold story of the richest woman in the world*.

With more than twenty years' experience, Adele is one of Australia's most awarded journalists. She has received eight Walkley awards, including a Gold Walkley for her joint Fairfax Media and *Four Corners* program 'Banking Bad'; two Gold Quill Awards, including one for her exposé of CBA's CommInsure; two Gold Kennedy Awards; a Logie; and the Graham Perkin Journalist of the Year award. She was recognised for services to journalism with an AM in 2019.

Banking Bad

ADELE FERGUSON

ABC
BOOKS

The ABC 'Wave' device is a trademark of the
Australian Broadcasting Corporation and is used
under licence by HarperCollins*Publishers* Australia.

First published in Australia in 2019
by HarperCollins*Publishers* Australia Pty Limited
ABN 36 009 913 517
harpercollins.com.au

Copyright © Adele Ferguson 2019

The right of Adele Ferguson to be identified as the author of this work has been asserted by her
in accordance with the *Copyright Amendment (Moral Rights) Act 2000*.

HarperCollins*Publishers*
Level 13, 201 Elizabeth Street, Sydney NSW 2000, Australia
Unit D1, 63 Apollo Drive, Rosedale, Auckland 0632, New Zealand
A 53, Sector 57, Noida, UP, India
1 London Bridge Street, London SE1 9GF, United Kingdom
Bay Adelaide Centre, East Tower, 22 Adelaide Street West, 41st floor, Toronto,
   Ontario M5H 4E3, Canada
195 Broadway, New York NY 10007, USA

A catalogue record for this book is available from the National Library of Australia

ISBN 978 07333 4011 6 (pbk)
ISBN 978 14607 1143 9 (epub)

Cover design by Darren Holt, HarperCollins Design Studio
Cover images: Rowena Orr by Eddie Jim / Fairfax Syndication; Kenneth Hayne ©
Commonwealth of Australia 2019, https://creativecommons.org/licenses/by/4.0/deed.en
Author photo by Rebecca Hallas
Typeset in Bembo Std by Kirby Jones

Printed and bound in Australia by McPherson's Printing Group
The papers used by HarperCollins in the manufacture of this book
are a natural, recyclable product made from wood grown in sustainable
plantation forests. The fibre source and manufacturing processes meet
recognised international environmental standards, and carry certification.

To those who choose not to stay silent

Contents

Prologue

'CAN YOU PLEASE GIVE me a call when you've got a minute, Adele? It's about the Commonwealth Bank. It's big. I have a whistleblower who wants to speak to you.'

It was 4 April 2013 when I received this phone message from Nationals Senator John 'Wacka' Williams. I'd come to know and trust Wacka after I'd written a series of stories that exposed some seriously dodgy behaviour in the insolvency industry, including fraud, standover tactics and links to the criminal underworld. An affable but hard-nosed politician, Wacka had received death threats and been the victim of smear campaigns after those investigations and had never flinched. This had cemented my deep respect for him. I hadn't thought anything could get much grubbier or more corrupt than liquidators and the insolvency industry, but Williams' phone message would blow this assumption out of the water.

The call came as I was getting ready to head to China on a work trip to cover the annual Boao Forum for Asia, a conference that brings together business people, politicians and academics to discuss policy and economic issues of the day. Prime Minister Julia Gillard was attending, along with the recently appointed Chinese president, Xi Jinping. I called Wacka back and he gave me the phone number of the whistleblower, Jeff Morris.

In between packing and finalising a late visa application for China, I rang and spoke to Morris, who'd worked for the Commonwealth Bank (CBA) until March 2013. He wanted to blow the whistle on CBA's malpractice; he also wanted to alert the public to the slowness of the country's corporate regulator, the Australian Securities and Investments Commission (ASIC), to investigate allegations he had already made.

After our call Morris emailed me over one thousand pages of documents, which I printed out before racing to the airport, hoping I wouldn't be late for my flight. What he had told me during that phone call and the material he had sent would lead me to uncover and expose misconduct in one of the country's most trusted and venerable institutions.

As I sat on the plane and went through the documents, I became increasingly shocked. They included internal bank emails, whistleblower correspondence with ASIC, and a series of customer files, which showed CBA had wilfully engaged in forgery, fraud and a management cover-up. The bank had put profit before people – a theme I would become all too familiar with over the next five years as I investigated other well-regarded financial institutions.

CBA wasn't some shonky fly-by-night company no one had heard of; it was the so-called 'people's bank'. Established by the Commonwealth Government in 1911, it had been allowed into our children's schools to sign up kids to savings accounts. It was an iconic institution that most Australians knew and trusted.

The most confronting document I read on that flight to China was a fax Jeff Morris had sent to ASIC warning it that CBA was engaged in a 'high-level conspiracy' to 'conceal repeated material breaches, corruption and gross incompetence of the bank's star financial planner, Don Nguyen, resulting in losses to clients of tens of millions of dollars'. Those 'material breaches' included forging clients' signatures, failing to provide essential documents such as statements of advice, and giving inappropriate recommendations. The most telling detail was that ASIC had ignored Morris's tip-off and done nothing for sixteen months.

Here was a scandal that involved the most profitable company in the country, its number-one financial adviser, a management cover-up and a regulator that had failed to act. It had the makings of a crackerjack story.

*

As soon as I arrived back in Australia, I rang Wacka and organised a meeting in Sydney with Jeff Morris and some other people Jeff knew who had battled CBA.

Weeks later, on 1 June 2013, the first day of winter, the story I wrote sent a hurricane through the financial services sector when it appeared on the front page of the *Sydney Morning Herald* and *The Age*. The public response to the article was phenomenal. It was the leading news item of the day, the next day and the next. Australians were appalled that CBA had shafted some of its most vulnerable customers and engaged in practices that were deceiving and illegal.

The initial articles focussed on CBA and one dodgy financial planner, but as the weeks went by the story got bigger. CBA's malpractice became a symbol of a toxic banking culture built on greed, targets and bonuses, where profits were put before people, and corporate regulators sat silent. Previous banking scandals had come and gone, but this one resonated with the public, and CBA couldn't fob it off as it had done in the past.

The banks' power rested not just in the profound wealth they were producing but also in the deep connection between the banks and the political establishment. Former heads of treasury, premiers, Reserve Bank governors, ASIC commissioners and ministerial advisers had all joined their ranks, taking up seats on boards and other key positions of influence. The widespread, aggressive and successful lobbying by the banks over many years was not unrelated to these appointments. The extent of the inter-linkages dwarfs any other sector. The meshing of the political class into the finance sector both reflects the power of the banks, and in turn contributes to the power of the banks.

But the Commonwealth Bank financial planning scandal pierced that veil.

Soon the story had multiple villains, hundreds of thousands of victims, and many superheroes. Jeff Morris's courage in blowing the whistle on what was going on at CBA made him one of those superheroes. He helped break the culture of silence and spurred other bank insiders to speak out. Many came to me.

A whistleblower from Macquarie Group contacted me with information about financial advisers cheating in professional development exams and misleading customers. A National Australia Bank (NAB) insider sent me an explosive cache of internal documents which revealed NAB had similar issues to CBA, including staff committing forgery and fraud as well as a cover-up by management. Then a whistleblower from the financial services giant IOOF Holdings sent me thousands of documents that disclosed misconduct, including insider trading, other types of market manipulation, misrepresentation of performance figures, and even the boss of its research division getting staff to cheat on his behalf in professional exams.

The Australian and New Zealand Banking Group (ANZ) was next. Documents I received revealed ANZ had bankrolled a high-risk, agricultural investment scheme, Timbercorp, which collapsed, with thousands of victims losing billions of dollars and owing massive debts.

When a call came from CBA's chief medical officer, Dr Ben Koh, that he was about to lose his job in the bank's life insurance arm after becoming an internal whistleblower, it was a watershed moment. Dr Koh revealed that CBA was putting profit before sick and dying customers. He said CBA was rejecting legitimate insurance claims by relying on outdated medical definitions. It didn't get much lower than that.

In March 2016, I presented the story in a joint venture with *The Age* and the *Sydney Morning Herald* and in an episode of *Four Corners*, called 'Money for Nothing'. In the program, Dr Koh described rampant misconduct, and a series of victims, some dying, told harrowing stories of fighting the bank after it had mercilessly knocked back their life insurance claims.

The revelations of 'Money for Nothing' provoked outrage. It was clear that vast numbers of executives across the financial sector had lost their moral bearing. A parliamentary inquiry into the life insurance industry was set up and the government ordered ASIC to launch an immediate investigation.

The CBA life insurance scandal was the final straw for Labor, which on 7 April called for a royal commission into banking, bringing it into line with Wacka Williams, who had been arguing for a royal commission since CBA's 2013 financial planning scandal. Yet the Coalition government remained against the idea and fobbed off these requests.

Then, finally, on 30 November 2017, the people of Australia heard the news so many had been pushing for. Prime Minister

Malcolm Turnbull – bowing to pressure from the National Party and at the behest of the banks themselves – ran up the white flag and called the Royal Commission into Misconduct in the Banking, Superannuation and Financial Services Industry. The uncertainty had become too great and the government needed to regain control of the situation by setting the terms of reference. Superannuation funds were added to the Coalition's remit, in the hope it would expose wrongdoing in the union-backed industry funds. The commission would have a tight budget and a short twelve-month timeline, and be prevented from looking at anything that might 'prejudice, compromise or duplicate' another inquiry or court proceedings.

Despite the government's attempts to constrain it, the banking royal commission managed to dominate the news. Its most prominent figures became household names: Commissioner Kenneth Hayne; senior counsels assisting, Rowena Orr QC and Michael Hodge QC. Their probing exposed rampant greed, systemic gouging of the living and the dead, bribery and corruption in mortgage lending, billions of dollars milked from retirement savings, dud life insurance policies, and financial advisers gorging on fat commissions at the expense of their customers.

Over the previous four decades, since the deregulation of the financial sector, it had been a free-for-all for bankers. Investors, addicted to high shareholder returns, played their part in a rotten system where banks and financial services companies got rich on the savings of the Australian people. It was only when reputational damage tore through these institutions, and share prices fell, that investors started to care about ethics and reputation. Bankers and executives from the financial sector, politicians and regulators lined up to issue apologies at the royal commission and via the media.

After the release of the commission's interim report on 28 September 2018, a grim-faced Anna Bligh, CEO of the peak banking body, the Australian Banking Association, fronted a Sydney press conference where she acknowledged: 'Our banks have failed in many ways ... failed customers, failed to obey the law and failed to meet community standards ... Make no mistake. Today is a day of shame for Australia's banks.'[1]

She was right. It was a day of shame, but it will take more than hand-crafted apologies to win back the public's trust, given the unconscionable behaviour of the banking and financial sector.

The damage done to people, the banking sector and Australia's economy is incalculable and will take years to play out. From the day the banking royal commission was announced to when it finished, a massive $59 billion was wiped off the market values of the big four banks (CBA, ANZ, NAB and Westpac), AMP and IOOF.

As veteran business reporter and presenter of Sky News Janine Perrett commented: 'I thought nothing could shock me anymore, but in my forty years as a journo, most of it covering business, I have never seen anything as appalling as what we are witnessing at the banking RC. And I covered the 80s' crooks including Bond and Skase.'[2]

What follows is the story ...

Part One

What goes on in the shadows

Four decades of misconduct, malpractice and misinformation

Chapter 1

Caught in a trap

The foreign currency loans scandal

IT WAS A BLISTERING afternoon in January 1985 when John 'Wacka' Williams went to see his bank manager at the local CBA branch in Inverell, a small town on the Macintyre River in northern NSW.

At 4 pm on the dot, palms sweating, wearing smart casual clothes, the thirty-year-old sheep farmer nervously walked into the bank for the appointment he'd made with the manager, Neville Dunbar, to ask for a loan. He needed $200,000 to help him through the drought that had stricken NSW in 1982, the worst dry spell in two decades, which had left him and his brother Peter struggling to pay the bills.

John Williams was known to most of his friends and family as 'Wacka' – a nickname his father, Reg, had given him when he was a toddler. In 1979, Wacka and Peter had sold the family's fifth-generation farm in Jamestown, South Australia, and moved to Inverell because the land was cheaper. They'd bought adjoining farms spanning 7000 acres of undulating countryside.

'It was tough,' recalls Wacka. 'We had a debt of $180,000 and the standard variable interest rates at the time were 15 per cent. We weren't making enough money to repay the existing farm loan we had with the bank as well as other living expenses, so we had to borrow more money to meet the interest payments and pay other debts.'

As he sat down with Dunbar, Wacka didn't realise he was about to be sold a pup. During the meeting, the discussion turned to the benefits of foreign currency loans – in this case one in Swiss francs – which were then offering substantially lower interest rates than standard variable loans. Wacka had heard about foreign currency loans from other farmers and had seen some ads on television, but he didn't know much about them.

An appointment was booked for him to go to CBA's head office in Sydney to organise the foreign currency loan. During that meeting Wacka was shown a series of historical graphs and charts, demonstrating the stability and reliability of the Swiss franc against the Australian dollar. 'They told me they were in touch with the markets all the time,' said Wacka, adding that the loans officer assured him the bank would keep him informed and help him manage the loan.

There was one catch, however. The bank said Wacka would have to borrow a minimum of $500,000 to be eligible for a loan carrying an interest rate of just 6 per cent. When Wacka asked 'What could go wrong?', the loans officer said to him, 'Absolutely nothing.'

By the end of the meeting, Wacka had committed to a AU$640,000 loan in Swiss francs – more than triple the $200,000 loan he'd originally asked for. He wasn't told about the risks involved in his foreign currency loan, or the skills he'd require to properly understand and manage it. This conservative farmer and grazier was about to become a property and currency speculator.

In the wake of receiving his bigger-than-expected bank loan, Wacka bought two units as investments, paid off his debts and then placed the remaining $100,000 in a CBA investment account. There, in theory, it would earn a much higher interest rate than he was being charged on the Swiss foreign currency loan.

What Wacka didn't realise was that Australian banks were in the process of transmogrifying themselves from service providers to sellers of products – with targets. It was a strategy that would change the way staff related to customers and shatter the special role of trust and respect bank managers had worked so hard to cultivate since Australia's first bank, the Bank of New South Wales, opened its doors in 1817.

*

Around the time Wacka took out his loan, sandwich boards were lining the streets, spruiking financial products and cheap loans. Creative TV ads and posters placed in bank windows promised instant credit. Unrequested credit cards were mailed to customers encouraging easy credit (and high interest rates for the banks).

The restructuring of the economy and the banks, which had led to this easy credit, can be traced back to March 1983, when the ALP's newly elected and popular leader, Bob Hawke, ended Malcolm Fraser's Coalition government's seven-year grip on power. Hawke's government would set the stage for a revolution in the financial markets.

In his election speech, Hawke offered the nation's voters 'a program to produce growth and expansion in the economy, achievable goals for re-building and reconstruction of this nation'.[1] To begin with, however, the new government had to grapple with a lingering recession that had left one in ten workers unemployed and resulted in double-digit inflation and a larger than expected budget deficit and wages breakout. So how would the Labor government turn the economy around?

The new Treasurer, Paul Keating, was sure the answer to this question was to open up Australia's economy to market forces. This was not a novel idea. US President Ronald Reagan and UK Prime Minister Margaret Thatcher had already gone down that road. Indeed, in the coming decades, deregulation and privatisation would become de rigueur around the world as the free-market economic rationalists gained a stranglehold on mainstream economic theory.

Over thirteen years, from 1983 to 1996, Hawke and Keating blazed a trail that paved the way for the Australian dollar to be floated, CBA and Qantas to be privatised, the end of collective bargaining, deregulation of the banking system, the entry of foreign banks into Australia, and the dumping of the country's centralised wage-fixing system. It was a tidal wave of economic change and it would herald the rise and rise of the banks.

Prior to 1981, the banks and the way they dealt with customers were regulated by the government. Banks weren't allowed to set interest rates on deposits or loans, including housing loans, which constrained the amount of funds available for lending. It also made them less profitable because lending rate controls made banks a cheaper source of funds than finance companies. After deregulation, banks were allowed to set their own interest rates and savings banks were given more flexibility to invest in higher-risk assets.

Keating 'fashioned a new Labor for the modern age that he called "the Big Picture" – redefining the market as a friend of the battler and reforming Australia's economic institutions to succeed in the international age'.[2] The ACTU–Labor Accord of 1983, under which the ACTU accepted wage restraint in return for a social wage for workers, which gave them universal health care and a basic income guarantee, would also play an important part in Australia's economic recovery.

But although Keating was admired by the financial markets and was named Finance Minister of the Year in 1984 by the magazine *Euromoney*, the regulators were weak and the changes set off an era of irresponsible lending. At the time, the stock market was booming and the debt binge was spiralling out of control as the banks offered huge lines of credit to entrepreneurs, including Alan Bond and Christopher Skase. According to Reserve Bank figures, between 1985 and 1989 bank credit in the Australian economy rose 20 per cent.

*

Deregulation included a change in policy to allow foreign banks to enter the Australian market, to increase competition in banking. Sixteen foreign banks came to Australia in 1985, immediately doubling the number of banks in the country. Feeling under siege, local banks looked for strategies to defend themselves and retain customers and staff. ANZ, for instance, announced it would revamp its passbook savings account, which had been offering 3.75 per cent on balances of up to $4000, with interest calculated on a minimum monthly balance. Now it would pay 12 per cent interest, calculated daily, for deposits of $500 or more. Concurrently, favoured staff at all banks were offered golden handcuffs and pay rises to price them out of being poached.

Soon, foreign currency loans, with terms of up to five years, were being marketed to mums and dads, small businesses – and farmers like Wacka Williams. Incentive schemes on all types of loans were introduced, which paid bank staff bonuses based on the number of loans they wrote. Ominously, bank staff weren't trained in the intricacies of the loans; all they knew was they had to sell them.

According to Evan Jones, a retired political and economics academic from the University of New South Wales, who has written extensively on this topic, thousands of foreign currency loans were sold post deregulation. Westpac flogged 50 per cent of them, followed by CBA, which sold between 25 per cent and 30 per cent of the loans; ANZ and NAB sold the rest. But few customers understood that the low interest rates attached to the foreign currency loans were a ticking financial time bomb, ready to explode if currency rates went the wrong way.

*

The ink had barely dried on Wacka's $640,000 loan before the Australian dollar started to lose value against other currencies as the current account deficit worsened and the US dollar surged. 'It was one or two weeks after I signed the loan that I realised the dollar was falling and wondered what it all meant,' says Wacka.

What it meant was that the size of his debt ballooned as the Australian dollar lost ground. Suddenly, it was a bloodbath for customers who'd been told by bank staff that the loans were safe. The banks reacted by demanding additional funds from borrowers to top up their original deposits. If the customers didn't have the extra funds, their assets – in the form of family homes, farms and/ or businesses – were seized then sold, sometimes at giveaway prices.

In an attempt to stem his losses, Wacka made an appointment to meet the loans officer at CBA's Inverell branch, Peter Neale, to discuss whether he could insure against, or hedge, the loan. Neale told him he couldn't.

Neale, who quit the bank in 1994 after twenty-five years of service, admits he didn't understand the loans being sold: 'I hadn't been trained in them so I asked the branch manager what he thought and our reading of it was it couldn't be hedged. I was wrong.' Neale's advice was similar to that given by banks to thousands of other victims of these loans as they spiralled out of control.

As things deteriorated, Wacka would turn on the television each day to check the exchange rate. The news got steadily worse as the Australian dollar continued to fall. 'The stress was terrible,' he recalls.

Over the next two years, between 1985 and 1987, the Australian dollar continued to plummet against the Swiss franc, going from a value of 2.2 Swiss francs to less than one. Wacka's $640,000 loan blew out to a crippling $1.5 million. It was at this time that he received a call from CBA's head office advising him to trade the currency. 'They said, "We want you to ring us every day. We've got an advisory room and we will trade the currency." The manager of the trading room told me he would get me back to my original debt in two years.

'I would get up every morning and ring the advisory room and say, "Should I go to Swiss francs? Should I go to Australian dollars?" and so on, and I reckon eight out of ten times I changed currency it was the wrong move and we lost more money.'

The results continued to be financially catastrophic. At one stage Wacka was trading AU$1 million on the instruction of CBA's foreign exchange dealers in Sydney. 'Every time I traded, they made money out of the trade.'

Things for Wacka went from bad to worse. He was being charged 25.25 per cent on an overdraft he had taken out, and the stress on him and his family was unbearable. At the time, Wacka was married with two young children under ten.

In 1987 CBA forced Wacka to sell the investment properties he'd bought in order to reduce his debt. One, a double-storey, three-bedroom brick unit on the beach front of Byron Bay, was bought cheaply by the local CBA branch manager for $80,000. 'It would be worth millions today,' says Wacka.

Then the bank asked Wacka and his brother to sell their farms. 'I pleaded with them to come up with a plan so we could keep the farms, and they just said no. To me it was a complete failure of five generations of work and I was the loser, I was the one who caused it all. That was on my conscience all the time.' To Neale it was the bank behaving like a pack of mongrels.

Farmers like Wacka started rallying together and in 1988 set up the Foreign Currency Borrowers Association, which gained more than two thousand members. Wacka recalls: 'We would meet in Sydney and share horror stories and support each other and give each other updates if anyone was taking legal action.'

When articles on foreign currency loans started to appear in the media, the banks spun the line that borrowers had been greedy and the banks had warned them about the risks of the loans. Later, CBA's chief general manager for credit policy, Barry Poulter, would say that the average foreign exchange loan was about $1.4 million, which showed CBA was not dealing with innocent small investors. Poulter's inference was that borrowers who'd taken out loans in foreign currencies were savvy investors who'd known what they were doing. What Poulter didn't mention was that many of the loans had started at a fraction of that amount. Poulter also denied the foreign currency loans were faulty, saying, 'There is nothing faulty about the product in the way in which one might consider a car which has a weakness in its braking system is faulty. There is no unknown defect in a foreign currency loan.'[3]

Wacka Williams was one of a number of customers who rejected this argument and decided to take on the bank. He fought CBA for five years, then signed a deed of settlement in November 1992. But in 1995 he learned that the bank's lawyers had misrepresented a statement by one of the key witnesses, Peter Neale, which prompted him to challenge the settlement.

During his legal battles, Wacka would set his alarm clock for an early start, leaving Inverell at 4.30 am to drive to Sydney to represent himself in the Supreme Court of NSW. 'I'd listen to the radio or think about what I was going to say in court,' he recalls. After the CBA meetings he'd drive back to Inverell, dropping in at the local pub to have a stubby before arriving home at 10 pm, having driven a round trip of 1200 kilometres in one day.

Despite Peter Neale giving evidence that CBA staff hadn't been trained about the loans and so didn't understand them, Wacka lost the case in May 1998, with the trial judge finding him to be dishonest. The judge also rejected Neale's version of events, saying, '[Neale] has plainly acquired an antipathy to the CBA.'[4] Wacka was ordered to pay $788,301 in favour of CBA, with interest accumulating at $204 a day. In the aftermath of the case, CBA took possession of Wacka's and his brother's farms.

Despite losing his case, Williams refused to give up and took it to the Court of Appeal. On 28 September 1999, he won. In a seventy-three-page adjudication handed down by the three judges, the Court of Appeal overturned the 1998 ruling and said the judge had erred in facts and findings on nine key issues. It also noted that CBA had withheld a critical internal memo written in 1986 referring to hedging facilities, which was damaging to the bank.[5]

Anne Lampe, an investigative journalist at the *Sydney Morning Herald*, wrote that Wacka had won a 'significant victory that cleared his name and restored his credibility'.[6] But it turned out to be a hollow win. The court found that the original trial had miscarried and that a new trial would have to be held. It said Wacka should be compensated for the cost of the appeal.

Wacka might have had his credibility restored, but he couldn't afford to go through another court case. He had lost his farm and his marriage had broken down. He moved into a second-hand caravan. Money was so tight that he rarely put the caravan's heater on, even in cold weather.

'[CBA] behaved like a pack of arseholes,' he says.

*

A year before Wacka started his proceedings against CBA, a senior auditor at Westpac, John McLennan, decided to quit. It was February 1986 and he'd worked at the bank for twenty years, becoming one of the bank's top ten executives. His final role at Westpac was heading an 'efficiency audit' team charged with eliminating waste in every department of the bank. It turned out that there were too many powerful interests defending cuts to their departments, and he wasn't able to change much. Nevertheless, he gained detailed insights into the workings of every division of Westpac.

Two years later, an accountant McLennan knew introduced him to an elderly couple who were in trouble with Westpac. Reg and Thelma Sonter lived in Laurieton, a coastal town in mid-north NSW, and had signed a AU$1.1 million foreign currency loan in Swiss francs with Westpac in 1985. The Sonters were an industrious and hard-working couple who ran a successful bus company, which they'd established in the late 1940s. Their company, which operated about thirty buses servicing the Laurieton area, had been virtually debt free when the Sonters had applied for a company loan, which they planned to use to develop a block of land they had purchased in the 1960s into a residential estate, hoping that would in turn provide a nest egg for their retirement.

Echoing Wacka Williams' experience, the Sonters had signed for a loan that was almost four times as much as they'd originally intended to borrow. The manager of the Westpac Laurieton branch had told them it was available only to 'valued clients' and they should take advantage of it, pointing to the relatively low interest rate on offer. The manager didn't tell them about the risks, or the bonus he would get for signing customers up to the loan.

As it transpired, soon after the loan was made, the dollar began to decline in value and the bank cut the Sonters adrift, saying they could not give them any advice. Senior representatives of Westpac refused to discuss the matter. Meanwhile the bank had set up an 'asset management' department to seize the assets of defaulting borrowers.

By the time McLennan got involved in 1998, the Sonters' loan had blown out to $2.4 million, pushing up the effective interest rate to 74 per cent. McLennan was shocked that Westpac had sold this elderly couple such a high-risk and complex loan without pointing out they could lose everything if something went wrong. It also struck him as the height of hypocrisy that Westpac could spend millions of dollars in marketing slogans describing itself as 'the bank you can trust' when it was selling dodgy loans to unsuspecting customers. What angered McLennan even more was that the Westpac Laurieton branch manager – who McLennan says would have had almost no knowledge of foreign exchange loans – had written to the Sonters saying the bank would look after them.

Westpac went in hard on the Sonters, threatening them with bankruptcy and asking them to sign an agreement to let the bank sell their assets as well as an indemnity clause clearing the bank of any wrongdoing. The constant pressure on the couple proved too great for their son, Glen, who sank into a deep depression then hanged himself a week before the Sonters' mediation with Westpac was due to occur. 'It was devastating for us all, but for the Sonters it was unimaginable grief on top of what Westpac was doing to them,' McLennan wrote later.[7]

In a desperate last-ditch attempt to save everything, McLennan advised the Sonters to take legal action against Westpac. They hired Garrett and Walmsley, a major commercial litigation firm, and McLennan helped them build a case. A statement of claim was made, which basically argued that the Sonters had been sold a 'defective loan'.

Westpac used every tactic to delay, muddy the waters and drag out the court case. It also withheld vital information that would have helped the couple. But eventually the bank was forced to present internal policy loan documents that substantiated everything the Sonters had said. In an out-of-court settlement in September 1988, Westpac agreed to write off all the foreign currency losses so that the Sonters' debt fell to about $800,000. Reg and Thelma were happy with the settlement, but they had been taken to the brink of financial ruin and the emotional costs were incalculable. Without the help of McLennan, who had given the lawyers invaluable insights into the inner workings of the bank and lists of documents to request, they would have gone under.

Despite these cases and growing public concern, the banks continued to promote foreign currency loans to customers and employees. Remuneration deals across the sector were restructured to offer incentives to staff, with lofty targets set and bonuses paid if targets were met. A culture of profit took hold and risk management became evermore lax. According to McLennan, there were no checks and balances, no quality controls. 'That was the beginning of the end,' he says. 'Staff soon learned to flog products to achieve bonuses and, as the saying goes, "When profit is the only motive, all forms of corrupt and immoral behaviour can be rationalised."'[8]

The Sonters' case put McLennan on the path to becoming an advocate for victims of foreign exchange loans. He set up a management consultancy in Port Macquarie, NSW, called Strategic Management Services, and in 1988 helped found the Foreign Currency Borrowers Association, which Wacka Williams joined. Over the ensuing decade, McLennan helped hundreds of bank victims win compensation of around $500 million.

What became clear was the banks, particularly CBA and Westpac, had become aware of the problems with foreign currency loans in the mid-1980s but had failed to warn borrowers. In fact, as with both Wacka and the Sonters, the banks had encouraged customers to take out bigger loans than they needed. When things turned sour, instead of helping, the banks seized whatever assets were left. They used legal action as a deterrent when customers lodged complaints or requested compensation.

*

It was against this backdrop of more and more customers going to the wall from bad banking practices that in 1987 Paul McLean was elected to Federal Parliament as a NSW senator for the Australian Democrats, after contesting seven elections in ten years. A self-described social actionist, McLean entered politics to take on tough issues on behalf of the Australian battler.

Within months of taking office, McLean began to hear disturbing stories about foreign currency loans and other types of bank misconduct. By now, bank share prices were trading at record highs. It was the time of 'greed is good' and power-dressing, yellow-tie-wearing stockbrokers and bankers taking clients out to lunch at topless restaurants and strip joints; when *Wall Street* character Gordon Gekko made his famous speech, saying: 'Greed is right, greed works. Greed clarifies, cuts through, and captures the essence of the evolutionary spirit. Greed, in all of its forms; greed for life, for money, for love, knowledge has marked the upward surge of mankind.'

But the boom came to an end on 19 October 1987, now known as Black Monday, when the US stock market plunged 22 per cent, its biggest one-day percentage loss ever, bigger even than the stock market loss during the Great Depression of 1929. The Australian Stock Exchange (ASX) followed suit, losing 25 per cent of its value – the worst-ever one-day fall on the Australian market. Investor confidence was shattered.

Within months of the crash, Paul McLean was contacted by one of his constituents, Donna Batiste, who wanted to expose a scam being practised by the big four banks. Batiste told McLean the banks were deliberately sending companies to the wall, then selling their businesses to favoured parties at knockdown prices. She also alleged that CBA had deliberately emptied her trading account to prevent her making interest payments on her business loan before taking her to bankruptcy court.

After McLean agreed to raise Batiste's case in parliament, hundreds of other victims of banking misconduct got in touch with him. He also came into contact with John McLennan as the two fought to expose further banking scandals. McLean lodged affidavits, spoke under parliamentary privilege and called for a royal commission into what was occurring. In his 1992 book, *Bankers and Bastards*, he described how his experiences with

Batiste and others led him to conclude that even at best the banks were 'greedy and heartless' and were involved in 'considerable malpractice and corruption'. He also realised there was little will among regulatory authorities to address these problems.[9] The Australian Government's regulator, the National Companies and Securities Commission (NCSC), had only a small budget of $5 million and a staff of eighty, which meant it could only pursue one major case at a time. Individual Australian states also had corporate watchdogs, but they too were resource-poor and had insufficiently experienced employees.

McLean's stories finally came to wider attention after two letters from the law firm Allen Allen & Hemsley to Westpac were leaked anonymously to Anne Lampe at the *Sydney Morning Herald*. The letters, sent in a fax, implicated Westpac's international currency trading subsidiary Partnership Pacific Limited (PPL) in illegal foreign currency loans, which involved lumping transactions together, mixing them up and deal switching. Allen Allen & Hemsley had been Westpac's legal representative for years, and a senior partner of the firm sat on the Westpac board.

The letters contained legal advice which was the result of the lawyers examining over 50,000 internal Westpac documents and interviewing staff. The advice showed that 'the PPL forex [foreign exchange] division was badly mismanaged' and that senior management had been aware of the 'gravity' of the situation by early July 1986 but had done nothing. One letter said management's failure to act decisively 'was a tragedy' that resulted in clients continuing to lose money. It also suggested that if customers took legal action they would likely succeed, and said, 'Many more documents have been examined and a number of them are very damaging ... all those reading these letters should read these documents – they are devastating.'[10]

Allen Allen & Hemsley's recommendations were that PPL should 'keep close and cordial contact with all potential claimants' – people like the Sonters; avoid litigation at any reasonable cost; make sure any concessions given to borrowers were made only in exchange for a complete release of legal action; and take 'all practical steps to avoid PPL's weakness being known outside PPL/Westpac boards and senior management'.

It was an explosive story, but Lampe knew Westpac would try to suppress it if she followed her normal practice and put questions about the letters' contents to the bank before publishing her report. The *Herald*'s lawyer also thought that Westpac would try to place an injunction on the article. He agreed that the document seemed genuine and gave the go-ahead for publication. Lampe's article appeared on 29 January 1991, with the headline 'Westpac arm faces forex suits'. The train of events that followed became known as the 'Westpac Letters Affair'.

Then the fireworks began. Westpac obtained injunctions in the NSW Supreme Court to stop publication of the letters. The court order demanded that Lampe and the *Sydney Morning Herald* hand over the offending letters on the grounds it was a 'stolen document' that belonged to Westpac. It also claimed copyright infringement and took legal action for compensation.

'Lawyers arrived at my home to serve me with breach of copyright action. I stayed inside while my husband asked a young Allen Allen & Hemsley lawyer to leave the premises and, when he didn't, turned the hose on him. He went away a bit damper than when he arrived,' Lampe recalls.

Trying every trick in the book to escape responsibility for its wrongdoings, Westpac then argued that the letters were subject to legal privilege – in other words, that information between a lawyer and a client is confidential. The bank then spent a fortune on media advertising and public relations campaigns, trying to justify its actions. Fairfax refused to run one of the ads on the grounds that Westpac was putting its side of the story in the ad at the same time as it was trying to suppress the other side of the story with an injunction.

On 4 February 1991, a week after the article was published and the *Herald* had been served with the injunction, Senator Paul McLean received a fax from an anonymous source in Belgium containing the same letters that Lampe had received. McLean had followed Lampe's exposé and knew about Westpac's injunction. Convinced the letters provided 'a window through which we could virtually observe malpractice as it occurred and see how their legal adviser and management reacted when they became aware of it,' he decided to put them into the public domain by tabling them in parliament.

But the Senate stopped him from tabling the documents after Westpac briefed the president of the Senate, Senator Kerry Sibraa. McLean then sent copies of the Westpac letters to all senators as well as to Prime Minister Bob Hawke, Treasurer Paul Keating and the leader of the federal opposition, John Hewson. Keating, through his parliamentary secretary, said the matters raised in the letters were best resolved in the courts. Hewson's office returned the envelope unopened.

McLean then sent the letters to the South Australian Upper House Democrat Ian Gilfillan, who read them into Hansard to cover their contents under parliamentary privilege, permitting politicians to speak about issues in parliament without risking legal action and allowing the media to report the items. However, the Westpac injunction in NSW meant that newspapers in that state, including the *Sydney Morning Herald*, couldn't write about the letters.

The more Westpac fought to suppress the letters, the more adverse publicity and outrage it generated. On 7 March 1991, Stephen Martin, chairman of the House of Representatives' Standing Committee on Finance and Public Administration's inquiry into banking and deregulation, commonly referred to as the Martin Inquiry, weighed into the debate and called on Westpac to table the letters at a special hearing of the inquiry to be attended by Westpac boss Stuart Fowler.

The Martin Inquiry had been called in October 1990, well before the Westpac Letters had burst onto the scene. Its purpose was to report on the deregulation of the banks and investigate claims by Treasurer Paul Keating that the banks hadn't been passing on official interest rate cuts to customers, pocketing them instead in what Keating described as 'a deliberate plan to recover bad debts amounting to about $10 billion'.[11]

Following the 1987 crash and with the economy wallowing in recession, banks had found themselves hugely exposed. They had loaned billions of dollars to companies like Qintex and Equiticorp, which had now gone broke and couldn't repay their loans. Witholding official interest rate cuts from consumers was a way for the banks to claw back some of that money. But customers were also doing it tough, and bank borrowers wanted to know why falls in interest rates hadn't been passed on.

With public opinion shifting firmly against the banks, Westpac allowed the letters to be tabled at the inquiry and dropped the various court injunctions with what Stuart Fowler famously described as 'the greatest reluctance'. Fowler also said, 'This campaign, timed to correspond with the commencement of [the Martin Inquiry], has been conducted by certain journalists, interest groups and others prepared to traffic in stolen documents.' He defended Westpac's actions and accused McLean of 'making outrageous claims' against the banks.[12] He also argued that the letters and the poor behaviour related to PPL, not Westpac, and that Westpac had sold PPL. Few Westpac customers had been affected, he said, and Westpac had paid compensation to those who had. In other words, nothing to see here.

The banks would wheel out similar excuses every time a banking scandal erupted – someone else was to blame, it was 'just a few bad apples', it happened in the past, few customers had been affected, compensation had been paid and it wouldn't happen again. These arguments belied what was really going on. Compensation was often avoided or low-ball offers made, and customers were obliged to sign gag orders. The misconduct was buried and nothing was learned. It destroyed people's lives. Some died waiting for banks to be held accountable. Others continued to fight, hoping for justice one day.

The *Sydney Morning Herald* business writer Max Walsh summed up the controversy as 'Westpac's Watergate'. In an article published on 11 March 1991, Walsh highlighted how the cover-up indicated a culture of arrogance and an inability to acknowledge wrongdoing. He also pointed out that the cover-up, not the original misdeed, had become the issue.[13]

But if Paul McLean had been disappointed by the way parliament hadn't backed his request to table the Westpac letters, as well as by the lack of action on the part of federal politicians, he would be equally disappointed by his treatment before the Martin Inquiry on 15 March 1991. He was given only three hours to discuss thousands of pages of documents, outline complex cases and attempt to prove fraud on the part of Westpac. It proved too difficult. Martin would later disparage McLean to journalists, saying, 'He had his day in court and couldn't deliver ... If people are out there with the impression that the banks are bastards, I believe that you have to be able to put up or shut up.'[14] Headlines at the time concurred, saying, 'Claims of fraud dismissed'.[15]

The Martin Inquiry did, however, recommend referring the Westpac Letters to the National Crime Authority and state fraud squads. Unfortunately, those recommendations were never followed up. No one was ever charged, despite the letters showing fraud and theft had taken place. Executives rode off into the sunset and the bank started to settle court cases relating to the mis-selling of foreign currency loans.

McLean, disillusioned and worn out by his battles, quit parliament in August 1991. He wrote a memoir, hoping it would do what parliament hadn't been able to do and 'change a financial system that is working against people but pretends it is working for them'.[16] But the book didn't fulfil those dreams, and McLean was again criticised for 'bank bashing'. After years of trying to do something about what he saw as the banks' bastardry, McLean moved to Tasmania and lived alone in a mud-brick cottage. He would re-emerge, years later, when Wacka Williams went into politics and another scandal blew up, leaving yet another path of destruction and financial ruin.

Chapter 2

Diversify or perish

The shift to financial services

IF DEREGULATION AND THE onslaught of competition from foreign banks into Australia's banking market were characteristic of the 1980s, the early 1990s would see the sector battling the rise of a new type of competition. Mortgage intermediaries such as Aussie Home Loans and RAMS, life insurance companies and global financial services companies all began offering home loans at lower rates. Customers were no longer blindly putting excess money into savings accounts; instead they were looking at managed funds and superannuation funds, which promised them better returns. And businesses had started looking overseas for cheap finance, primarily in US bond markets, where interest rates were lower and money easier to access.

The traditional role of a bank as an intermediary between borrowers and lenders was being eroded. Banks realised that if they didn't adapt, their profits would shrivel. They began offering new products and services, and expanded domestically and overseas to build on their economies of scale. NAB purchased four banks in the United Kingdom: the Clydesdale, Yorkshire, National Irish and Northern banks. ANZ tried to diversify into life insurance and superannuation with a $3.6 billion proposal to merge with National Mutual. It was blocked by Treasurer Paul Keating on the grounds that it wasn't in the national interest, but it triggered a strategic alliance between the ANZ and National Mutual. Westpac soon did the same with AMP, while CBA didn't have much room to grow because it was owned by the government.

In this new era of deregulation, Keating was becoming increasingly frustrated. He feared CBA couldn't be a 'gutsy competitor' if it didn't have sufficient capital. He became convinced it had outlived its time as a government-owned enterprise. 'It was the natural thing to do …' Keating said of his desire to privatise CBA. 'Basically it was a post office bank with the deposits of pensioners and it had the cast of mind of a post office bank.'[1] But Keating knew that privatising the 'people's bank' would be a tough sell within his party. Privatisation remained a vexed and unresolved issue between the right of the party, who were in favour, and the 'true believers' on the left, who vehemently opposed such sell-offs.

Keating's chance to privatise CBA arrived with Black Monday, the day of the 1987 stock market crash, when the State Bank of Victoria, owned by the Victorian Government, was undone by the disastrous antics of its free-wheeling merchant bank subsidiary Tricontinental. Tricontinental had lent money to high-risk operators and entrepreneurs during the 1980s. When these entities defaulted on their payments after the crash, Tricontinental ran up losses of $1.3 billion by 1990 and bad and doubtful debts to the tune of $2.7 billion.

The Victorian Government couldn't afford to save the bank. But there was a risk that if the public got wind of the State Bank's dire financial situation it would trigger a run on the bank, sending it broke, and with it the Victorian economy. Keating pounced, telling the Labor Caucus, 'If you allow me to sell a quarter of the Commonwealth Bank I will fund what would otherwise be the collapse of the State Bank [of Victoria] and the decimation of the Victorian economy.'[2] While the left wing of the party hated the idea of privatising the 'people's bank', the ramifications of the State Bank going under would be intolerable.

The chairman of CBA was Keating's good friend, the highly regarded and well-connected Morrish Alexander 'Tim' Besley, who'd become CBA chairman in 1988 after a phone call from Keating in late 1987. Besley, who had worked in Treasury before moving into the private sector, agreed with Keating that Australia's financial system was 'uncompetitive and rigid', and needed modernising.

When Keating approached Besley and Don Sanders, CBA's chief executive, about buying the State Bank, Sanders was reluctant, but Besley was keen. Besley recalls Keating saying to him, 'Let's crash through.'

Keating still needed to win over CBA's union, the Commonwealth Bank Officers' Association (CBOA), which had a strong membership base among the bank's senior executive. He summoned Peter Presdee, the state secretary of CBOA, to Canberra with four other union officials for a meeting in August 1990 to discuss the partial float and privatisation. Says Presdee today, 'It was a smart move to get us in a room and win over the union. The last thing they wanted was union opposition.'

When Presdee heard Keating's arguments – including that the Victorian Government didn't have the money to bail out the State Bank – he realised it would be hard to argue against privatisation: 'We were told if it didn't happen there would be massive job losses in Victoria and a loss of confidence in the banking sector and the economy. I didn't want that on my conscience, so I agreed.'

*

When CBA released the details of its partial privatisation on 8 July 1991, it was billed as the 'sale of the century'. A lot was riding on the float. It would be the government's first privatisation and it wanted it to go off without a hitch.

The government had decided to sell 30 per cent of the bank at $5.40 a share, to raise more than $4.5 billion. The target market was first-time investors; 1.25 million prospectuses were printed and distributed throughout the bank's vast branch network and ads appeared on TV. Ironically, when the shares were about to be listed on the Australian sharemarket, Keating wasn't there to celebrate. He'd been moved to the backbench after a failed leadership challenge and John Kerin was the new Treasurer.

A series of interviews was given ahead of the float, detailing a new logo and corporate identity. Passbooks and chequebooks and all CBA stationery were redesigned, and branches throughout Australia were repainted in time for the listing.[3]

But there were other, less cosmetic changes in the works. 'Until then, the bank had been government-coddled, if you like. It needed sharpening up. There were still people who played business golf on Wednesdays, it was fully unionised, and it had to change,' Besley says. According to Besley, the public-service culture was entrenched right up to the board. About half the CBA workforce thought the bank existed for commercial reasons, Besley says, while the other half saw it as operating under a social charter. 'The most important things were to clarify [that] we operated on a commercial basis, ensure there was a group of very good commercial people and that our objectives were very clear.'

The salary of the chief executive – along with those of other senior public servants – had previously been set by a tribunal in

Canberra. That was about to change, along with the pay structure of almost every front-line bank employee. 'Targets and incentives were introduced which changed the culture overnight,' remembers Presdee. 'The bank went from having a primary aim to provide the people of Australia with a good service to a primary aim to look after shareholders.'

Besley needed to find a new chief executive who was equipped to manage a bank with a majority government shareholder and hundreds of thousands of retail shareholders – and who could change the public-service culture of the bank's staff to a more commercial mindset. One of the applicants for the CEO role was forty-two-year-old executive David Murray, who'd started at CBA as a teller and gained an MBA while working his way up the ladder. Ambitious, serious and ruthless, he'd played a major role in the bank's commercialisation and had strong ideas about the strategic direction of the bank.

In his interview, Murray expressed an unwavering commitment to changing the bank's brown-cardigan public-service image and turning it into a formidable competitor. He was confident he could bring this about even if the bank was 'half-pregnant' – with a mix of private ownership and government control. He'd been running the retail bank for the past year, had been involved in the complex merger with the State Bank of Victoria, and had a blueprint for what had to be done to modernise CBA. He also outlined a vision for the bank to transition from a savings bank to a diversified financial services provider and expand into Asia.

Nevertheless, Besley says Murray seemed startled when he told him, 'The board wants you to be the chief executive.' Murray replied, 'It's a bit early, isn't it, for me?', to which Besley responded, 'It's not. You're it. You're in the deep end.' Besley thinks Murray was a great pick.

Murray might have worked at the bank for years, but he behaved like an outsider. He wasn't one for small talk, had a bone-dry economic outlook that included a belief that the economy was best served by small government, light-touch regulation, free-market banking and an emphasis on innovation and technology. 'He is a great lateral thinker and doesn't suffer fools gladly,' Besley says.

Besley and Murray made a formidable team. Besley was the polished and diplomatic chairman, while Murray, who'd grown up in country NSW, was blunt.

The 'people's bank' was fast becoming a relic. An institution from a bygone age.

*

Murray quickly set about restructuring operations and shedding staff to cut expenses. He justified this to the sharemarket by saying, 'The Commonwealth Bank cannot stand alone with uneconomic services and/or high costs and continue to provide the community with the reliable service it has come to expect. Nor can it compete with a public-service mentality.'[4]

Comments like this didn't go unnoticed by the union or Presdee, who recalls, '[Murray] was ruthless and hardnosed and was determined to change the culture into a private bank piranha and establish shareholder value.' Flat fees of $1.50 a month were slugged on passbook and Keycard savings accounts with balances below $250, and other fees were introduced. Murray moved the bank further and further into financial services, setting up a stockbroking arm, CommSec, and moving into funds management and insurance. The sky was the limit.

Less than a year into his job as CEO, Murray told staff of plans to slash the 42,000-strong workforce. Technology was disrupting the way people did banking, and Murray wanted to encourage customers to make more use of automatic teller machines (ATMs) and EFTPOS. 'It was a huge blow for everybody,' Presdee recalls.

The union wanted all redundancies to be voluntary, but CBA wouldn't agree. 'Everybody was nervous about their future, and they had every right to be,' Presdee says, adding, 'The relationship between the union and the bank became increasingly toxic, which is a shame. It was never like that before.'

At the same time as their jobs were under threat, staff were increasingly pressured to sell new products. Peter Neale, who had worked at the bank as a loans manager since 1969 and had advised Wacka Williams on his foreign currency loan, recalls that after CBA's privatisation the culture of the bank changed and staff 'were pushed to sell, sell, sell'. 'If a couple came in for a home loan we would have to see if we could get them to take out a credit card, a personal loan, insurance on the house, life insurance. It was tough,' he added. As one example, Neale says he personally struggled to sell a $5000 credit card to a young couple who had just taken out an $80,000 loan. 'I was happy to inform people, but I wasn't prepared to write things into a loan that some wacko in head office was forcing us to do.'

Having moved from Inverell in 1990, Neale was working out of a CBA branch in Goulburn, in rural NSW. After CBA's privatisation, Neale recalls being given targets to meet each month. 'They had shareholders to accommodate and they had to move products off the shelves and staff were pressured to do it. It was something ridiculous like having to sell 150 loans a month,' he says. 'I'd get a call from administration in Canberra asking why I hadn't met my quota. I'd say, "Goulburn has a population of 24,000; if you subtract children from the number, and other things, you are left with an income source of 10,000 people and you have ANZ, Westpac, Advance Bank [which was later bought by St George then Westpac] all trying to write loans. How in God's name can you expect us to meet that target? It's impossible."' On 28 September 1994, Neale resigned, unable to agree with the bank's policies.

*

Murray wasn't the only one shaking things up. All the major banks recognised that having an extensive network of thousands of branches was a costly way of delivering services. In particular, it was no longer economical to retain branches in small country towns, where they often had to compete with other bank branches. But the closure of branches in small towns would become a massive, divisive and highly emotive issue, not just for communities but for the unions. People felt that the banks were mercilessly ripping the lifeblood out of their communities.

There were protests and anger in small towns everywhere – towns such as Stanhope, west of Shepparton in Victoria, where locals held a rally after CBA flagged the closure of its branch. Jim Thompson, who was the manager of the shire of Bet Bet in central Victoria in 1994, called on the media to cover the impact of branch closures. He told *The Age* the closure of the Dunolly branch in December 1993 had a devastating impact on the town. 'The nearest Commonwealth Bank is now at Maryborough, twenty-three kilometres away, and that makes it difficult for people without transport,' he said. 'The Commonwealth is supposed to be a people's bank, a government bank, but it seems that these economic rationalist decisions are made in Sydney and Dunolly is irrelevant.'[5]

By 1995 Murray had overseen the closure of more than 200 branches from about 1600 and cut staff to 35,000. To further reduce the power of CBOA, in 1996 he hired Les Cupper, who was well known for his success in busting the unions in the mining sector, to run the bank's human resources department. During Cupper's tenure he would offer non-union individual employment contracts to bank workers, a move that would make it easier to introduce new sales and targets.

For many, Murray was an enigma wrapped in a riddle. He had spent two decades living and breathing the culture of the bank, yet when he rose to power he was able to flick a switch and radically change it. Presdee saw Murray's behaviour as being motivated by a fear of failure. 'I think Murray wasn't going to be a failure, so he wanted to build a bank he thought would survive deregulation and technological advances.'

The bank that the Fisher Labor government had created in 1911 as the 'people's bank' was transformed into an institution where the raison d'être was making bigger and bigger profits at any cost. Between 1998 and 2000, CBA's profit totalled $5.4 billion – more than half the total proceeds received by the Australian public through its partial privatisation.[6]

Chapter 3

A soft touch

Resisting the regulators

THE HILTON, BRISBANE. IT was November 1991, just a few months after the part privatisation of CBA, and Allan Fels, the chair of the competition watchdog, the Trade Practices Commission (TPC), stood before a room packed with journalists and photographers. Fels, known for his distinctive drawl and piercing eyes, had spent the morning on the phone ringing around media outlets – working up interest, promising a bombshell.

Clutching his press release, a serious-looking Fels waited for silence before outing the institution in question as Colonial Mutual, one of the biggest and most respected life insurers in the country. Colonial Mutual, Fels alleged, had engaged in five years of deceptive and misleading conduct by targeting Aboriginal people and poorly educated Australians to sell dud insurance policies.

'Unconscionable, misleading or deceptive conduct will not be tolerated,' Fels thundered as the cameras rolled and journalists scribbled notes furiously.

Fels said that experienced Colonial Mutual agents had sold policies to people who couldn't afford them, promising them they would get their money back in two years and that the policy could buy a car or fund a Harvard University education for their children. In Fels' view, the case highlighted the need for stronger protection of 'less financially sophisticated' consumers when they were buying life insurance and superannuation products. He also said he intended to institute proceedings against Colonial Mutual in the Federal Court.

It was the first time a regulator had used the media so effectively to name and shame a big financial services firm, and it confirmed the fears of some of the business community about Fels, an economic rationalist and academic who'd been appointed to the role of TPC chairman in July 1991 and was also the head of the Prices Surveillance Authority. Big business had tried to derail his appointment; the peak business body, the Business Council of Australia, even wrote to Prime Minister Hawke urging him to pick someone else.

Fels was seen as trouble within the business community and disliked for his use of the media to air his views – or scandals. He had gained a reputation at fifty as a 'media tart' after putting powerful oil companies, the book industry and the aviation industry into the headlines when he was chair of the Prices Surveillance Authority, a regulator that had been almost invisible before Fels came along.

Fels' revelations about Colonial Mutual would also mark a growing appetite among the media to cover bad behaviour by financial institutions. There had already been the foreign currency loans scandal and the Westpac Letters Affair. The Martin Inquiry into deregulation, which reported in the same month as Fels fronted the media, had also heard some gruesome misconduct stories. Now there was confirmation that it wasn't just banks doing the wrong thing in the pursuit of profit and targets.

Colonial Mutual's life insurance scandal couldn't have come at a worse time for the industry. Three months earlier, on 20 August 1991, the Labor government had introduced the compulsory superannuation guarantee charge, requiring employers to pay 3 per cent of each worker's salary into a superannuation account from July 1992, with the employer contribution to rise to 9 per cent by 2002. It would democratise super which, until then, had been a product used mainly by the wealthy.

It was also a decision that effectively placed Australia's retirement savings into the hands of fund managers, most of which were owned by insurance companies, including Colonial, AMP and National Mutual. Life insurance companies played a major role in the provision of superannuation services, from managing employer-sponsored and industry-productivity funds through to the sale of personal superannuation. According to the TPC, $56 billion of the funds managed by life insurance companies related to superannuation contributions.

For these companies, which were about to join the race for management of an estimated $600 billion of retirement savings by 2000, bad publicity like that sparked by the Colonial Mutual affair could result in unwanted scrutiny and more regulation, particularly if Fels was on the case.

More to their liking was the appointment earlier in the year of Fels' regulatory counterpart, Tony Hartnell, as the founding chairman of the new national corporate watchdog, the Australian Securities Commission (ASC), which was set up after it became apparent from a string of company collapses and bank scandals that the current regulatory system wasn't working. In January 1991, the ASC replaced the NCSC and the patchwork of state agencies, which had been little more than a fig leaf for regulation.

The new regulatory body promised to be far better resourced than its predecessor.

Others, mainly those in favour of stronger regulation, felt Hartnell was too close to big business and was taking a softly-softly approach. Before becoming chairman of the ASC Hartnell had been a senior partner at Allen Allen & Hemsley – the law firm that had penned the infamous Westpac Letters. In contrast to Fels, Hartnell saw the role of the ASC as being 'to establish a climate of compliance, ethics and responsibility'.[1] The ASC had criminal and civil law available to it, but from his earliest interviews Hartnell made it clear his preference was to use civil action rather than criminal prosecutions to enforce compliance of corporations. Civil action required a lower burden of proof and was therefore quicker and more efficient, he said.[2]

This frustrated the Commonwealth Director of Public Prosecutions (DPP), Michael Rozenes, whose job was to pursue criminal action in the courts. The tension between Hartnell and Rozenes culminated in an extraordinary public outburst in September 1992 at a parliamentary committee hearing when Rozenes claimed the ASC had one rule for the rich and another for the poor when it came to decisions about civil and criminal sanctions. It was a brutal attack that Hartnell denied. He defended his preference for civil proceedings in 'appropriate cases' and said there was no disagreement between him and the DPP over 'serious' fraud that merited criminal action.[3] After Hartnell's term expired in late 1992, he returned to Allen Allen & Hemsley, before starting a new law firm, Atanaskovic Hartnell, specialising in corporate and finance law.

Fels had a different style. He was all about public statements and using fear tactics to keep companies in line. To obtain firsthand accounts of the life insurance scam, he had sent a team of TPC investigators to the outback for two months. The stories the investigators came back with were powerful – and appalling. Colonial targeted people in low socioeconomic areas and misled them into buying products they didn't need and couldn't afford. Aboriginal people on welfare payments, foreigners with limited English and people who had only primary-school education were all easy prey. The agents organised premiums to be automatically deducted from welfare payments and pensions to make sure they got their commissions.

Some agents were flogging hundreds of policies a week and getting rich on the commissions. The more policies they sold, the more they earned. It was open season, as the laws governing superannuation and life insurance were flawed, leaving customers vulnerable to exploitation. There were no tribunals, for instance, where customers could lodge a complaint if things went wrong.

The behaviour of the life insurance agents was so egregious that the Australian Government announced a full-blown inquiry into the sector in March 1992 and appointed Fels to chair it. In December 1992, the final report from the inquiry, *Life Insurance and Superannuation*, was released. It laid bare deep conflicts in the industry, showing that life insurance agents felt their primary responsibility was to the life insurance companies that employed them, not to the customers who bought their products. As a result, many products they recommended were not appropriate. Nevertheless, most customers believed the agents were acting in their best interests, not realising they were paid a commission for the products they sold.

The report also found an alarming number of consumers were losing money on insurance products because of high fees and charges, hidden penalties and inadequate disclosure of information at the time of sale. It recommended that commissions should be disclosed to customers. It said insurance policies were generally complex and opaque, and their wording lacked consistency between companies, making it impossible for customers to compare products. Finally, the report noted that 'insurers have not controlled the conduct of their agents or implemented steps to stop bad agents being recycled from company to company and that the market continued to deliver poor value for money to a high proportion of customers'.

The insurance and superannuation industries rejected the report and its recommendations. Using the Life Insurance Federation of Australia conference, AMP's chief executive, Ian Salmon, who was also a member of the Business Council of Australia, denounced the TPC as a 'creature of the consumer movement' and said its policies were 'anti-business and anti-competition'. He concluded: 'There seems to be no need for a watchdog that increasingly wants to bite everyone within reach.'

Others in the sector tried to use fear to hose down Fels. Mercantile Mutual slammed the TPC report as 'on balance, completely unnecessary' adding, 'If the TPC interferes too much in the mechanics of the industry they could damage one of the ways the country can generate long-term capital.'

This would be a recurring theme throughout the decades. Indeed, it would take until 1 January 2018 – more than twenty-five years – before some of Fels' recommendations, such as greater transparency in commissions, would be addressed.

*

It wasn't just the life insurance sector that had learned to mobilise powerful lobby groups to delay or water down reforms. The banks had recently mastered this strategy too.

When the Martin Inquiry had released its own report in 1991 – wittily titled 'A Pocket Full of Change: Banking Deregulation' – it had called for a new code of practice to be developed for the banks, one that would be 'contractually enforceable' by bank customers and would be subject to ongoing monitoring by Fels' TPC. It also recommended a banking ombudsman.

Banking executives immediately went on the attack. The first to fire a pre-emptive strike was Don Argus, chairman of NAB and a representative of the high-profile banking lobby group the Australian Bankers' Association (now the Australian Banking Association), who was nicknamed 'Don't Argue' because of his forthright and forceful personality. On the eve of the release of the Martin Inquiry report, Argus used a speech at the Australian Bankers' Association annual dinner in Canberra to claim the industry was being 'suffocated' by new regulation. He told the crowd of bankers and politicians that a new code and other possible legislative changes would cost hundreds of millions of dollars.

'[A] free and competitive market contains the most powerful inbuilt mechanism for consumer protection,' he railed, adding, 'Loss of business is a powerful disincentive to shoddy behaviour.' Besides, he argued, the sector couldn't afford to comply with the code – it was facing headwinds from every direction. 'There's an imminent squeeze on bank revenues, margins and profits as a result of continued low inflation, a slow reduction in non-performing assets, the de-gearing of corporate balance sheets, and the diversion of savings from banks into superannuation,' Argus said.[4]

It was targeted lobbying at its best and most sophisticated, and Argus won. The code was downgraded from a mandatory code into a voluntary code and some key recommendations were removed. Proposed responsible lending requirements were also diluted. A credit assessment 'obligation' was imposed on the banks.

But it failed to set any specific standards, rendering it virtually useless. The industry had fought back and Canberra had buckled. A banking ombudsman with a narrow brief, and a watered-down banking code of practice was the sum total for reform.

The result of all this was to effectively give the green light to the banking sector to do whatever it wanted. Over the next twenty years there would be a number of iterations of the banking code, but they clearly never went far enough. The power imbalance between customers and the banks grew starker and more dangerous. The importance of the customer was forgotten in the quest to build market share and profits.

With the Martin Inquiry behind them, and self-regulation in place, the banks were now within reach of the rivers of gold that would flow after the opening up of superannuation. But the banks were still minnows in this area in comparison to the insurance companies, which had a century's life insurance business behind them, and weren't about to give up access to the new funds sloshing around without a fight.

The compulsory superannuation legislation spawned a huge number of funds and almost guaranteed sloppy practices would arise in the market.

*

The new *Superannuation Industry (Supervision) Act*, which came into effect on 1 July 1993, made it clear that banks would have to hand over their own staff pension funds to external managers if they didn't start offering funds management themselves. As a result, the banks began chasing mergers and acquisitions, seeking to expand rapidly and create synergies by cross-selling bank products and financial products and economies of scale, and spreading their tentacles further into funds management. A new buzzword emerged, 'bancassurance', or 'vertical integration', meaning the cross-selling of customers' banking and insurance – a practice that would dominate the next two decades.

Meanwhile, Allan Fels was busy meeting bank chiefs, who were determined to soften him up in the hope that with enough political lobbying the so-called 'four pillars policy' would be scrapped. The four pillars policy, which prevented the four big banks – ANZ, CBA, NAB and Westpac – merging with each other or buying attractive insurance companies like AMP, had been introduced by Treasurer Paul Keating in May 1990 when he rejected a proposed merger between ANZ and the country's second biggest life insurer, National Mutual. In a press release explaining the rejection, Keating drew on national interest, saying, 'It is vital for the efficient application of the nation's savings that there should be a reasonable diversity of institutions and effective competition in banking, in life insurance, and more generally in the provision of financial services.' It was the government's judgement, Keating said, that a merger between a major bank and a major life insurer would hurt competition.

Fels regarded the proposed mergers between banks and insurers as a case of the 'nirvana fallacy', he says. 'Every CEO dreams of taking over another bank but what they really want is an empire twice as big as before. They said it was about savings and removing duplication but I didn't buy it.'

Whatever the case, there was a constant stream of bank chiefs visiting Fels at the TPC's head office in Canberra. One of Fels' most frequent guests was Bob Joss, an American with an MBA and PhD in economics, who had moved to Australia to become the CEO of Westpac in early 1993 with a board mandate to fix the bank and return it to its former glory. Westpac had suffered in the early 1990s after a series of debtors with big commercial property loans defaulted after the stock market crash, and it was struggling under a mountain of debt, a $1.6 billion loss and a new shareholder on its register – billionaire Kerry Packer.

Joss was an abrupt departure from previous Westpac chief executives. He had come from the Californian-based bank Wells Fargo, and the salary he demanded was more than the combined salaries of the other three big bank CEOs. His five-year contract promised a pay packet of $38 million to $45 million if he met all his share price and performance targets.

Joss became known as the bank executive who pioneered options packages, and his salary triggered a 'me too' response in banking circles, with other bank chiefs demanding similar aggressive performance-based remuneration structures which they could extend down the ranks of management.

Together with increasing pressure from institutional shareholders to deliver greater returns, these new mega salaries accelerated the move towards even more aggressive sales programs designed to boost profits and, in turn, increase share prices. It became a case of: 'Why sell two banking products to a customer when you can sell them four?'

Salary packages were structured to ensure performance was based on shareholder returns, and by the mid-1990s incentives were being attached to sales, further entrenching that culture. For boards and management, the higher the profit, the bigger their bonuses.

*

Of course, another way to increase a bank's returns was through cost-cutting. As David Murray and executives at the other banks had done, Bob Joss accelerated cost-cutting initiatives, including retrenching thousands of middle managers, selling operations overseas and renewing Westpac's focus on retail banking. Branches were closed and new transaction fees introduced. To ensure Westpac was employing the right people, psychometric tests were introduced to identify extroverts with a bent for sales.

Between 1993 and 2000 about 1800 bank branches closed across the banking sector, equating to a loss of about 40,000 banking jobs. Technology was the convenient excuse. 'Banks now are open 24 hours a day, seven days a week, rather than 10 am to 3 pm,' the Australian Banking Association told the *Sydney Morning Herald* in 2000.[5]

Prior to the deregulation of the financial system, fees charged to customers had been almost unheard of. But during the 1990s they boomed. According to the interest-rate comparison company Cannex Australia (now called Canstar), the average base fee among the four major banks rose 75 per cent between 1993 and 1998. Over-the-counter fees soared 276 per cent and ATM fees increased by 112 per cent.[6] Retail banking was now all about cutting costs, fees, sales and shareholder returns.

Bob Joss had extensive funds management experience and, like executives at the other three major banks, was keen to promote vertical integration so that more customers could be sold a variety of products. It was a no-brainer: traditional banking was seen to be in decline, and funds management was growing at double-digit rates.

Joss was also keen to dismantle the four pillars policy, hence his intense lobbying of Fels. The four pillars might have been a sacred cow, but smaller banks and fund managers weren't. To this end, the 1990s would see a number of institutions swallowed whole. In the wake of CBA's purchase of the State Bank of

Victoria, Suncorp bought Metway Bank in 1996, Advance Bank bought the State Bank of South Australia in 1995, Westpac bought WA-based Challenge Bank in 1996 and the Bank of Melbourne in 1997, and St George Bank bought Advance Bank in 1997.

Colonial Mutual made the biggest acquisitions in the 1990s, buying up the State Bank of NSW in 1994, Prudential, Legal & General in 1998, and then the Trust Bank of Tasmania in 1999. There was even talk that Colonial would march on Bankwest and then one of the big four banks.

*

All of this presented challenges for the industry regulators, which at the time were going through a phase of reorganisation and reconsolidation. In 1997, the Wallis Inquiry, headed by businessman Stan Wallis, was tasked with reviewing the post-deregulatory environment and ensuring the right systems were in place for the oncoming technological changes and moves by the banks into superannuation. There were many overlapping supervisors, including the ASC and the Insurance and Superannuation Commission. The Reserve Bank was the prudential supervisor of the banks, while credit unions were regulated by the states. Industry participants complained there was too much administrative red tape.

Wallis was handpicked by the Howard government, which had taken office the year before. Wallis was a corporate blue blood sitting on the board of the country's biggest financial institution, AMP. He was never going to rock the boat. Although he took a leave of absence from AMP while he completed the inquiry to try to improve the optics of his appointment, it really didn't matter.

Not surprisingly, the Wallis Report recommended the continued support for light-touch regulation with the added twist that the regulator needed to be mindful of the compliance costs on the institutions it regulated.

The financial services sector embraced the findings of the Wallis Report, which also included recommendations to streamline regulatory reporting by creating two mega-regulators, the Australian Prudential Regulation Authority (APRA) and the Australian Securities and Investments Commission (ASIC), both established on 1 July 1998. They would become known as the twin-peaks regulators.

APRA would be the prudential regulator for banks, credit unions, superannuation funds and insurers, and the other prudential regulators would either close or, in the case of the Reserve Bank, be stripped of its prudential supervisory powers. Importantly, APRA was funded largely by the industries that it supervised, which arguably put it in a compromising situation as the policeman being funded by those it policed. ASIC replaced the Australian Securities Commission (ASC) and was given a broader remit to cover consumer protection in financial products and services, as well as financial advice.

In his final report, Wallis said: '[ASIC] should adopt a flexible approach to regulation. No one model of regulation should be imposed on the whole system. Where industry standards and performance suggest that the most practicable method involves self-regulation or co-regulation, such methods should be preferred.' He also recommended: 'In all cases, the cost effectiveness of regulation should be subject to ongoing stringent assessment.' It was music to the industry's ears.

Under Wallis, APRA and ASIC would adopt what's known as a disclosure-based approach to regulation, which operated on the assumption that companies would always provide full details and conditions of products to consumers, who could then make an informed decision. Essentially it was caveat emptor or buyer beware. Where any breach of a regulation was detected, companies were expected to own up to the relevant regulator by sending it a breach notice. Rather than a fine, this usually resulted in a negotiated settlement, often involving a donation to a charity or community cause, or an enforceable undertaking, whereby the company simply agreed to implement a set of changes to rectify the problem.

It was light-touch regulation indeed, and although APRA and ASIC considered it an efficient approach, for financial products it was a disaster in waiting. Successive scandals would make it obvious that disclosure was of little value if investors didn't understand or read the long and convoluted product disclosure statements (PDSs) and other documents they were supplied, which were often written by corporate lawyers in deliberately complex and opaque legal language; nor could it work where a system had thrived by being allowed to exploit its customers' lack of financial literacy. Buyer beware principles simply helped fuel the culture of greed and entitlement inside the banks.

And it didn't end there. To ensure the sector continued to call the shots, the Wallis report recommended the creation of the Financial Sector Advisory Council (FSAC), a non-statutory body comprised of leaders from the financial services sector to advise on 'developments in the financial system and their implications for regulatory arrangements and on the cost effectiveness and compliance costs of regulation'.

If it wasn't so serious, it would have been a joke.

*

In the meantime, Allan Fels had become the chairman of the Australian Competition and Consumer Commission (ACCC), another national regulator formed by the merger in 1995 of the TPC and PSA. Its mandate was to prevent anti-competitive behaviour, including outlawing mergers or collusion that could stifle competition, and protect consumers from unfair practices, such as false advertising and faulty products. From day one, Fels adopted an enforcement-style approach to regulating rather than a disclosure-based arrangement. If there was a breach of the law, the ACCC went in hard, using a court-enforceable undertaking, legal action or fines. As noted, Fels also enjoyed public naming and shaming in the media.

While the big banks were doing mating dances with smaller banks and financial institutions in order to bulk up, NAB chief executive Don Argus had his sights on the main game – merging with one of the other big four banks. The NAB board had sent Argus to Britain and the United States to study the markets. He came back believing NAB's future was to become a global giant big enough to take on other foreign banks. To this end he beefed up NAB's presence in the United Kingdom and the United States while lobbying endlessly in Australia to get the four pillars policy overturned.

NAB's ambition to topple the four pillars dated back to the early 1990s when ANZ was in serious trouble and Argus visited Treasurer John Kerin with a plan to merge with ANZ. Argus says he still has the letter from Kerin, rejecting the proposal. 'We tried twice with ANZ but I also think a problem was that Charlie Goode [chairman of ANZ] didn't want to do it initially because he was new to the chairmanship.'

Throughout his reign at NAB, Argus never gave up trying to dismantle the four pillars. Before the 1996 federal election,

NAB became one of the largest donors to the Liberal Party. That generosity failed to sway John Howard, who decreed that the four pillars policy would stay.

Not to be defeated, Argus tried again in 1998 with Operation Edwin, which brought together some of the country's best lobbyists to find a way to win over the public, the government and Fels to the idea of abandoning the four pillars policy.

Operation Edwin was cloaked in secrecy. Four teams worked on the project, all using different code names, so nobody except one coordinator had complete knowledge of what was going on. Former TPC chairman Bob Baxt was hired by NAB to advise executives on the issues and ways to win over Fels, who Argus believed had it in for the banks. To help with political strategy, Ron Burke, general manager of group corporate relations at NAB and one of Argus's key advisers, hired Prime Minister John Howard's own research and advertising team from the previous two federal elections: Toby Ralph, Mark Textor, Ted Horton and Darcy Tronson. Corporate adviser Mark Burrows was put on the payroll to conduct detailed financial analysis on the pricing of the bid and the types of concessions the bank could make. Richard McKinnon, the head of investment advisory at NAB, was put in charge of the project to win over the government and the TPC. An advertising campaign was prepared, including television ads.

Operation Edwin's initial target was ANZ, and plans were put in place for NAB to announce a $20 billion merger with ANZ after the release of NAB's annual results on 5 November 1998. I was working at *BRW* magazine at the time and learned that Argus would prefer a friendly merger with ANZ but was prepared to go hostile if ANZ spurned NAB's advances. The plan was that, once the deal was publicly announced, NAB would launch a multi-million-dollar television, newspaper and radio campaign to educate the public.

I heard from multiple sources that NAB was so serious about a takeover of ANZ that it had already printed a 'Part A statement' – a formal document that outlined the proposed offer – in case it had to make a hostile bid. NAB had set the price and had been lobbying various politicians around the country, saying either that they would not close branches or that they would open branches in the politicians' electorates.

Howard put a stop to the NAB–ANZ merger at a meeting with Argus in mid-October 1998. It came days after a visit by ANZ chairman Charlie Goode to Howard's office. Goode was a vocal supporter of the four pillars policy and held a lot of sway in Liberal circles. He sat on the Victorian Liberal Party finance committee and was a trustee of one of the main fundraising trusts of the party.

A few weeks later, on 15 November 1998, Argus called a meeting of senior executives and told them Westpac was the new target.

By early February 1999, the talks between Westpac and NAB had fallen apart and Joss had resigned as chief executive of Westpac. The Westpac and NAB merger was blocked by the Westpac board. A source close to the board at the time said, 'No one would get into bed with NAB. Culturally, it is a weak fit because NAB would want to dominate everything. It would make a powerful institution, but it would destroy Westpac. Intrinsically, Westpac is in favour of mergers to strengthen the organisation, as long as it doesn't destroy the culture.' Although Joss hadn't stormed out of the bank over a disagreement with the board, it is believed he was disappointed with the decision not to merge with NAB.

Business commentator Alan Kohler wrote in September 1998 that the benefit to bank shareholders would have been at least

$10 billion per merger if the four pillars policy had been removed: 'That's because if NAB and ANZ merged, management would be expected to cut at least $1 billion a year of costs out of the new group (about a third of ANZ's total costs). If combined revenue stayed the same profit would increase by that amount. Capitalise that extra profit at existing price–earnings ratios and the new whole is worth at least $10 billion more than the sum of the two parts.'

Kohler went on to say that all the other publicly stated reasons for having bank mergers, including to create 'national champions' that can compete globally, or just to satisfy the rampant egos of the executives, came a distant second to the money. 'Put simply, the prospect of creating more than $20 billion in new value for Australia's bank shareholders through two mergers that allow staff levels to be cut by another 30,000 or so is impossible to resist.'[7]

Yet resist they did. Argus left NAB without breaking the four pillars policy. It is a regret that lingers with him today. 'The frustrating thing is there was never a valid argument given to me as to why [overturning the policy] didn't make sense,' Argus says. 'It would have saved shareholders a lot of money on expensive technology initiatives, and the synergies would have been great.'

With the idea of dismantling the four pillars now on the back burner, vertical integration was about to be put on steroids.

Chapter 4

Bigger is better?

Incentives, targets – and deception

LESS THAN THREE MONTHS after taking over as chairman at CBA, John Ralph strode into Melbourne's prestigious Grand Hyatt, in the upmarket Paris end of Collins Street, with the company's CEO, David Murray, for a dinner that would change the course of Australian corporate history.

It was 10 February 2000 and Ralph and Murray had booked a private room in the swank hotel to discuss a friendly takeover of Colonial Mutual, the Melbourne-based company that had hit the headlines almost a decade before for its systemic mis-selling of life insurance products to vulnerable consumers. Over an eight-year period, Colonial Mutual's boss, Peter Smedley, had turned an old-fashioned, non-performing life insurance institution into a modern financial services powerhouse. Under Smedley's leadership Colonial had demutualised, listed on the stock market, spent billions of dollars snapping up small banks and life insurers, and pushed into the Asian market to create a sprawling empire. During that time, following its move into banking and the bolstering of its presence in superannuation, life insurance and investment products, Colonial had seen its customer base swell from 350,000 to more than three million. Smedley had been a trailblazer in the art of cross-selling financial products to customers. And he had built an empire that Murray now wanted.

Since becoming chief executive of CBA, Murray had gained the respect of the investment community for his cost-cutting. But he knew that if he was to keep growing the bank, its profit and its share price, he needed to make a spectacular and transformative acquisition. Six months earlier, he had hired corporate advisers to do the numbers on Colonial. Now it was time to strike.

The timing of the dinner was no accident. Days earlier, Smedley had indicated at a press conference that Colonial was interested in making a takeover bid for Bankwest. Murray believed that if Smedley bought Bankwest it would kill any chances he had of buying Colonial, an acquisition that would create the biggest financial services giant in the country and be the biggest corporate takeover in Australian history, with a likely offer price north of $8 billion.

Murray and Ralph waited patiently for the arrival of their dinner guests – the brash and confident Smedley, and Colonial's chairman, David Adam. They knew their offer for the insurance giant had to be generous enough that Smedley and Adam would find it hard to refuse. Still, they were aware it wouldn't be easy to win over Smedley, who had earned a reputation as a pugnacious and fierce negotiator and was likely to fight hard to keep Colonial in his grip.

Murray and Ralph's message to their dinner companions was clear: the two organisations together would create a financial leviathan that would dominate the Australian landscape. They promised that if CBA took over Colonial they would give Smedley a generous exit package from executive duties but allow him to stay on the new board.

By the end of the dinner Smedley and Adam had agreed to take a formal offer to the Colonial board the following week. When they did so, the board put the offer from CBA to one side and put out feelers for a better one, approaching NAB, ANZ and others who had expressed interest in buying Colonial. But the offers from the other banks were hastily put together and less attractive. CBA had offered seven of its shares, which were trading at $22, for twenty Colonial shares, which were trading at about $6. The offer was set at a healthy premium of more than 40 per cent, valuing the bid at $10 billion. Realising CBA's bid was the best, Smedley hopped on a plane to Sydney to close the deal.

The next step would be winning approval from the competition tsar Allan Fels. Murray and Smedley set up a meeting with Fels for 6 March 2000. Fels recalls Murray and Smedley walking into his office and both being fairly aggressive, particularly Murray. 'They wanted an urgent decision and I wasn't going to give it to them.'

Fels was familiar with Colonial and CBA. He was also familiar with the various leaks in the newspapers about an impending announcement. 'I knew the merger wouldn't raise any competition issues, but I made it clear I wasn't going to rush it,' he says. This was one of the biggest mergers ever and he didn't want to mess it up. The ACCC's decision would depend on whether merging CBA and Colonial would substantially reduce competition. It didn't have a mandate to go any further than that. That meant it couldn't look at whether the merger would result in inherent conflicts of interest that would be to the detriment of customers. Fels told Murray he would wait for CBA's official submission then make a decision eight weeks after that.

On the morning of 10 March 2000, Smedley and Murray held a press conference to unveil the deal. CBA's takeover of Colonial would displace NAB as Australia's biggest bank and AMP as Australia's biggest fund manager. Smiling like the cat that has just eaten the cream, Murray told the large gathering of journalists and banking analysts, 'The scale and breadth of the merged entity will result in strong growth in all aspects of financial services, increased choice for customers, expanded distribution channels and growth of international revenue.'[1]

He went on to pitch the merger as CBA becoming a 'full service' behemoth offering everything from retail banking to insurance and financial planning. He outlined what the impact of the transaction would be on the makeup of the bank. Traditional banking, including deposits and loans, in the newly merged group would account for about half of its activities, compared with 92 per cent previously. Insurance and funds management would account for about one-third of business, compared with 3 per cent previously.

'Over recent years, the Commonwealth Bank has been building towards these objectives, but the merger will help us to achieve that vision far more quickly than by organic growth,' he told the assembled journalists. 'We believe the imperative for stronger savings in Australia implies very strong growth prospects for funds management and superannuation.'

The message Murray was sending to the nation through the press was: 'If we sit here and do nothing, the Australian financial services industry will be a branch office of the rest of the world, and that is not acceptable.'

Murray was hailed as a hero. *The Australian*'s business commentator Mark Westfield wrote, 'Two men, two banks and too clever for their rivals.'[2] Another article in *The Australian*, headlined 'The Mega bank "good for the nation": Jobs to go, but chief defends deal', pitched the merger as being in the national interest because the combined group would have 'scale, efficiencies and scope of activities to provide more choice to more customers on a more cost-effective basis'.[3]

Other media and banking analysts wrote reports lauding Murray for his cost-cutting initiatives, which would make the new entity even more profitable: 2500 jobs were expected to go and there would be 450 branch closures. Warnings by the union that it would be devastating to rural jobs and services were barely acknowledged in media reports. If the banks could boost profits through cost-cutting or acquisitions, it would translate into share price gains. That, in turn, would feed into the burgeoning salary packages of senior executives, who were increasingly being judged on shareholder returns.

Three months after the bid was announced CBA's shares had jumped almost $6 to $28 a share. The apparent success of the CBA–Colonial merger opened the floodgates for other acquisitions as the investment community put pressure on ANZ, NAB and Westpac to follow suit. A month after CBA's deal with Colonial was completed, NAB announced a $4.5 billion merger with MLC. AMP was also on the prowl for major purchases, as were Westpac and ANZ.

*

Smedley wasn't about to play second fiddle to Murray. After the CBA deal, he picked up a $15 million payout and an annual life pension of $840,000. He decided not to take a seat on the board.

Peter Beck, an actuary who was head of strategy at Colonial and part of the team that had sold Colonial to CBA, stayed on and headed the life insurance division newly rebranded as CommInsure. Beck recalls being surprised when CBA's head of human resources asked him whether he was 'crafty'. 'I'm South African, and crafty has a certain meaning and connotation of being dishonest, underhanded, even deceitful. I said if you're asking me am I smart, the answer is yes. But it struck me as a very unusual question to put to someone,' he remembers.

Beck saw a lot of 'craftiness' at CBA during his five-year stint, and was particularly struck by the focus of executives on the fortunes of CBA's share price, shattering any illusions that the selection of appropriate products for customers factored into their decision-making. 'They would take a lot of costs out of the business just to grow the share price,' he says. Often that meant reducing the numbers of risk-assessment and compliance staff. 'Everything was about the impact on the share price.' The reward system for senior executives at CBA also heavily influenced the culture: 'They became "crafty" at finding ways to enhance profits to the detriment of customers and staff.'

According to Beck, CBA lawyers had a lot of power and influence. 'I remember the head of legal telling me how close he was to Murray, which was essentially a message not to mess with him because it would get right back to Murray,' Beck recalls. 'It was a very litigious culture.'

Consequently, CommInsure was always ready to fight insurance claims. Says Beck, 'They were [often] just small claims that customers believed they were covered for, but there were technical angles in the contract we could use to avoid paying.' In particular, home and contents insurance claims were frequently referred to the legal department.

In 2005, Beck was ushered into a meeting and told his position had been terminated, after twenty-four years with Colonial and CommInsure. The way a company treats its staff on the way out says a lot about its culture. CBA offered Beck a resignation benefit equivalent to his own 5 per cent contribution with interest, as opposed to the 10 per cent contribution the company had made all those years. In dollar terms, he would receive $1.5 million instead of $4.5 million. CBA did this on the basis that Beck was fifty-three when he was terminated, and he would only officially become eligible for his entitlements when he reached fifty-five – despite the fact it was standard practice to grant full entitlements after ten years' service.

Gutted at what CommInsure had done, Beck wrote to the head of human resources, then the fund trustees, then the external complaints body the Superannuation Complaints Tribunal – all without success. He then wrote to the new chief executive of CBA, Ralph Norris, asking him to pay his due benefits and saying, 'It is hard for me to understand how after twenty-four years of service I am expected to be content with around one-third of my full entitlement.' Norris wrote back, replying that while he had 'carefully considered' Beck's letter he was unable to meet his request.

Beck eventually launched action in the NSW Supreme Court and won his case in 2015. But before he could pop the champagne, CBA lodged an appeal, which Beck lost in April 2016. APRA had – to Beck's astonishment – backed him by writing a letter of support that set out how CBA had incorrectly interpreted 'accrued benefits'. But it turned out to be useless, because APRA failed to follow up by giving evidence or joining the case, which meant that the court wouldn't let Beck use the APRA letter.

The battle cost Beck $600,000 in legal fees. Now in his sixties, Beck is still negotiating a cost settlement with CBA. He has to pay the bank's estimated $1.2 million court costs.

*

One of the first things CBA did was merge its funds management business, Commonwealth Investment Management, with Colonial First State, which manufactured financial products such as property funds, managed share funds and super funds. Colonial First State was run by funds management guru Chris Cuffe, who after joining Colonial First State in 1993 had built it into one of the top three entities in the investment industry, boosting funds under management from $100 million to more than $50 billion.

With its newly expanded base of ten million customers and a greater range of products, CBA began installing commission-driven life insurance brokers and financial planners inside bank branches. This vertical integration enabled the aggressive cross-selling of financial products to millions of loyal banking customers. Fees were based on funds under management rather than how much value was added to the funds, and were charged at every stage of every process. More than ever, the mantra was sell, sell, sell.

While Colonial was already renowned for its entrenched sales-driven culture based on commissions, fees and incentives – Smedley prided himself on measuring the number of products per customer that the business could sell – what was less well known was that CBA had also been working towards a similar culture from as far back as 1995. Intent on increasing sales and cutting costs to make bigger profits, Murray had introduced a sales system developed by US consultancy Cohen Brown, which pitched itself as providing the banking industry with a 'new' way to sell customers more financial products.

Staff were coached in the Cohen Brown method via extensive video training and manuals. They were told that selling wasn't something to switch on or off, it had to be all-pervasive. Tellers were encouraged to spend more time with customers, spruiking them as many new products as they could. One Cohen Brown manual stipulated: 'Always discover and sell to unknown needs. Simply asking a client "Is there anything else I can do for you?" is totally insufficient as a mechanism of helping clients and increasing cross-sells. Nine out of ten times the answer is no. Rarely will [clients] call you if anything changes in their financial lives even though they promised to do so. Leave nothing to chance. Practice the Cohen Brown rule on an ongoing and continuous basis … [and] become a financial missionary for your markets.'[4]

The strategy caught on at other banks. Andrew J. Macey, who runs specialist finance services at Westpac, worked at NAB in the mid-1990s when the Cohen Brown method was introduced there too. In August 2017 in a LinkedIn article titled 'When incentives go wrong' he discussed the impact of Cohen Brown on the culture inside NAB. He recalled regular gatherings around a TV for training videos. 'I remember Cohen [Brown] exhorting that "I had the power and the responsibility!" It felt, so … foreign … so … um … American?'[5] In 2003, Cohen Brown's website featured a review from Trevor Eddy, then head of sales development at NAB, saying: 'Referrals increased by 1000 per week, with a 42 per cent increase in lending sales, a 19 per cent increase in deposit sales, in a very tough market, and a 36 per cent increase in insurance and risk sales.'[6]

Few disputed the impact of Cohen Brown on improving sales and increasing profits. But in the hands of Australia's big banks, it was used to create a culture of aggressive selling that too often resulted in poor outcomes for customers. Such single-minded focus could lead to a lack of oversight elsewhere. In 2003, it was revealed that a CBA branch manager in Karratha, WA, Kim David Faithfull, had systematically stolen $20 million from the branch's general ledger account between 1998 and August 2003.

Every two weeks representatives from the bank's area office had visited the branch to check that the sales and service techniques were being implemented. But they were so concerned with sales that they completely missed the fraud. Justice Kevin Hammond, the chief judge of the WA District Court told the court he found it 'curious' that CBA hadn't noticed the money missing until a suicidal Faithfull left a note for staff members, admitting his crimes.[7]

Another branch manager, who quit after CBA bought Colonial, recalls how CBA rewarded a bank teller who beat sales targets each week, unaware that this was being achieved through deception. 'She received awards and movie tickets because she consistently opened twenty-plus new accounts each week,' the former manager says. 'She might have a brief conversation with clients to ask if they wanted whatever new style of account that was being flogged at the time. The customers would politely decline, but this woman would open the accounts anyway without a signature and deposit her own funds. Sales targets were exceeded, and she was the sales hero. It all unravelled when a client received their first statements and came into the branch to advise they had never opened the account and asked who put the $2 in to open it.'[8]

While high-flying executives drew massive salaries thanks to the huge inflows of funds from compulsory superannuation, bank tellers not only struggled to meet monthly sales targets, but also faced the constant threat of job cuts. CBA's 'Which New Bank' program closed yet more branches and slashed 3700 jobs, to achieve savings of $1.5 billion. One of those who lost her job was branch manager Ann O'Farrell. In a controversial cover story in *BRW*, she described the culture. 'Every bank has customer service targets; they are part of the business,' O'Farrell said. 'But I would say in the Commonwealth Bank they are being grossly misused. People in the bank think about targets, not the service.'[9]

The branch closures resulted in a series of staff strikes, but Murray was defiant, telling *BRW*, 'This is the most important change at the bank since privatisation a decade ago. If we deliver on this, we will be the most competitive bank in the country.' When Murray stepped down as CEO in 2005, the company's shares were trading at a record high of $42. In just over a decade he had taken CBA 'from a partly privatised company with a market capitalisation of $6 billion in 1992 to a fully integrated financial services provider with a market capitalisation of around $50 billion in 2005. Shareholder value has grown … with Total Shareholder Returns (including gross dividend payments) of more than 24 per cent per annum (compound annual growth).'[10] Hawke and Keating would no doubt have seen CBA's spectacular growth as a vindication of their decision to turn the people's bank over to the private sector.[11]

By now the banks not only dominated the wealth management industry but their massively increased market values meant they also ruled the Australian stock market, accounting for a third of a typical balanced Australian equities portfolio. The banks' power was supreme, and the rising batch of executives and boards knew it and thrived on it. Arrogance and a sense of infallibility ran riot.

*

Ralph Norris succeeded Murray as chief executive at CBA in 2005. Like Murray, Norris was a 'true believer' in the Cohen Brown sales model, and wasted no time in what he described as 'reinvigorating' it.

The New Zealand–born Norris had been the managing director and CEO of CBA's New Zealand subsidiary ASB Bank from 1991 to 2001, during which time the company had expanded its footprint across New Zealand and grown 'its profitability six-fold and increased market share by 60 per cent'.[12] Norris attributed part of his success to the Cohen Brown model, which he introduced to the bank in 1994. He liked to point out that ASB's level of cross-selling was more than double CBA's.

One of his first moves as CEO of CBA was to hire Cohen Brown to review service levels and sales. 'We are not achieving the customer service levels that we had anticipated,' he told the media and investors in his first month after taking the top job. 'I'm taking that very seriously.' In other words, not enough products were being cross-sold to customers, largely because staff hadn't fully embraced Cohen Brown.

When releasing a record half-year profit in February 2006, Norris again spoke about Cohen Brown, telling analysts and the media that the Cohen Brown mantra was 'not so much about sales targets [but] about actually being able to satisfactorily meet the needs of our customers through stronger needs analysis'. He noted that CBA's share of business lending had fallen by one-third in the previous decade, due to an inability to 'initiate customer leads', along with some other issues relating to the centralisation of loan approvals. To change that, everyone at CBA needed to embrace the Cohen Brown method. When Norris released a new blueprint for CBA on 31 March 2006, he claimed the changes would deliver profitable market-share growth, productivity improvements and higher dividends.

As NAB and CBA further absorbed the Cohen Brown mindset, they adopted its concept of 'Onebankism', which aimed to break down traditional silos within banks. Under Onebankism, bank tellers and other bank employees were required to refer customers to other parts of the business, such as private banking, business banking, financial planning or life insurance. At CBA, the CEO and top executives were front and centre of this new approach and Cohen Brown reported that it 'moved quickly down and out through the ranks, gathering energy and sweeping the entire organization into its reach'.[13]

Bank staff had to attend meetings each morning and give a commitment to the group to achieve their targets. A 'debrief' meeting was held each afternoon. Some former CBA employees later reported that when staff didn't achieve their targets they were belittled in front of colleagues. One bank employee says managers patrolled the work area like stormtroopers to make sure staff were pushing products to customers at every opportunity. Some bank staff felt the training was a form of brainwashing.

By 2007, the feedback from CBA staff in Financial Services Union surveys was alarming. Only 15 per cent thought management had realistic expectations about targets. A massive 80 per cent didn't believe they could reasonably expect to achieve their targets. When asked if their work–life balance suffered because of targets, 75 per cent either agreed or strongly agreed. The question 'I don't feel pressured to make inappropriate sales to try and meet my targets' produced a result of 33 per cent disagreeing and 32 per cent strongly disagreeing, which was higher than the average across all banks. Even more worrying was the response to a question about whether 'targets bring out the best in me' – 83 per cent of respondents disagreed. Furthermore, 26 per cent of those surveyed admitted they were aware of inappropriate lending practices being undertaken to achieve targets.

I first came across the impact of Cohen Brown in 2013 when I wrote a series of articles about the aggressive sales at CBA. The series triggered hundreds of responses from CBA staff. Many described it as a cult-like sales technique that placed staff under intolerable pressure and resulted in serious mistakes. One former employee who'd left CBA in the early 2000s recalled branch staff going home and leaving the strong room open because they were too engrossed in their end-of-day sales debrief meeting. 'Tellers' errors went through the roof,' he said. 'A quick and accurate balance of the cash at the end of the day was for years the standard tellers aspired to. Now it was about how many new business referrals you got and whether you got your target for the day, forget about balancing the cash; cash was left out at night, customers' deposits were lost and nobody cared. It was all about the tellers getting referrals and meeting targets. Tellers who failed to reach their referral targets were managed out of the bank.' Some CBA staff suffered nervous breakdowns and some started taking antidepressant medication.

The Cohen Brown method featured so heavily in CBA's strategy during Ralph Norris's reign that I decided to contact the company's co-founder and CEO, Marty Cohen, in late 2018. I wanted to talk to him about the Cohen Brown method, including a patent filed in 2006 titled, 'Systems and methods for computerised interactive training', which contains an example of a telephone script that physiologically conditions staff to respond in a certain way. The patent talks about supplying a positive tone and visualisation when the right answer is achieved and a negative tone and visualisation when the answer is wrong. 'A positive tone is generated and/or a text acknowledgement appears, indicating that the correct phrase was identified by the trainee,' the patent says. 'Then a "negative tone" is played, and a graphic and/or text message is provided, indicating that the answer was incorrect.' The user is scored 'based in part on the number of errors and/or opportunities that the user identified and optionally on the user's response to the question'.

In an email exchange, Cohen told me he is no longer using this type of 'methodology', but he doesn't think there is anything wrong with the practice of 'negative reinforcement'. 'Any director or choreographer in the performing arts clearly tells the performers when they have done it right or they have done it wrong,' he said. 'If people are not aware of their incorrect behaviours, etc, then they cannot possibly change them because they don't know that the behaviours are indeed problematic.'

Cohen believes the insurance and financial planning malfeasance that occurred at CBA had nothing to do with Cohen Brown. 'The bottom line is that I stand by my comments to you that Cohen Brown had absolutely nothing to do with the egregious financial activities that occurred at CBA or any other bank in Australia,' he said. 'It is the duty of bankers to CREATE AWARENESS of opportunities. This has nothing to do with product pushing … instead it is simply about creating awareness.'

Cohen asserts that his company has been 'erroneously besmirched in the Australian press, where it was stated that we created "aggressive sales cultures". We have never used the word "aggressive" in any of our literature or presentations because we absolutely do not believe in being aggressive with customers. We believe in helping customers and caring about customers by first understanding their needs before offering solutions.'

Whatever the case, an aggressive sales culture and an army of financial planners and bank tellers who were pushed to cross-sell products created perfect conditions for conflicts of interest and misconduct to fester. As long as the sharemarket boomed, inappropriate advice went undetected. But during downturns, such as the dot com bust and the Global Financial Crisis (GFC), flawed business models and dodgy advice would be exposed.

Chapter 5

Giving with one hand ...

Misleading advice and margin calls

ON 20 JANUARY 2009, Senator John 'Wacka' Williams swung his car into the Golden Ox restaurant in Margate, a north-eastern suburb of Brisbane. Five days earlier, CBA had put a financial advice company called Storm Financial, run by husband and wife team Emmanuel and Julie Cassimatis, into receivership to recover corporate debts of $10 million. It was a minuscule amount, given that CBA's action would ultimately leave more than three thousand investors, mostly retirees, exposed to losses – and debts – of $3 billion. CBA had been the largest lender to the many elderly clients who had signed up to the Storm Financial business model and without its backing Storm would never have grown to the size it did.

Wacka had been asked to address a meeting of the victims of Storm Financial's collapse by John McLennan, the former Westpac Bank executive turned whistleblower who'd helped Wacka when he was a victim of CBA's foreign currency loan scandal a decade earlier. Tired and hot after driving six hours from his home in Inverell, Wacka thought back to meetings he'd attended twenty years earlier as a victim of the CBA foreign currency loan scandal.

He braced himself for the worst before entering the restaurant. He'd missed dramatic scenes earlier in the day when the owner of the Golden Ox had called the police and an ambulance to come to the restaurant in an attempt to contain the highly stressed crowd of retirees.

Inside the Golden Ox, Wacka was confronted by crowds of deeply distressed Storm Financial victims, some of the women hysterical and the men trying not to choke up. 'There must have been about four hundred people who turned up to hear me talk,' Wacka recalls. 'These people were in their sixties and seventies and were facing eviction from their homes onto the streets after working hard all their lives.'

Their worlds had been turned upside down the previous month when CBA, sweating over the GFC and having to digest the $2.1 billion acquisition of Bankwest it had made in October, told hundreds of Storm Financial clients who held margin loans that the bank had made a margin call and sold their holdings in Storm Index Funds. Some were told the value of their funds – in many cases, their entire life savings – had fallen so much they were now worth less than the debt they owed on them. Most didn't understand what was going on.

A margin loan allows an investor to borrow money for investments, using the purchased equities as security. Such products are not for the faint-hearted – although they can help investors increase their returns, they can also magnify their losses. For example, if the value of the equities drops significantly, the lender can make a margin call, which requires the borrower to put more money into the account to cover the loss. If clients can't inject the extra cash, they are forced to sell some of their shares. Normally, a margin call occurs only when the value of the equities in the portfolio falls below a set amount, at which point, by law, the borrower must be notified and given the opportunity to top up the account. In the case of Storm, however, the margin call had happened as much as six weeks earlier – without the clients' knowledge.

'In layman's terms, the banks simply sold these people's portfolios down without prior warning, snuffing out their income streams and forcing many distressed investors to sell their family homes in order to meet their [loan] commitments to the bank,' Wacka says. 'Many Storm clients could easily have met their margin lending commitments if they'd been given the basic courtesy of a phone call to alert them that they needed to top up their account. If margin calls had been made in a professional and orderly manner, most of these investors would be watching their portfolios performing strongly today (given the market's rally since then) rather than staring at financial ruin.'

Wacka told the meeting that probably the best he could do was arrange a Senate inquiry into what had gone wrong and how it could be fixed.

*

Wacka's fight with CBA had been one of the worst periods in his life and destroyed his marriage. But he was never going to stay down long: he had set up his own business selling nuts and bolts to farmers and met his soul mate, Nancy Capel, a journalist who owns independent newspaper *The Bingara Advocate*, based in northern NSW.

In the years after his battle with CBA, Wacka had secretly dreamed about running for office but never had a chance to act on it. He'd joined the National Party in 1982 and increased his involvement in the party over the years. Then in April 2006,

aged fifty-three, Wacka told Nancy he wanted to run for the
Australian Senate. He entered Federal Parliament on 1 July 2008,
during the GFC.

Wacka had been a federal senator for only a few months when
he fronted the Golden Ox meeting. One of the main reasons
he'd become a politician was to help battlers and small businesses,
just as Australian Democrats Senator Paul McLean had done two
decades earlier. A few days after the Margate meeting, Wacka
invited McLean, who was living in virtual seclusion in Tasmania,
to Inverell to help him get his head around Storm.

It soon became apparent that Storm had been built on a
flawed business model and the banks, including CBA, Macquarie,
Westpac and Bank of Queensland, were complicit in its collapse,
as they had facilitated the loans and margin lending facilities.
The investors had been encouraged by Storm Financial advisers
to mortgage their homes or superannuation in order to generate
a lump sum to invest in the sharemarket via Storm-badged
Colonial First State managed funds and Storm-badged Challenger
managed funds. Clients were then advised to take out margin
loans to increase the size of their investment portfolios. This one-
size-fits-all advice model based on getting new clients into debt or
persuading existing ones to go even further into debt proved to be
highly inappropriate for the retirees, who should never have been
put into such risky products. Many lost everything and ended up
owing a fortune.

'If you had a million-dollar house and you owned it you could
borrow half a million dollars from Colonial, then you might
borrow another $2 million and invest it in Storm index funds, and
the earnings off those shares or index funds would [theoretically]
pay your interest on the loans, plus give you $50,000 a year to
retire on,' Wacka says. 'And of course, Storm [and] Cassimatis

76

got tens of thousands of dollars for every client they took on.' Clients were charged a hefty upfront fee of 7 per cent of the total geared amount as well as trailing commissions – commissions that continued after the investments had been made. For the Cassimatis family, the fees helped build a lavish empire, including a private jet and a five-storey mansion with Waterford crystal chandeliers, lifts, swimming pools and panoramic views over Magnetic Island. Before the GFC hit, their estimated wealth was $450 million.

The Cassimatises shared some of the spoils with Storm's best clients. Annual cruises to exotic places became legendary and were subsidised by the banks and other sponsors. Investors were whisked off for two weeks to Europe, Alaska and Canada, or South Africa. The trips were designed to promote the success of the business and attract more investors. They also highlighted the close relationship with the big gorillas of the financial world, including CBA, whose representatives would often attend the events.

While the market was rising, everything went well. When the sharemarket tanked, the strategy unravelled. As the value of Storm index-fund investments plunged below the equity level required to maintain the margin loans, CBA pounced, putting Storm into receivership and calling in the loans. Thousands of ordinary Australians were affected – including the many retirees persuaded by Storm to invest. They lost savings, businesses and homes – some of them were forced to live in tents, caravans, even pre-fabs beneath the elevated Queensland homes of their children. Some died early or committed suicide.

The *Financial Review*'s Duncan Hughes later travelled to Townsville to cover the Storm Financial collapse and interviewed many victims, including Steve Reynolds, a Vietnam War veteran on a totally and permanently incapacitated annual pension of

$30,000 per year. 'Over a glass of beer in a backroom of the Townsville RSL Club, the father of two daughters explained how his home and income were geared to $1.2 million through a combination of a Bank of Queensland home loan and a Colonial margin loan,' Hughes recalls. 'The documents were prepared by Storm and he was told where to sign in a ten-minute signing session conducted at its nearby headquarters.'

Like so many Storm victims, Reynolds had no financial experience and was hoping to provide some security for his children. He was sixty when he signed the deal in 2008; within six months, he had lost $420,000 in borrowed money and had to put up his home for sale. He moved to a hut in Bali in late 2016, after losing everything and finding it too expensive to live in Queensland.

Phil Green, a forty-seven-year-old public servant, married with two young children, earning $46,000 a year, ended up with debts of $1.8 million courtesy of CBA. The home loan application prepared by Storm failed to take into account the interest payable on his six-figure margin loan. Jack Dale, an air-worthiness controller and his wife, Frances, a school teacher, retired in 2002 in Cairns. In 2004 their financial planner moved to Storm and advised them to invest their super funds of $340,000 and apply for a $260,000 margin loan with CBA's Colonial Mutual, bringing their total investment in Storm to $600,000. They were then advised to take out an additional loan on their family home. It was the first time they had invested in the sharemarket. By November 2007, their margin loan exposure was $1.8 million. At the age of seventy-two, they lost their home and were forced onto Centrelink payments. 'We are on the edge of disaster if anything untoward, such as a health issue, should happen; if that were to come up we do not know how we would handle it,' Jack Dale told a parliamentary hearing in September 2009.

Misconduct, particularly in relation to valuations and risk management, was rampant across Storm and CBA. As was later revealed in an affidavit lodged with a parliamentary inquiry into Storm Financial, one former Storm employee who had worked in the Aitkenvale branch in Townsville claimed that a vacant suburban block in the outback township of Charters Towers in Queensland was revalued by CBA's computerised property valuation system, VAS, in March 2008, at $350,000 – just eight months after another valuation had priced it at $50,000. The tiny Aitkenvale branch became CBA's biggest home loan writer in the country, as staff overstated income and asset values to make customers eligible for bigger loans than they could afford. Some customers claimed documents had been forged so that they could be shifted to higher-risk investments.[1]

Sadly, the regulator had been too slow to act. At least two months before Storm collapsed, ASIC had been told the company was in serious trouble and that investors faced heavy losses. ASIC obtained a letter written by Cassimatis instructing investors to dump Storm index funds and switch to cash. The peak lobby group, the Financial Planning Association (FPA), also obtained the letter and quickly launched an inquiry that resulted in Storm's expulsion as a member. But ASIC didn't start an investigation until December 2008. By then the markets had plummeted further, CBA had called in its margin loans, and it was too late to help Storm investors.

*

I was working at *The Australian*'s Melbourne bureau as the Storm scandal unfolded, and was appalled by the behaviour of both Storm and CBA, and by the heartbreaking stories of Storm clients. But another scandal was waiting to be uncovered closer to home.

Tricom and Opes Prime were two relatively large and well-known stockbroker firms that touted a variation on margin lending, known as securities lending. Their operations were largely facilitated through ANZ's equity finance business. Unlike a margin loan, where the investor at least owns the shares they've borrowed to buy, a securities loan strips away the investor's beneficial ownership of the shares, leaving the client as an unsecured creditor, behind the banks, if the stockbroker hits financial trouble. The attraction is that the securities loans allow investors to leverage small-cap, high-risk stocks that would be excluded from margin loans. But most of Tricom's and Opes Prime's clients didn't realise they had signed up for securities lending rather than a margin loan.

Tricom hit the skids in late January 2008 – the beginning of the GFC – after the sharemarket plunged 5 per cent, triggering margin calls among its 29,000 clients. Tricom's main creditors, largely ANZ, panicked and froze $1.5 billion in assets held by the broker. Tricom was forced to dump shares on the sharemarket so that ANZ, as the secured creditor, could retrieve its money. An insider was feeding me information about the pandemonium going on, which I then reported on.[2] Selling such a large number of shares in an already volatile market wreaked havoc, and thousands of investors were hit with margin calls as the share price of smaller stocks went into free fall.

Tricom's problems undermined confidence in Opes Prime, as they both offered a similar product, had a similar legal structure, shared the same financiers and did business together. In March 2008 Opes Prime collapsed as ANZ moved to rapidly sell the stockbroker's share portfolio, exposing more than 1200 clients to huge losses. Twenty-three companies were placed in trading halts while they rushed to find buyers to prevent their share prices collapsing.

Adding to the intrigue was the fact that Opes Prime was the broker of choice for the criminal underworld. When it collapsed, some shady figures began to emerge, including figures linked to money laundering, sharemarket manipulation and other illegal practices. Back in 2006, ANZ had made the fateful decision to extend its share lending facilities beyond the blue chips and members of the ASX200 to all ASX-listed shares. Previously, margin lending had only been used with blue-chip stocks such as BHP Billiton and the banks, but there was no law to enforce this and, as with the US sub-prime mess, financial engineers started targeting small-cap stocks, which were easier to manipulate. This opened up opportunities to invest in the bottom end of the market.

Colourful Melbourne identity Mick Gatto flew to Singapore in a bid to find more than $1 billion worth of assets some of his clients believed were hidden by Opes Prime. 'I have a good track record of tracking things down,' Gatto told me. 'You can run but you can't hide, and you can quote me on that.'[3] Nobody ever got to the bottom of what Gatto was up to, but his involvement turned the spotlight on Opes Prime and what it had been doing, all under the auspices of one of the biggest banks in the country, ANZ.

Two of Opes Prime's founders, Laurie Emini and Anthony Blumberg, were jailed in 2011 for breaches of directors' duties over their role in the collapse. ASIC entered an enforceable undertaking with ANZ and Merrill Lynch, to enable 1200 Opes Prime creditors to receive thirty-seven cents in the dollar. In return, ASIC wiped the slate clean on all pending and future litigation against ANZ and Merrill Lynch. ASIC did the deal before it had even completed its investigations into Opes Prime.

*

Covering the GFC was like riding a rollercoaster every day, as more revelations came out about the failings of the global banking system, largely driven by the greed of banks and other financial institutions and enabled by lax regulators. The entire financial system was over-leveraged – meaning loans were secured by undervalued stock – but nobody seemed to have seen the crash coming.

At the time, I was regularly ringing close contacts, including banking analyst Brett Le Mesurier, for his company's take on the collapse of the major financial services company Lehman Brothers and what it meant in the Australian context. The message I was getting was that Macquarie Bank was bearing the brunt of the market's concern. Its shares had fallen 7 per cent – a substantial decline, but not catastrophic.

The real activity was happening in the credit markets. Subordinated debt – debt that ranks below other loans or securities in the event of a company collapse – ended the day of the Lehman crash at 500 basis points, or 5 per cent. (In financial markets, interest rates are described in terms of basis points, where 100 basis points is equivalent to 1 per cent.) Macquarie's senior debt – debt which is senior within a company's capital structure and is therefore first to be repaid ahead of bond and equity investors – soared to a spread of 320 basis points. That meant Macquarie would have to pay increasingly higher prices to persuade investors to buy its debt – the lifeblood of any financial institution – if the crisis continued. In comparison, Citigroup's senior debt was trading at an interest rate spread of 300 basis points, while J.P. Morgan's senior debt was trading at a spread of 200 basis points. The high interest spread on Macquarie's debt was a clear sign that investors were worried that Macquarie was carrying too much risk on its balance sheet.

The response of the credit markets to Macquarie's debt, coupled with a report Le Mesurier had written two months earlier on Macquarie's funding profile, prompted me to write a column in *The Australian* warning: 'The reality is that by March next year Macquarie needs to refinance $45 billion of debt. While most of it will be relatively easy, more than $5 billion could prove difficult to get away at a decent price and decent length of time.'[4]

On the same day, Macquarie issued a statement to the ASX trying to calm investor concerns by suggesting the article was false. ASIC also issued a statement to say that it was looking into alleged false rumours about a number of companies, including Macquarie Group. 'Pushing false rumours designed to harm a company, such as by forcing a share price down, is illegal,' it said.[5] The practice was known as 'rumourtrage'.

At 1.30 pm that day, Le Mesurier told me he'd received a call from the compliance department of his employer to say that ASIC investigators wanted to talk to him as soon as possible. They organised a time of 3 pm that day.

Le Mcsurier was taken aback by the speed of ASIC's approach, particularly given his research had used Macquarie's own disclosures on their funding profile. During the meeting, he was asked what his analysis was based on; he explained that he'd thought Macquarie's disclosures did not put sufficient focus on their reliance on short-term funding. He was also asked about my article, specifically how I had come by his report and the reason I had written the column. He was further surprised when a journalist from the *Financial Review* rang him later that day and asked him about the ASIC interview, even mentioning the time of 3 pm. The meeting was supposed to have been confidential, but someone was clearly keen for it to be leaked.

The whole point of my story was that if Macquarie was to continue its operations in the same manner, then refinancing would be an issue. The fact that the Australian Government subsequently guaranteed the debt of Australian financial institutions shows those fears were well founded.

The reaction to my column provided me with my first lesson in the close relationship between the regulator and the banks. Here was ASIC, the slow, timid regulator when it came to the banks' misconduct in the case of the Storm Financial victims – yet it could respond on the same day to a negative article on Macquarie.

It was also my first real taste of the role of the media in protecting the banks. Eric Beecher, the co-publisher of online newspaper *Crikey* wrote an op-ed piece lambasting my article as 'highly speculative, highly questionable, highly irresponsible and highly damaging'. He went on to say, '*The Australian* and its owner could be singly responsible for undermining confidence in Australia's largest investment bank and, as a result, in the Australian financial marketplace.'[6] It was a surprising attack.

What Beecher left out was that Macquarie – whose shares had, by then, plunged 38 per cent to their lowest level in five years – was a major sponsor of his other online website, *Business Spectator*. Greg Baxter, the media adviser to News Ltd, which owns *The Australian*, wrote in a letter to *Crikey* that was published on their website, '*Crikey* was incredibly agitated yesterday about coverage in *The Australian* of one of Eric Beecher's advertisers, Macquarie Bank.' He said 'coming to the defence of an advertiser is admirable in management, but not such a good look editorially'.[7]

Former *Crikey* editor Stephen Mayne then weighed in, writing a separate *Crikey* piece in which he called my article 'reckless', saying, 'In the current environment you just can't say a bank has $45 billion repayable in nine months if it's not true.'[8] He went on to write in his Mayne Report, '*The Australian* has been running a vicious campaign against Macquarie ... and for the past three days the paper has been recklessly fear mongering about its financial strength.'[9]

J.P. Morgan then published a report saying Macquarie had $46 billion of borrowings that it needed to refinance within a year. Beecher was silent on that one.

Over the following days, the rumour mill went into overdrive. Stories emerged that I was being investigated by ASIC for 'rumourtrage'. A major market integrity investigation known as Project Mint was established, focusing on false rumours and their effect on market prices. It was spearheaded by a senior ASIC commissioner, Belinda Gibson.

The rumours settled down and everyone got on with their business until a story appeared in the Fairfax papers on 14 January 2009 suggesting ASIC had stepped up its investigation into 'false rumours spread last year about the financial position of Macquarie Group'.[10]

In an attempt to get some answers and an insight into ASIC and why it had so quickly launched an investigation into me, I lodged a Freedom of Information request to ASIC in December 2018. The FOI request confirmed that ASIC had launched its investigation on the same day my story was published. Most of the documents were redacted, including who had made the allegation that I had committed a criminal offence. They revealed that on 24 September 2008 Belinda Gibson and five ASIC investigators had held a meeting to discuss me and the article and the findings of one of its staff, Dennis Ho, who had analysed the numbers underpinning my article. He had determined that it was based on credible evidence. A decision was made at that meeting to drop the case.

I also discovered through the FOI process that a high-profile journalist had been actively forwarding my Macquarie articles to Gibson. It made two things clear to me: ASIC could act decisively when it suited its agenda and the media had a lot to answer for when it came to protecting the banks.

The collapse of Tricom, Opes Prime, Storm Financial and other financial organisations showed that the world of banking hadn't changed since the foreign currency loan scandal that embroiled all the banks. In all these cases there were attempts to play down the scandals, even cover them up.

*

When parliament returned from the summer break on 11 February 2009, Wacka Williams fulfilled the promise he'd made to the gathering at the Golden Ox in Margate and sought a notice of motion in the Senate to establish a parliamentary inquiry, which was successful. Labor was in government and decided to take it out of Wacka's hands, appoint Bernie Ripoll as the chair, and run it in the Parliamentary Joint Committee on Corporations and Financial Services. The inquiry had a mandate to investigate recent financial collapses including Storm and Opes Prime, and the roles of CBA, ANZ and ASIC in those events.

As the inquiry wrapped up on 23 November 2009, Wacka gave a speech in parliament that summed up his feelings: 'My time on this committee inquiry has left me with indelible memories of the wholesale human suffering experienced by the victims of these corporate collapses ... The victims of the Storm collapse can never be adequately compensated for the anguish, heartache, anxiety and psychological suffering they have been forced to endure. Sadly, suicides and threats of suicide have been part of the fallout from the collapse of Storm Financial.'[11]

By that time, law firms dealing with class actions had waded in and launched actions against CBA, Bank of Queensland, Macquarie and others. CBA paid out compensation of $270 million, Macquarie Bank agreed to pay $82.5 million to victims and the Bank of Queensland signed off on a $17 million compensation deal for victims of Storm.

*

It took the justice system another eight years to finalise proceedings against the owners of Storm Financial. In March 2018, Emmanuel and Julie Cassimatis were each fined $70,000 for breaching their directors' duties and disqualified from managing corporations until 2025. An ASIC press release reported, 'It draws to a close ASIC's Storm-related litigation, which has included investors receiving compensation in relation to losses suffered on investments made through Storm.'[12]

It might have been over for ASIC, but it wasn't for anyone else. A month later, Cassimatis filed an appeal, which was heard in February 2019 before the Federal Court, which reserved its judgement. Emmanuel and Julie Cassimatis told Tony Raggatt at the *Townsville Bulletin* their fight was 'just beginning'. 'I promised my clients that I would battle for them and ourselves till my last breath and I have been doing that,' Emmanuel Cassimatis said, adding that the appeal would be fought on the basis that Storm had been solvent and as directors he and Julie had acted honestly and in accordance with the wishes of shareholders.[13]

Chapter 6

Profit before people

Unmasking CBA's rogue planners

JEFF MORRIS WAS DESPERATE. His wife was ill and he needed a stress-free job close to home to help look after his young children. A job as a financial planner at the local Mosman branch of Commonwealth Financial Planning seemed ideal.

He was overqualified for the role, having worked in a number of high-powered jobs in his twenty-five-year career, including as vice president of investment bank Bankers Trust, but this was not the time to focus on his career. In any case, it was March 2008, financial markets were still performing well, CBA was hugely profitable and its reputation was unblemished. What could go wrong?

A lot, as it turned out. A month earlier, on 29 February 2008, ASIC had written a damning letter to Tim Gunning, the general manager of wealth management at Commonwealth Financial Planning and Financial Wisdom, after conducting surveillance over a six-month period in 2007. The letter said ASIC had interviewed senior staff and reviewed 496 examples of advice selected at random from fifty-one financial planning representatives. Of those fifty-one representatives, it had rated thirty-eight as 'critical'.[1]

For an adviser to attract a 'critical' rating, there had to be evidence of 'fraud and dishonest conduct', 'deliberate or reckless failure to disclose fees, costs, charges, relationship and warnings' and 'no evidence of appropriate advice'. In response, CBA had dismissed twelve of the thirty-eight representatives and reported seven to ASIC, ASIC's letter to Gunning noted. That meant it had kept twenty-six dishonest advisers on its payroll. Given it was a sample of fifty-one advisers, it should have raised alarm bells that the division had systemic issues.

ASIC said there seemed to be a 'correlation' between the amount of business that representatives wrote and CBA not terminating their employment. In other words, if a star adviser did the wrong thing, the bank turned a blind eye.

What was even more worrying than the nondisclosure of fees and commissions and the poor record-keeping was the fact that, according to ASIC, CBA's compliance framework 'wasn't adequately detecting serious misconduct'. ASIC was 'particularly concerned about the findings from this surveillance, given many of them had already been put to CBA in 2006, after a smaller surveillance was undertaken of its Bankstown branch and Financial Wisdom's Cairns branches'.

In other words, ASIC had gone inside CBA in 2006, and conducted surveillance and found serious problems with the bank's systems, files and some of its financial planners. But instead of taking action, ASIC had left it to CBA to sort out these issues. By 2008 the problems had become worse. Yet ASIC's only response was to write a stern letter to Gunning.

*

Against this backdrop of festering misconduct, Morris was inducted as a CBA financial adviser. What he encountered was the sales- and profit-focussed culture that had flourished under David Murray and Ralph Norris. Monday mornings would begin with a sales meeting and watching CBA television appearances featuring chief executive Ralph Norris or some other senior executive extolling planners to ramp up sales figures. As Morris recalled, 'The poor branch manager would have to go through this terrible American sales process as to how we were going to shoot the lights out on some sales target or other.'

Practice managers, whose job was to manage the financial planners, would ask the planners for details of their past week's sales and their next week's pipeline of business. At the weekly meetings certain products were identified for the planners to flog. Sometimes it was life insurance, sometimes managed funds or some other CBA financial product.

Financial planners were hired on small base salaries with the lure of being able to earn hundreds of thousands of dollars a year in fees, bonuses and commissions. Each month a league ladder was emailed to all the financial planners, at branch, state and regional levels, with their rankings listed from highest to lowest. These rankings were based on revenue written and showed how each planner fared against their target and against each other. Planners who didn't meet their targets had to submit to management a 'Diary Review for Appointments' with an explanation of why they had failed to meet the targets and how they proposed to do better next time. Those who hit their targets celebrated at places like Otto, an Italian restaurant in Sydney's harbourside Woolloomooloo, before moving on to a seedy strip joint in Kings Cross; in Melbourne such celebrations often ended at Spearmint Rhino, a strip joint in Melbourne's King Street.

It was a pressure-cooker environment where probity and ethics fell by the wayside – and ASIC knew all about it.

*

On 30 October 2008 – seven months after Jeff Morris joined the Commonwealth Bank – he met three colleagues at the Buena Vista Hotel in Sydney's Mosman to exchange horror stories about what was going on at CBA. The catalyst for the meeting was their shock and dismay at the news that one of CBA's star financial planners, Don Nguyen, had received a promotion.

Nguyen was known around the traps as 'Dodgy Don'. His legendary ability to sign up new customers had placed him at number one in the bank's internal financial planning league table in 2007. That year, he had signed up $39 million of customers' money for the bank – more than three times his target.

But Dodgy Don had been caught charging improper fees to customers, putting them in inappropriate high-risk products and paying cash backhanders to bank tellers to get them to send clients his way. He had even been caught selling a life insurance policy to a dying man who could never claim. The bank had suspended him in June 2008.

During his suspension, Nguyen's clients poured through the branch's doors in a state of anxiety about their loss of income, which had fallen more than 50 per cent in many cases. Some were on walking frames, others had heart conditions, emphysema and dementia. Morris had been asked to deal with them, and it had shaken him up.

'It was obvious to me from looking at some of Don's [client] files there was a systemic problem with his advice that needed to be addressed,' Morris recalls. 'Rather than do the right thing and just put their hands up and compensate the victims, I could see from their reactions to the complaints that management was going to force these non-expert clients to prove their claims on an individual basis. They were working on the assumption that none of the clients would ever be able to "join up the dots" [to see the systemic nature], and [they] could thus be fobbed off individually. I realised with a shock that the organisation would almost certainly get away with it unless somebody intervened and blew the whistle on them.'

To Morris's consternation, he had learned before the 30 October Buena Vista meeting that not only had Don been reinstated, he had been promoted to senior planner. As the four men downed beers and discussed what to do about Nguyen, they agreed to become whistleblowers and call themselves the 'Ferrets' to protect their identities.

Morris went home that night and wrote a letter to ASIC, on behalf of the Ferrets, detailing their concerns. He outlined corruption and misconduct at CBA and how innocent people were losing their life savings. In the letter he warned there was a 'high level conspiracy at Commonwealth Financial Planning to conceal repeated material breaches/corruption/gross incompetence of planner Don Nguyen resulting in losses to clients of tens of millions of dollars'. Morris wrote that Nguyen, who had been with the bank since 1999 and controlled an estimated $300 million in investments for 1300 clients, had a history of dishonesty breaches, which resulted in questionable advice to clients. He said CBA had chosen to turn a blind eye to Nguyen's behaviour because he brought in millions of dollars in sales.

Morris also described the aggressive sales culture at the bank: 'In the current difficult climate planners are now being threatened with the sack if they don't meet their sales targets.' He concluded his letter with an urgent message for ASIC to hurry up and investigate because customer files were being 'cleaned up'.

The evidence was compelling. Yet ASIC would take sixteen months to launch an official investigation.

*

Meanwhile, it was business as usual at CBA. In December 2008, just weeks after Morris had written to ASIC and Nguyen had returned to work from suspension, Nguyen and one hundred of the bank's top financial planners were flown to Auckland for an annual three-day bash in honour of the bank's biggest earners, the so-called 'diamond alliance'. Dressed to the nines in 1980s fancy dress, the bank's elite picked up awards and trophies for a job well done.

What was particularly galling to Morris was that very day CBA had announced to the market that it had frozen seven CBA-owned Colonial First State mortgage funds containing $3.3 billion worth of investors' money. In other words, it had suspended the right of 61,000 investors to withdraw their cash from the funds.

CBA was one of several Australian financial services firms to freeze redemptions on such funds, some of which had suffered a surge in withdrawal requests following the Rudd government's move to guarantee bank deposits (but not mortgage funds) as the GFC gathered steam. Yet it had been CBA advisers who had persuaded many of these customers to switch from the safety of term deposits to mortgage funds with higher interest rates, mainly because these funds gave the financial planner and the bank a fee and trailing commission (0.44 per cent) that they didn't get from a humble term deposit. In many cases, it was part of a last-ditch effort by planners to reach their sales targets and boost their funds under management so that they could earn their end-of-year bonus – and qualify for the international three-day conference.

As Morris and the other Ferrets saw what was going on, they became increasingly despondent about ASIC's inaction. They kept writing, and ASIC kept fobbing them off. In March 2009 ASIC told them: 'As advised the issues raised in your complaint [have] been referred to ASIC's Financial Advisers team. It appears that the issues are still currently being considered and we will contact you in due course.'[2]

Frustrated, the Ferrets tried to work out how to get ASIC motivated. Abandoning anonymity and marching into ASIC was canvassed and rejected. Some Ferrets had begun to suspect that a too-cosy relationship with the bank, rather than mere incompetence, lay behind ASIC's inertia. Instead, on the morning of 2 June 2009, Morris walked into CBA group security, the bank's internal fraud and investigation unit, and blew the whistle on management's attempt to cover up the Nguyen scandal. He didn't tell them he had already written to ASIC or that there were other whistleblowers involved.

A few hours after the interview concluded, at 2.51 pm, an email was sent from a senior manager in the compliance department to CBA managers with the subject line: 'Don Nguyen Case'. It said, 'Group security have asked that any new information be forwarded through to [a CBA lawyer] in legal prior to being forwarded to them. This is so that we have legal privilege over the documents in the event of any legal proceedings.' That meant any incriminating documents could thereby remain secret. It was an attempt, in other words, to use 'legal privilege' to conceal documents in the event of lawsuits – or regulatory action – in relation to Nguyen.

The email showed Morris that group security couldn't be trusted. So, to force CBA to act, Morris followed up with another, anonymous email to group security and senior CBA management, titled '"Dodgy" Don Nguyen Conspiracy'. It named names and included a copy of an internal file note one of the Ferrets had found in a bin. Dated 15 October 2008, it was a transcript of the meeting at which Nguyen had not only been reinstated after his suspension for 'fraudulent activity' but promoted to senior planner and given a book of more clients to work his magic on. This primary document confirmed the Ferrets' allegations about a management cover-up.

'More bombs exploded at CBA as the group security men started to bounce managers around interview rooms seeking answers,' Morris recalls. He was sitting at his desk when he heard one of the managers in his area bleating to another about how he'd been hauled into group security: 'They had everything, the file note, every email I've ever written.' Morris then overheard the same manager asking Nguyen to come in for an 'update' meeting with the head of Commonwealth Financial Planning at the Colonial Centre.

In July 2009, Nguyen resigned, citing ill health as the reason for his resignation. That enabled him to lodge an income protection claim, estimated at $70,000 a year, with CBA's life insurance arm, CommInsure. Nguyen was allowed to resign and keep an insurance payout that he would be allowed to collect for years, while his clients were fobbed off with little or no compensation, and other former staff, like loyal executive Peter Beck, are still fighting for entitlements they believe they are rightly owed.

A team was brought in to go through Nguyen's customer files, along with the files of other dodgy planners, but to the Ferrets' increasing astonishment, senior management at CBA didn't fire anyone. Instead it allowed some of the wrongdoers to collect their hefty bonuses and move to other financial institutions, where they work today. Others were kept on and promoted and still work at CBA.

By February 2010 Morris and one of the other Ferrets had had enough and decided to go in person to ASIC's head office in Sydney's CBD to see if that would get the regulator to act. It worked. Three weeks later ASIC wrote to CBA to say it was planning to launch an investigation. Morris remembers the office around that time. 'ASIC giving them the heads up they were coming in resulted in files being sanitised or suddenly disappearing. Liquid paper was in demand,' he says.

Around the same time, class-action law firm Maurice Blackburn started sniffing around and sending CBA victims to ASIC. John Berrill, who was a senior partner at Maurice Blackburn, had been contacted by victims of Don Nguyen. After hearing their stories and seeing the evidence, he believed the bank had a case to answer; he also believed ASIC needed to investigate. 'A number of cases had come through and they were all shocking,' Berrill recalls. 'People had lost millions of dollars because of the poor advice of Nguyen.'

*

Inside the small windowless office, Jeff Morris, a burly man with a big presence, was scribbling furiously. Wearing an old college tie, 1980s-style red braces and a pair of jeans, he looked up nervously as Wacka Williams pushed open the door and greeted him loudly.

It was 20 May 2013, and I had gone along with Wacka to meet Morris and a small group of other CBA victims, people I'd been reading about in the documents Morris had sent to me just before I'd gone on my work trip to China. I'd emailed Morris while I was in China to let him know the material – which included allegations of forgery, fraud and a cover-up by CBA – was chilling.

As Morris spoke, everyone in the room leaned in to hear the details of his incredible story – of how ASIC had taken sixteen months to act on inside information provided by Morris and other whistleblowers exposing rampant misconduct at Commonwealth Financial Planning.

Next to Morris sat Jan Braund, an impeccably dressed, no-nonsense elderly woman with silver hair, bright red lipstick, a matching red jacket and a lot of accessories. A retired occupational therapist, Jan talked about the ordeal CBA had put her through, and how she was facing destitution after a lifetime of hard work. She had brought along print-outs of unauthorised transactions carried out by Don Nguyen, as well as copious notes she'd made detailing an ordeal nobody should have to go through.

Wacka was visibly taken aback by what he heard. Rubbing his face, he kept shaking his head. It was a lot to digest. The iconic CBA had peremptorily dismissed Jan's serious allegations of misconduct and wrongdoing in its planning arm and had tried to fob her off with a low-ball compensation offer.

Jan explained how she had lost all her life savings while caring for her ailing husband, Alan, who had crippling vascular dementia. 'Not since my daughter's death at the age of six,' Jan said to us, 'have I felt the awful, unpleasant, exhausting, emotional and physical pressure associated with the fact that I would soon be dealing with Alan's demise, financial insecurity and writing letters to CBA and ASIC.'

Jan told the room how her troubles had begun in 2002 when she and Alan had sold their home. A former Qantas pilot and a CBA bank customer since 1950, Alan wanted to put $1 million into a conservative retirement account. The bank had referred them to Don Nguyen. As Jan found out later, Nguyen had subsequently used her signature, without her permission, to facilitate product switches from conservative financial products to high-risk, high-fee-paying CBA products. She said some of the transactions took place while she and Alan were overseas, when it would have been physically impossible for her to sign the transaction authorisations. She added that she had the passport stamps to prove it.

By 2009, the Braunds' wealth had fallen from $1 million to $350,000 and Alan's dementia had taken over their lives. 'I just can't tell you how devastated I was,' said Jan. 'At that stage, I'm carrying a man that doesn't know who he is, where he is, what he is, where he's going – nothing – only to be told our financial future was absolutely gone, and I couldn't do anything about it.'

She said CBA had tried to downplay the scale of Nguyen's misconduct, which included forging her signature and switching funds. It initially offered her $200,000 in compensation, then $215,000. In one letter, written on 3 February 2012, the bank told Jan that although they 'regard[ed] that allegation very seriously' the matter was closed because she was receiving compensation. The letter continued: 'This means that all switches, including any which may have been made without your proper authorisation, have been unwound for the purpose of calculating your compensation. Therefore, through our compensation calculation you will have suffered no negative financial impact as a result of this alleged conduct.'

In August 2012, Jan agreed to an $880,000 settlement, which was still short of what she had lost by that time.

Next to Jan sat Merilyn Swan, whose piercing blue eyes darted back and forth as she started to describe the nightmare her parents, Merv and Robyn Blanch, had endured with CBA. Her parents had been customers of the bank for sixty-five years. Merv had even introduced CBA's school banking program into Coolah

Central School in north-west NSW when he'd been the principal there, back in 1961.

In March 2007, eighty-two-year-old Merv had decided it was time to see a financial planner. Robyn was eleven years younger than Merv, and he wanted to make sure she'd be well looked after if anything happened to him. The couple went to their local CBA branch and signed up with Nguyen. He told them he usually didn't deal in such small amounts because he was one of the bank's top financial planners, but he would make an exception in their case. The Blanches felt lucky to have him investing their life savings of $260,000. Nguyen told them he would put their money into eight moderate-risk CBA investment funds.

Within twenty-two months, this couple, who had been self-funded for twenty-five years, had lost almost 70 per cent of their savings and been forced to live on the cold charity of Centrelink. Merilyn recalled how the stress had taken years off her parents' lives. 'One day I went to visit them and saw my dad sitting with his head in his hands and he said: "I can't believe what has happened." He was humiliated, he suffered depression, he'd had a stent put in his heart and had psoriasis due to stress.'

Her parents had received a letter from the bank saying their money was not sitting in eight moderate-risk bank products as they had been told but had been put into nine CBA products, most of which were high risk. Then another letter arrived blaming their financial ruin on the GFC, claiming the advice Nguyen had given them was appropriate. Yet the bank couldn't explain how $25,000 of the Blanches' money had been invested in the mystery ninth product, so it offered a $6700 settlement.

It was an insult. At that point, with the GFC in full swing, the Blanches had lost $160,000.

Merilyn decided to get involved. She rang the bank and was asked if her parents had kept original documents. She pretended they hadn't and asked the bank to send copies to her. When she compared her parents' original statement of advice with the one the bank had sent, there were striking differences. 'One document contained several pages that weren't in the original documentation. And it also contained four tables that were not in the original statement of advice,' she recalled.

She believed that someone at CBA had changed the tables to make it appear that the Blanches had been given more information than they actually had – thereby minimising how much compensation the bank had to pay.

Once the bank realised the Blanches had kept the original documents, its offers of compensation multiplied. Within six months, the bank had increased its offer from $6700 to $95,000, but without any admission of liability. In many respects it was an identical story to the one Jan had just told. Exhausted, the Blanches accepted the offer, which again was well below what they had lost, and then laughed with amazement and disbelief when a CBA representative rang them to see if they wanted to invest the compensation payout with the bank.

When Merilyn finished speaking and handed the floor back to Morris, there was a palpable feeling in the room that things were about to get very serious. The time to do something to expose CBA's malpractice was fast approaching.

There was also a sense of trepidation at the prospect of becoming potential targets of the big bank. The members of the group had already experienced firsthand how CBA could play hard and dirty. I'd spoken to Morris numerous times ahead of the 20 May meeting. I knew he'd shopped the story to a number of politicians and journalists, including some from *The Australian* and the *Sydney Morning Herald*. None had acted, telling him it was too complicated, too risky, too much work, too this, too that. Whatever the reason, one of the biggest stories of the past decade had remained untold – until now. A whistleblower like Jeff Morris is rare. And this story was too big to ignore.

However, Morris was recovering from a nervous breakdown after receiving a death threat from a co-worker. The stress had led to the collapse of his marriage. There was also the complication of a deed of release he'd signed weeks earlier, which prevented him disparaging CBA. By that stage the bank knew he was a whistleblower and had been glad to see the back of him.

Sitting in the room, having absorbed the testimony of Morris and the others, I was dumbstruck. One hundred and one thoughts swirled around my brain, including how my bosses would react when I briefed them. I knew if I didn't get the story right, not only would Jeff Morris be in trouble, but the newspapers would be sued by the country's biggest and most powerful corporate giant.

It was a controversial time at Fairfax. Weeks earlier I'd been served with a subpoena from Gina Rinehart's Hancock Prospecting company requesting my contacts, in relation to the unauthorised biography I'd written about her the previous year. I was faced with every journalist's worst nightmare: comply with a court order to hand over documents and sources that I had promised would be kept confidential, or face a jail sentence for contempt of court. The fact that Rinehart was also the biggest shareholder in Fairfax added to the stress. And now here I was, in a stifling room, ready to do battle with CBA, with Rinehart already breathing down my neck.

Wacka suggested if the story stacked up it should come out before Federal Parliament resumed on 3 June. That way he could grill ASIC at a senate estimates committee hearing scheduled for that week. I decided the best day to run it would be Saturday 1 June, assuming I could get all my ducks in a row.

With the clock ticking, I asked a colleague at *The Age*, Chris Vedelago, to help investigate the story and the many allegations I'd heard. Chris was a gun commercial property writer who was keen to move into investigative journalism full time. He jumped at this opportunity.

Chris and I went line by line through the various versions of the documents CBA had sent to the Blanches and compared them to the Blanches' original documents. Sure enough, they were alarmingly different in significant ways. We looked at Jan's allegations and checked her passport against the timeline she'd given me, which proved she had been out of the country, as she'd said, when she supposedly signed documents.

We spoke to other victims, who corroborated everything we'd been told. We triple-checked Morris's story, as well as everyone's confidentiality agreements and deeds of settlements. The last thing we wanted to do was to create any more anxiety for everyone – these people had been through enough already. Morris asked us to leave out the personal ordeal he'd been through, including his nervous breakdown and his separation from his wife. We made sure that in the story he criticised only ASIC, not CBA, to ensure he didn't breach his deed of release. Merilyn spoke on behalf of her parents. Jan managed to keep to her letter of settlement with the bank by commenting only on her personal experience, leaving us to do the rest.

In the course of our investigations, we found that at least six other CBA financial planners around the country had been banned by ASIC, including Ricky Gillespie, who'd received a lifetime ban for forging his clients' signatures.

On 28 May, Chris and I decided it was time to lay our cards on the table and let CBA know what we had, including documents, emails and the testimonies of a whistleblower and victims. Four days out from our intended 1 June publication date, we sent CBA three pages of detailed questions, including queries about the operations and culture of Commonwealth Financial Planning, its handling of the Nguyen affair, and whether bank staff engaged in a cover-up or withheld information about potential criminal acts from ASIC or the police.

CBA's reply was short and terse, and failed to answer any of our questions. Instead it rolled out the same old 'bad apple' excuse banks had used countless times before: 'Don Nguyen was employed as a financial planner in Commonwealth Financial Planning from October 2003 until his resignation in July 2009. In 2008, following complaints from [his] clients to the Commonwealth Bank and to Australian Securities and Investments Commission (ASIC), we became concerned about the advice provided by Mr Nguyen. Those concerns were investigated and saw Mr Nguyen suspended from duty. Mr Nguyen subsequently resigned whilst under investigation.' The bank reiterated its commitment to compensating the 'small number' of clients who it said 'still' had unresolved claims and encouraged 'dissatisfied' clients to contact the Financial Ombudsman Service.

Meanwhile our story was legalled, edited and re-edited. I was instructed by one of the paper's editors to call the media person at CBA to let him know the article was going on page one and ask them if they wanted to add anything else to their brief statement. The bank declined.

The article duly appeared on page one of the 1 June edition of the *Sydney Morning Herald* and *The Age* under the headline 'Profit above all else: how CBA lost savings and hid its tracks'.

I woke up at 6 am to the sound of my phone pinging as emails started to flood in from current and former CBA staff, along with victims of CBA and other banks. By the end of the day, Chris and I had received hundreds of emails, documents and leads. We were overwhelmed by the response.

We already had a corker of a follow-up story for the following week, featuring Joe Hockey's mother-in-law, as well as the grilling of ASIC in the Senate by Wacka, but the responses we received immediately gave us enough material to write a bank story every day for weeks.

The story of Joe Hockey's mother-in-law was symptomatic of so many that were reported to us. It came to us via Glenn Burge, a senior Fairfax executive, who was friends with the future treasurer's brother-in-law Tim Babbage. Burge had been asked to help Babbage's mother, Patricia Babbage, who had been ripped off by a CBA planner and complained. Unaware of her political connections, the bank had given her a low-ball compensation payout at a time when she was fighting bowel cancer.

Patricia Babbage's planner, Chris Baker (who was later banned for five years by ASIC), had put her life savings into high-risk products and wiped out much of her wealth. By June 2009 her retirement savings had fallen from $200,000 to $92,000. Burge gave me a copy of the correspondence with the bank, which showed Burge had managed to increase her compensation payment from $43,286 to $67,092 by telling them who he was and where he worked. It was still far less than she had lost, but she was too ill to keep fighting, so she accepted.

When the story appeared in the *Sydney Morning Herald* on 5 June 2013 with the headline 'Hockey's mother-in-law stung by rogue financial planners', the bank went into meltdown. A senior media spin doctor, who is still at the bank, rang me and screamed down the phone. I put the call on loudspeaker so that Chris Vedelago could listen in and respond to some of the rants and threats.

After the barrage of abuse, the PR had a go at Jeff Morris, who he described as 'unreliable and unstable', saying Morris had a 'history' and the bank had a thick file on him. He said that if we knew what he knew we wouldn't listen to anything Morris said. Chris belted back: 'All right, send it to us.'

Realising we weren't buying his smear, the spin doctor hung up.

The first week of June was frenetic, as was the rest of the month. The newspaper articles Chris and I had written exposing the wrongdoings at CBA sparked massive public outrage and condemnation of the bank's behaviour. The same day the scandal around Joe Hockey's mother-in-law broke, ASIC was scheduled to appear in front of the Senate Estimates Committee in Canberra, a regular event where regulators front parliament to answer questions. A line of ASIC commissioners and media flacks filed into the chamber, including ASIC deputy chairman Peter Kell. After a quick opening speech by Kell on matters ASIC had been dealing with, Wacka launched straight into questions about the financial planning scandal.[3]

> Wacka: On 30 October 2008 bank staff or whistleblowers, call them what you like, tipped off ASIC about alleged wrongdoings in the Commonwealth Financial Planning and sent a four-page fax. I believe in that fax it said there was some urgency in ASIC securing the files as they were being cleaned up. Are you familiar with this case?
>
> Kell: Yes. I am happy to give you a brief outline of the matters.
>
> Wacka: Are you familiar with the fact that on 30 October 2008 you received a fax —

Kell: I am not going to comment on these issues. I would like to take the opportunity to outline what we have achieved here. It is a very significant outcome for —

Wacka: We will get to that. I only have 10 minutes. Why did it take ASIC 16 months to follow up on that fax and numerous emails from the whistleblowers and to act in relation to the Commonwealth Financial Planning files?

Kell: I am not going to comment on the exact time that was involved in —

Wacka: I can give you the exact time, if you like —

Kell: Can I respond to your question, please?

Wacka: Yes.

Kell: … What we achieved here was an enforceable undertaking that completely changed the way the Commonwealth Financial Planning operated … It has set a new benchmark for raising the standard of financial advice and has meant tens of millions of dollars in compensation for hundreds of investors.

Wacka: I disagree with you because it took you 16 months to actually act on this. When Jeff Morris, the whistleblower, in frustration went actually around to ASIC … that staff member said, 'If you had not come in today, this would not have landed on my desk and nothing would have happened,' … and 'I can tell you that the report you sent in has been bouncing around here for months and months and months and nobody else knew what to do with it.' The point I am making, Mr Kell, is that you were told of wrongdoings and 16 months later when the whistleblower actually went to your office then you acted …

Kell: As I just mentioned a minute ago, we have obtained tens of millions of dollars for hundreds of investors. You disagree that this is a good outcome. We will have to disagree on that ...

Kell's tone was dismissive and defensive, and he dodged far too many questions from both Wacka and other senators. The series of articles on ASIC's failure to respond to the whistleblower hadn't been missed by the committee, particularly by Labor Senator Doug Cameron, who at the time was sitting in his office watching the interchange. In outrage he stormed into the hearing and in a thick Scottish accent demanded that Kell stop demurring:

Mr Kell, you do not seem to take a breath when you are answering a question, and it really is quite annoying, I must say. You can answer these questions much more quickly. I am not telling you how to answer the questions. But I watched your responses to Senator Williams. Please do not do that to me. This is a very serious issue for ASIC. It is a serious issue for the government. All of the senators are concerned about it. Do not take me on a waltz around the merry-go-round.

Days later, on 20 June, Kell achieved a rare feat – he united the Nationals (Wacka), Greens (Christine Milne), and Labor (Cameron) to co-sponsor an inquiry into the performance of ASIC by the Senate Economics References Committee. That date will go down as a landmark moment. The ensuing Senate inquiry into ASIC and CBA would change the course of history and become the first brick in the wall for a royal commission into banking and the financial services sector.

Chapter 7

'Banking Bad'

Out of the newspapers and onto TV

A SCANDAL LIKE THE Don Nguyen cover-up, which had a big bank as its villain, an inspiring whistleblower, a regulator that had failed, and victims Australians could relate to was a powerful combination. It built a momentum that was unstoppable. Tip-offs flooded in and the stories kept coming.

CBA had navigated its way relatively unscathed through the Storm Financial scandal. It had even weathered complaints about Bankwest when that subsidiary had foreclosed on more than one thousand small-business customers and farmers who had commercial loans valued at $8.2 billion.[1] Bankwest had been acquired by CBA in October 2008 after its parent, the British HBOS Insurance and Investment Group, had collapsed, leaving UK taxpayers to fund a £17 billion bank bail-out. It was the first big deal stitched up by future CBA boss Ian Narev and at $2.1 billion, which was half Bankwest's pre-GFC valuation, it was seen as cheap. The purchase had been approved by the ACCC (well after Allan Fels had left), and received the blessing of the Reserve Bank, APRA and the Rudd government, something that would have been difficult to achieve if it hadn't been seen as the bail-out of a failing bank.

It also put Narev in the box seat to become the Commonwealth Bank's CEO in 2011, when Norris retired. Narev had joined CBA in 2007 at the request of fellow New Zealander Ralph Norris, who had appointed him to run CBA's mergers and acquisitions division. Narev was the first non-banker to run CBA: he had a background in law and management consultancy and had been a child actor in his youth. He had a keen intellect and set targets which he made sure were met. Emotion didn't come into his decisions.

Shortly after the merger, the bank initiated an internal review of Bankwest's loan book. The GFC was driving down property values and slowing the economy, and the recommendation of the review was to reduce the bank's exposure to commercial property loans by $1.8 billion. Properties were revalued and any loans that were deemed impaired or high risk were terminated. CBA was brutal.

Its actions triggered a series of parliamentary inquiries, spearheaded by Wacka Williams, who had received a number of complaints from business owners and farmers who had been foreclosed despite never missing a payment. The first, in March 2012, was a Senate Economics References Committee inquiry into post-GFC banking. It received more than 150 submissions from Bankwest customers, which told stories of a bank that engineered defaults. CBA and Narev denied the allegations, but they lingered.

CBA saw such stories as a minor irritation. Its typical response was to admit nothing and deny wrongdoing, as it had done with all the other scandals. But now, as the financial planning stories raised by Morris and Wacka Williams started to gain traction, and the Senate inquiry into ASIC was underway, CBA went on the offensive. Narev, his dapper chief legal counsel David Cohen, and one of the bank's spin doctors, who still works at the bank, demanded a meeting with a senior editor on the *Sydney Morning Herald* and *The Age*. The editor later told me that the CBA executives had accused me of being unprofessional and attempting to threaten a former manager of Nguyen's to speak up – or else. The executives told the editor CBA would pull advertising whenever a bank story was written.

Meanwhile, CBA executives and spin doctors were briefing journalists on other papers in an attempt to disparage and diminish my stories. A business commentator at *The Australian* wrote: 'Parliamentary scrutiny of regulators is by definition a good thing but this inquiry smacks of nothing more than grandstanding.' It went on: 'As the problems in question occurred in 2009, all the financial-planning staff involved at the CBA has gone, the management has changed and ASIC has an entirely new commission. The central character in the investigation, Don Nguyen, has gone and ASIC has helped his former clients recover about $23 million out of $36 million. That is not a bad recovery … Once again, the question worth asking is what is to be gained from this inquiry, given all that has changed since.'[2]

From that point on I was told I had to send draft copies of my stories to the editor for review, along with any questions and responses from CBA, a move designed to pressure me to stop writing about the bank. I duly sent in my drafts. To the editor's credit, he never changed anything in the copy, but he had swallowed the same spin: it happened in the past, compensation has been made, move on. It was pressure I didn't need.

In the face of what was going on, I decided to ask Marian Wilkinson, one of the country's best investigative reporters, who worked at ABC's *Four Corners*, whether the flagship program would be interested in doing a story about the CBA scandals.

I told Wilkinson there were numerous people willing to speak publicly, including the whistleblower. I felt the story needed to be given more attention than it was getting. She encouraged me to do it and organised a meeting with the executive producer of *Four Corners*, Sue Spencer. Spencer took a big risk in deciding to go ahead. I had never done TV before, but she saw the potential of the story and had the courage to back it – and me.

In February 2014, I took leave from the *Sydney Morning Herald* and *The Age* and went to work for *Four Corners* in Sydney for the next seven weeks. It was a steep learning curve, but I was determined not to squander the opportunity.

'Banking Bad' aired on 5 May 2014.[3] I watched the program nervously in the hotel room I had been camping in. My husband had flown to Sydney to share the moment with me, and I can still remember my heart almost stopping with excitement and trepidation when 8.30 pm came and host Kerry O'Brien introduced the story.

It was a forty-five-minute exposé of the human cost of conflicted remuneration and the brutal behaviour of CBA. It attracted one of *Four Corners'* biggest audiences of the year, with more than one million viewers tuning in. Many cried as they watched Merilyn Swan sifting through documents on the floor of her home in an attempt to help her aging parents. They saw Jan Braund talk about the ordeal she had been put through, and admired the bravery of Jeff Morris as he took on the bank and the regulator.

Then there was Teghan Couper, the beautiful daughter of scaffolder Noel Stevens, who told the story of how her father had spent the last six months of his life fighting for justice after CBA rejected his life insurance policy two days before Christmas. Stevens had worked hard all his life but had few savings. What he did have was a water-tight life insurance policy with Westpac, a policy which he had held for seven years, which was worth almost $300,000 and was guaranteed to pay him out if he ever got sick. But in late 2010, a teller at his local CBA branch called him and asked him to see a financial planner. When Stevens went in, the financial planner advised him to switch his policy to CommInsure and he agreed. It was a win for the bank – it scored a new policy holder and an annual premium of $1,482, the teller pocketed a referral fee of $444.60, and the planner received an $815 kickback plus an ongoing annual commission. But it was a disaster for Stevens.

A year later, when he was diagnosed with pancreatic cancer, the bank refused to pay his insurance claim on the basis that he had been dishonest about his medical history. On the form filled out by the financial adviser, Stevens had answered 'no' to a tick-box question asking if he had a drinking problem, but notes the bank had obtained from the Frankston Medical Centre from November 2009 said, 'Drinks eight stubbies every night. Counselled about alcohol.' The bank scrutinised Stevens' bank statements, logging his alcohol purchases from liquor outlets. It then used what it had found to deny his claim. Scandalously, at the same time it continued to charge him premiums on a policy that was void. If Stevens had remained with Westpac, he would have been paid out in full.

Stevens took legal action. It was a David-and-Goliath battle: a dying man with $10,000 to his name taking on a multi-billion-dollar corporation in the courts, giving testimony from his bed while he was high on morphine to dull the pain, to fight for something that was rightfully his – a $300,000 insurance policy payout that he wanted to leave to his daughter. Days before he died, Stevens won the case and the bank was ordered to accept the claim.

But it didn't end there. As his daughter, Teghan, was arranging her father's funeral, she was told CBA was appealing the decision. Teghan fought the bank and won the appeal.

This tragic yet ultimately inspiring story demonstrated to me how far the so-called venerable institution, CBA, was prepared to go to avoid paying out a valid life insurance claim – the bank pressed on even after its legal costs overtook the claim total of $300,000.

When the *Four Corners* program ended, I felt a surge of pride. Text messages started pouring in, congratulating the team. Sue Spencer called to say how much she'd enjoyed it. It was a special moment, a highlight of my career.

The day after the show aired, CBA went into damage control. Branch staff were briefed to stop people closing their accounts in protest. It was the beginning of a long journey. 'Banking Bad' would become a game changer, and have a cascade effect that would culminate in a royal commission.

*

There was a fresh scandal at CBA that we had discovered during our research for 'Banking Bad' but which hadn't made it into the final cut of the program – a scandal that CBA had managed to keep secret throughout the Senate Economics References Committee inquiry into the performance of ASIC, established in June 2013. It involved a separate financial planning division at CBA, Financial Wisdom; shoddy financial advice that devastated the lives of hundreds, possibly thousands, of customers; and a cover-up by the bank.

One of the businesses operating under CBA's Financial Wisdom umbrella was Meridien Wealth, and among its star financial planners was Rollo Sherriff, who worked out of the seaside town of Cairns, in the heart of tropical Queensland. Sherriff had started his career in the 1990s selling Colonial life insurance with his business partner, Michael Irwin. Together they set up Meridien Wealth, and targeted cane farmers, retirees and families in Cairns and Port Douglas. Sherriff and Irwin quickly built a name for themselves as top-gun advisers, based on the amount of financial products they sold. After CBA took control of Colonial Mutual and Financial Wisdom in 2000, the solid reputation of the bank drew in more customers for Sherriff and Irwin and emboldened existing clients to increase their exposure to the planners' investment schemes, which involved gearing up and investing in high-risk, high-fee-paying CBA products, including margin loans.

As the sharemarket rallied in the lead-up to the GFC, everyone was making money. But Sherriff's clients didn't realise they were sitting on a time bomb, and soon many of them were in trouble. One of the saddest cases was Bob Nissen, who had sought advice from Sherriff in 2006 to get his finances in shape. At the time, the sixty-year-old's daughter, a paranoid schizophrenic, was becoming increasingly dependent on him. 'I told [Sherriff] the priorities were to look after my daughter [and] get my house sorted out because it was falling down around my ears,' he said. Nissen signed up with Sherriff, believing his life savings would be safe. 'Because of the Commonwealth Bank I thought it was rock solid, you can't go wrong there.' Sherriff advised him to gear up and invest in mainly high-risk, high-fee-paying CBA products. Then in June 2008, even as the GFC was starting to gather momentum, Sherriff advised Nissen to gear up some more by re-mortgaging his house and borrowing $150,000 from CBA. Nissen agreed. He subsequently lost everything and to make a living had to work gruelling twelve-hour days, seven days a week, two weeks on and two weeks off, in the mines at Cloncurry, near Mount Isa, with men less than half his age.

During our investigation into Financial Wisdom and Meridien Wealth it became clear that Financial Wisdom was a mirror image of Commonwealth Financial Planning. Sherriff was operating at the same time as Don Nguyen and others were riding high there. Under pressure from CBA investors to make the Colonial Mutual acquisition work, CBA had been reluctant to dump planners who earned them big money. Rollo Sherriff was one of the biggest individual writers of margin loans in Queensland, at a time when the bank was competing with other financial institutions and trying to grow its market share. Meridien Wealth had amassed a base of three thousand customers and had more than $135 million in funds under management, which was largely invested in Colonial products. It was all too lucrative for CBA to pull the plug on.

It wasn't just CBA that was behaving this way. Armies of advisers at AMP and other organisations were all at it. These companies had paid a fortune to expand into wealth management and were under immense pressure to sell as many bank products as possible. Even their own compliance departments – which are supposed to make sure financial planners are giving appropriate advice – could do little to resist this pressure. Rod Gayford, who had worked at ASIC before becoming a compliance manager at CBA, said that compliance at the bank was seen as the 'business prevention unit'.[4] Compliance officers were not allowed to do their job. They weren't allowed to interview clients, and if inappropriate advice was discovered, or a planner was rated critical risk, the usual response from the top was to give the adviser another chance. It created a culture where performance was rated above all other criteria and misconduct had no consequences. Everything was covered up, and usually ASIC was missing in action.

In the case of Meridien Wealth, CBA first became aware of Sherriff's practices in the early 2000s, when he was found to have given poor advice to clients. It was forced to compensate a number of these clients after they lodged complaints. Sherriff's conduct caught the attention of the professional body, the Financial Planning Association (FPA), which culminated in a decision in October 2004 to withdraw his status as a certified financial planner. It was a gutsy move on the FPA's part, but it was short-lived. CBA came down hard and backed Sherriff, threatening legal action if the decision wasn't reversed. The FPA thought better of taking on the bank, and reinstated Sherriff in March 2005.

Meanwhile, CBA quietly compensated a number of Sherriff's customers in the early 2000s. They included Mareeba car dealer Kevin Day and his wife, Ellen, who had lost more than $1 million of their hard-earned money and been left owing $150,000 in loans, after being leveraged into margin loans by Sherriff. In distress, Day had turned to ASIC for help, but the corporate regulator sent him polite replies and tuned him out. Day then took Rollo Sherriff to court, but CBA stepped in and fought the case on Sherriff's behalf.

Day spent five years battling CBA before settling. By then his wife had cancer and his legal bills had mounted to $110,000. As part of his settlement, which went nowhere near what he'd lost, Day signed a confidentiality agreement and tried to get on with his life. But he never got over the ordeal or the belief that CBA had ripped him off. He kept 30 kilograms of documents in his attic, hoping that one day he might use them, and after he saw our exposé in 2014 he dusted them off and got in touch with me. But despite subsequent assistance from Jeff Morris, he never obtained a satisfactory settlement, and in 2015 he sadly passed away.

*

As part of our investigation into Financial Wisdom, my colleague Mario Christodoulou and I sent a series of questions to CBA asking how much compensation the bank had paid to clients burned by scandal. When I received the response, I noticed the figure differed from the one it had given to the Senate at the 2013 ASIC inquiry. It was a big deal because it meant CBA had misled parliament and, as ASIC had relied on CBA's figures in its submissions, so had the government regulator.

I wrote a column for the *Sydney Morning Herald* and *The Age* pointing out the deception.[5] According to well-informed columnist Tony Boyd, when the chairman of ASIC, Greg Medcraft, read it, he went ballistic at the bank. According to Boyd, Medcraft phoned Ian Narev, telling him to come to his office and explain the disparity. Narev rushed there with his two lieutenants, general counsel David Cohen and the iron-fisted head of the bank's scandal-ridden wealth management arm, Annabel Spring. Spring, according to Boyd, blamed the misreporting on a 'stupid mistake' someone had made inside the bank.[6]

On 17 May, in response to being misled, ASIC revealed it had amended the licence conditions for CBA's financial advice businesses and that the licence would be suspended or even revoked if the bank breached the new conditions. ASIC also instructed CBA to re-examine the case for compensating the victims of Rollo Sherriff and other advisers at Financial Wisdom and Commonwealth Financial Planning, which it did.

*

After the scandal on Sherriff broke, numerous former staff, compliance managers and other victims called or emailed me. One of them was Darryl Tenni, who told me about his father, retired Queensland sugar farmer Myles Tenni. Myles had invested $800,000 of the $1.2 million proceeds from the sale of his sugarcane farm in the late 1990s in CBA products and then taken out a further $800,000 in margin loans to invest in more CBA products, based on advice received from Rollo Sherriff. By 2004, he had lost most of his money.

Like Kevin Day, Myles Tenni had complained to CBA. He, too, had been fobbed off. Somehow, though, Tenni had scraped together enough money to hire accounting group William Buck to investigate whether he had a case for 'negligent advice' from Financial Wisdom. The report he received concluded that if he hadn't made further investments using a margin loan – as advised by Sherriff – his initial $800,000 investment would have gone up by 30 June 2004, instead of falling $333,941. This contradicted CBA's response to him, which had said that although 'the funds weren't invested appropriately' it hadn't cost him money. He applied for compensation after the bank was forced to revisit old claims as part of its licence agreement with ASIC and was offered $625,000, which he accepted in 2016 – more than fourteen years after losing the money. He believed the bank owed him far more than that, including compensation for all the pain and suffering.

In February 2010, by which time his status as a big writer of business had slipped, Sherriff left Meridien Wealth, just as the bank launched an official investigation into his conduct. A month later, on 18 March 2010, a senior manager of advice and regulatory affairs employed by CBA lodged a breach report to ASIC. By the end of March, Sherriff had declared himself bankrupt.

Further revelations about Sherriff's practices, including pressuring clients into buying shares in a company of which he was a director, resulted in a request from a liquidator to ASIC to pursue more detailed investigations. ASIC refused. A Freedom of Information request, lodged as part of our research, revealed that on 4 November 2013 Joanna Bird, who was then senior executive leader of ASIC's financial advisers' team, had sent emails to Peter Kell, ASIC's deputy chairman, with a summary of reasons to withdraw from action in relation to Rollo Sherriff. The request was declined and they did not release the details of those reasons.

ASIC stood by its decision not to pursue Sherriff and CBA. In a statement it released at the time of *The Age* and *Sydney Morning Herald* article about Sherriff and Financial Wisdom, it said it had considered a range of factors before deciding not to take action, including Sherriff's decision to leave the financial services industry.

When I tracked Sherriff down on the phone in Cairns in 2014, he denied any wrongdoing and blamed his client losses on the GFC. He told me while he was 'regretful clients suffered losses', the financial advice he'd given had been properly delivered. He said he had lost money too.

Haunted by what had gone on at Meridien Wealth, one of the partners, Peter Percali, who had repeatedly informed CBA about Sherriff over the years, tried to help clients with compensation claims. But, he told me, he was ultimately silenced by the bank. Percali said CBA pressured him to sell Meridien Wealth. He owed money to the bank, so he agreed to sell in exchange for debt forgiveness, but the deal meant he had to sign an agreement preventing him from assisting Meridien Wealth clients. He described that arrangement to me as blackmail.

Over the years I have kept in touch with many victims of Financial Wisdom, including Bob Nissen, who is now living in poor health on the pension and struggling to make ends meet. He said he received his last payment from CBA two years ago, but it wasn't enough. 'We recovered about two-thirds of our losses,' he said in an email.

He still remembers 2008 and the GFC, when he watched his savings being wiped out and his life almost fell apart. 'I was desperate, I was panicking,' he says. 'There were some nights I couldn't sleep, worrying, "What am I going to do?" It all disappeared.'

Nissen has gained a new appreciation of what constitutes misconduct. 'You grow up thinking a criminal looks like a beagle boy in the cartoons but in reality they are over forty, wear a suit and live on the North Shore. It is human nature that there are some people who if temptation is in front of them cannot resist and will ignore the effect on others … These people missed something as a child. Take care. You are doing a great job … Bob.'

Chapter 8

Reluctant concessions

CBA in damage control

My *Four Corners* program 'Banking Bad' and the subsequent articles in the press had unsettled the banks. But Australia's financial services sector was rocked to its core in June 2014 when the Senate Economics Reference Committee released its report on its inquiry into the performance of ASIC, concluding: 'The committee is of the view that a royal commission is warranted.'[1]

A call for a royal commission into CBA to investigate fraud, forgery and allegations of a cover-up inside its financial planning arm was the most explosive of the recommendations of the scathing 553-page document. The committee – chaired by Labor Senator Mark Bishop, with other members including Wacka Williams, Greens Senator Peter Whish-Wilson and independent South Australian Nick Xenophon – made sixty-one recommendations, including that CBA should reopen its existing compensation program for financial planning victims and review offers already made.

The report aimed to right the wrongs of the CBA scandal, and investigate other institutions, including the Macquarie Bank's financial advice division, Macquarie Private Wealth. It also sought to rebuild public confidence in the regulator. Nevertheless, a royal commission was required, the committee said, because it was not convinced that ASIC could be trusted to achieve these goals: 'The committee is now of the view that the CBA deliberately played down the seriousness and extent of problems in Commonwealth Financial Planning in an attempt to avoid ASIC's scrutiny, contain adverse publicity and minimise compensation payments. In effect, the CBA managed, for some considerable time, to keep the committee, ASIC and its clients in the dark. The time is well overdue for full, frank and open disclosure on the Commonwealth Financial Planning matter.'[2]

The report's criticism of ASIC was withering: 'ASIC has limited powers and resources but even so appears to miss or ignore clear and persistent early warning signs of corporate wrongdoing or troubling trends that pose a risk to consumers … ASIC needs to be respected and feared [but it] has shown that it is reluctant to actively pursue misconduct within Commonwealth Financial Planning and Financial Wisdom; rather, it appears to accept the information and assurances the CBA provides without question.'[3] The committee found it particularly troubling that ASIC was consistently described in submissions and various testimony as being slow to act or as a watchdog with no teeth.

It wouldn't have been a surprise to ASIC, which had taken a shellacking during the inquiry. At one stage ASIC chairman Greg Medcraft had raised his hands and chanted 'mea culpa' as Mark Bishop, Wacka and Peter Whish-Wilson got stuck into the poor treatment of whistleblower Jeff Morris and ASIC's cosiness with the bank.[4]

Mark Bishop had become convinced that the entire sector needed to be further scrutinised. Then a senator based in Perth, he had been involved in hundreds of Senate inquiries by the time he came to chair the probe into ASIC. At the outset he'd had low expectations, believing the inquiry would be unremarkable. But he had soon changed his mind as he listened to the whistleblowers, lawyers and victims who gave evidence. By the end of the inquiry he was convinced the major banks regularly engaged in grossly negligent behaviour, fraud and unacceptable business practices to the detriment of thousands – possibly millions – of customers, virtually unimpeded by the so-called corporate cop. It became clear to him that the problem with CBA was cultural during one particular exchange with the bank's legal counsel David Cohen, who summed up the rampant misconduct as 'inappropriate'. Bishop now says he saw that as a 'fuck you to the Senate':

> Bishop: Does the term 'inappropriate advice' capture
> the seriousness of misconduct at Commonwealth
> Financial Planning? If I wear a brown tie and grey
> suit, my wife will say to me: 'They don't match. That's
> inappropriate.' … Do you think 'inappropriate advice'
> captures the seriousness of what occurred here: the
> fraud, the doctoring of files, the lying to clients, the
> cheating, the lack of oversight by senior executives? Is
> 'inappropriate' the exact, correct description?
> Cohen: … 'Inappropriate' covers the fact that some of the
> behaviours, which I think you are alluding to, from some
> of our people just were not the appropriate behaviours,
> were not the behaviours that we expect today …
> Bishop: … In my mind, 'inappropriate' is not systemic
> fraud, is not systemic theft, is not loss caused by systemic
> bad behaviour. When my three-year-old writes on
> the wall, that is 'inappropriate' and you tell her off.
> 'Inappropriate' is not the word here, is it?
> Cohen: We believe it is.[5]

Recalling the exchange, Bishop says, 'It made me think these guys don't get it, refused to get it, and so the only way they would get it was a royal commission.'

*

The release of the Senate report couldn't have come at a worse time for Tony Abbott's recently elected Coalition government. The new Minister for Finance, Senator Mathias Cormann, had been briefed on the report's contents by Bishop ten days before its release. He knew it was going to be contentious.

Cormann had an exquisite problem. In December 2013, three months after winning the election, the Abbott government had unveiled its much-trumpeted but controversial plan to wind back legislation known as the Future of Financial Advice (FoFA), which was due to come into force on 1 July 2014. The FoFA reforms had been devised by the previous Gillard Labor government to boost protections for consumers after the disastrous failures of Storm Financial and Opes Prime in 2009, and partly in response to the landmark November 2009 report of the parliamentary inquiry into financial products and services in Australia chaired by Bernie Ripoll. It had recommended, among other measures, the banning of commissions for financial advice, along with other forms of conflicted remuneration.[6] In addition to these bans, FoFA stipulated that advisers must act in their clients' best interests, send customers annual fee disclosure documents, and seek client approval every two years to continue to charge ongoing fees, known as 'opt in'. The banking and financial sectors hated FoFA. Seeking to protect their cosy set-and-forget regime, they sought to portray FoFA as nothing more than costly red tape that would make financial advice unaffordable for everyday Australians. They complained they would need to spend a fortune on new systems to comply with the FoFA laws.

The Coalition government, then spruiking 'small government' measures such as 'Red Tape Repeal Day', sided heavily with the industry. Its plan was to scrap the 'opt in' requirement of FoFA for ongoing advice and require only new clients to be provided with annual fee disclosure statements, leaving existing clients in the dark. It would also allow commissions to be paid for so-called 'general advice', meaning bank tellers could still earn kickbacks for selling or referring bank products.

These efforts to dilute the FoFA reforms could not have looked worse, given what had emerged in the parliamentary committee report about culture and misconduct in CBA and the financial advice sector. The Coalition realised that getting FoFA amendments through parliament would be a problem, as Labor and the Greens controlled the Senate at this point, and even after the new Senate was sworn in on 1 July, it would have trouble passing legislation unless it could win over eight new independent senators.

With just days until the industry had to comply with the 1 July FoFA reforms, Cormann announced he would simply bypass parliament and make the desired changes to FoFA through regulations, which, unlike legislation, don't require a vote. It was a questionable move because regulations are only supposed to be used for minor matters, such as tweaking existing legislation, not winding back significant legislation, but it would give the Coalition breathing space until a deal could be struck with the new crossbenchers – specifically, members of the Palmer United Party – and a more conventional procedure could be implemented to change the legislation.

Labor and the Greens both vowed to get the numbers to disallow or torpedo the proposed regulations. They, along with

Industry Super Australia, the umbrella body for union-backed industry superannuation funds, believed it would fundamentally change the primary FoFA legislation, which was a massive overreach by the government. They were sure it would either be disallowed by the Senate or challenged in the courts.

CBA didn't help the Coalition's cause at all. On the day the regulations were introduced and Mark Bishop's report was released, CBA chief executive Ian Narev was holidaying with his family in Bali and chairman David Turner was missing in action.[7] The release date of the Senate report had been known for months, yet the CBA executives had planned to be away. It was gobsmackingly arrogant and short-sighted, and displayed an alarming disconnect with wider society.

Cormann, in an attempt to mitigate the damage, issued an insipid statement saying, Narev would have 'more to say by way of a considered response to the Senate estimates report' and that he expected him to 'present a credible process to quickly resolve any outstanding legitimate issues from aggrieved customers'.[8] It was pure spin. Behind the scenes, Cormann and other Coalition politicians were furious at CBA's arrogance. Here was the government trying to water down FoFA (by now being called 'WoFA', a play on 'woeful'), in a move that would benefit CBA and the other banks – but CBA was doing nothing to help.

Meanwhile, Narev was fielding calls from Canberra urging him to launch a compensation scheme to pacify the public. At pre-dinner drinks at a Wesfarmers centenary celebration on 2 July at Melbourne Town Hall, Treasurer Joe Hockey was shaking his head at the arrogance of CBA and Narev. There, as he mingled with other invitees who included the business and political *Who's Who* of Australia, Hockey told attendees that 'poor Matthias' was desperately trying to get Narev to do something.

The pressure was mounting. Former Victorian Premier Jeff Kennett admitted he generally 'loathed' government inquiries but said in a *Herald Sun* column, 'I support a royal commission into the activities of the CBA advisers, its leadership and the CBA's conduct' because of 'the importance today and in the future of the financial services industry and confidence in it'.[9]

Even the country's peak body representing financial planners, the FPA, turned the tables on the Coalition government, sending out a letter to members saying 'enough is enough'. The FPA announced it would support a royal commission unless CBA agreed to certain conditions. 'The past few weeks we have seen unprecedented events unfold before our eyes,' FPA chairman Matthew Rowe wrote to members. 'Like many of you, I am appalled at the damage done to many customers of the Commonwealth Bank Financial Planning business as well as the actions of some in CBA management ... I believe we only get what we accept or tolerate, and on behalf of our members, we are no longer willing to accept what has been made public about the Commonwealth Bank's management practices.'[10]

The FPA called on CBA to establish an independent review committee into client compensation, examine the professional standards and ethics of CBA financial planners, and fund ethics training for all CBA and Financial Wisdom financial planners. It suggested the bank invite an FPA Board representative to join the independent review committee into client compensation and ensure all the bank's planners were members of a professional body. 'Anything less than this and the FPA will fully support a royal commission.'

On 2 July, FPA chief executive Mark Rantall added his voice, calling on CBA to pay full compensation to all impacted clients. The next day CBA summoned Rantall and Rowe to discuss their requests. Rowe says when they arrived, they were surprised to see a roomful of bankers and lawyers.

The air was tense. One senior executive launched into a tirade. 'We will smash you,' Rowe recalls the executive saying, 'We have an almost limitless balance sheet with which to protect our reputation.'

Rowe says he sat there thinking, 'Oh shit.'

With nothing to lose, Rantall hit back, saying to the room, 'The subtlety of your threat is not lost on us, but before we go on could you please tell us about Stuart Jamieson from WA?'

Rantall explained that the FPA had a whistleblower file on Jamieson, a former CBA adviser. He told the room the FPA was about to ban Jamieson and suggested CBA might want to notify ASIC. The room went silent. Jamieson was another scandal CBA had mishandled and tried to bury.

Stuart Jamieson had left CBA in May 2012 after the bank had uncovered repeated misconduct. CBA allowed him to resign instead of terminating him or filing a breach report with ASIC, which enabled Jamieson to get picked up elsewhere in the industry. It wasn't until September 2013, when the Fairfax Media and Senate scrutiny was most intense, that CBA lodged a breach report on Jamieson with ASIC, which resulted in him being banned as a financial planner for five years from October 2015.

The reference to Jamieson might have halted momentum for a moment, but CBA had other means of putting pressure on the FPA. It removed all sponsorship from the FPA Congress and FPA events. It also stopped paying members' fees on behalf of advisers via salary sacrifice. 'We were two blokes from a small not-for-profit professional body who had just picked a fight with the largest corporation in Australia – and they let us know it,' Rowe recalls.

*

On 3 July, Narev jetted into Sydney to front the media with a well-rehearsed mea culpa and a commitment to reopen its compensation scheme. It had taken Narev seven days to address the explosive report from the Senate. 'Poor advice provided by some of our advisers between 2003 to 2012 caused financial loss and distress and I am truly sorry for that,' he told the media conference.[11] He reminded everyone that the scandal was in the past and said an 'air of defensiveness' had been replaced by a 'spirit of openness'. The belated response from Narev couldn't hide the lack of contrition among senior executives and the board over the damage and hurt it had caused customers, or the lack of comprehension of the depth of anger brewing against it.

I bought a bottle of champagne to celebrate a small victory. My colleague Ruth Williams and a few others were there to share the hope that now Narev had been hauled back kicking and screaming to re-launch a compensation scheme, victims of the bank just might have an opportunity for recompense.

To keep up appearances Narev invited a few of the people he clearly saw as 'troublemakers' to separate meetings at his office at CBA headquarters in Sydney, where they were served coffee with the CBA logo sprinkled in chocolate on top. His first call was to Jeff Morris. It was 9 am on 4 July and it was a call Morris had waited six years to receive. Morris had offered to meet with Narev when he still worked at CBA, but Narev had declined.

Others on Narev's list included Wacka Williams, Merilyn Swan, Jan Braund, Senator Sam Dastyari and me. My meeting with Narev was short but to the point: any victims who had contacted me should be referred to the bank to be dealt with expediently and outside the glare of the newspapers or *Four Corners*. I left the meeting thinking, 'He must reckon I'm stupid.'

Wacka and Morris went to their meeting together. Morris recalls one of the bank's media advisers, Andrew Hall, busy taking notes. He also remembers the meeting taking an interesting turn when Wacka suggested the bank's new compensation scheme would have a lot more credibility if Morris was put in charge. 'Narev ignored the suggestion,' says Morris, 'then started talking about how we should be really impressed with the plaintiff law firms they had signed up to help customers.' Morris knew then the scheme was designed to ensure he couldn't be involved. 'The bank didn't want me anywhere near it, so they signed up the law firms,' he says, adding that he offered to meet Narev again to discuss some ideas on how to improve the scheme. Narev agreed but Morris again knew it would never happen. 'When we left, Narev put his hand up and said, "Trust me, I would be a fool if I played games with this scheme." That's exactly what they did,' Morris says.

Merilyn still remembers her meeting with Narev. She thought his apology seemed genuine – until she was about to leave the meeting. 'I turned to leave his room and he couldn't resist saying, "You have to remember investing is a buyer beware activity,"' she recalls. 'I was utterly stunned. Despite the overwhelming evidence that had been exposed through the media, *Four Corners*, and the parliamentary inquiries, he clearly seemed to think Mum and Dad were primarily responsible for their own plight,' Merilyn says. 'This confirmed what I already knew, that all of Narev's apologies were simply hollow PR exercises and he slept soundly every night.'

Sam Dastyari's adviser, Cameron Sinclair, recalls Narev saying to them at their meeting they wouldn't believe how many bank customers were trying to rip off CBA. 'I left thinking that my impression of him had been made irreparably worse.'

Dastaryi had been summoned to meet Narev because, on 1 July 2014, Labor Senator Mark Bishop had retired from politics and the diminutive thirty-one-year-old Dastyari had replaced him as chairman of the Senate Economics References Committee. Dastyari was fiercely ambitious and could see that banking and the financial services sector was a topic that resonated with the public, so he seized it as his own. He rang me to introduce himself, assuring me he would continue the good work of the committee and push for a royal commission by exposing further misconduct. Anything he could do to help, he said; he was the go-to man.

One of Dastyari's first jobs was to get the numbers in the Senate to 'disallow' or block the regulations Cormann was proposing to introduce. If he could do that, the 'original FoFA' would be reinstated and the industry would have to comply with the law. As it was, he was short two votes. If he couldn't find them, the industry would win the day and the regulations would become the rule of law.

*

Morris and two of the three other Ferrets reunited at the Buena Vista a few days after the Bishop Report into ASIC and CBA was released. They raised their beers to the Ferret who had recently died in his sleep at the age of thirty-six.

'Then, as now, the cleansing ales brought clarity,' Morris said. 'ASIC was a complicit non-participant. Not interested in taking on the big players, not really interested in doing their job at all.'

He was right.

As Morris and the other Ferrets parted on the footpath, they agreed that the journey they had begun six years earlier had a long way to go yet.

Chapter 9

Flawed schemes

Timbercorp, ANZ and the future of financial services

WITH THE INK BARELY dry on the Senate report calling for a royal commission into CBA, a fresh scandal was exposed across the front pages of the *Sydney Morning Herald* and *The Age.* This time it was about Macquarie Group.

It was July 2014 and a whistleblower working within the so-called 'millionaires' factory' had watched the CBA scandal unfold and wanted to help blow the lid on similarly poor behaviour at Macquarie. He made contact with me and Wacka Williams, saying he was concerned that Macquarie Group customers weren't being properly compensated for poor advice and – in a familiar refrain – that ASIC wasn't doing its job. 'We [the Macquarie Group] have a legal and moral responsibility to shareholders to protect and inform them.'

Around the same time, another source gave me an explosive confidential document, an assessment by an external consultant of client files, which showed that Macquarie's team of financial advisers had serious compliance problems. The stories mirrored what had happened at CBA: investors had lost their savings and struggled for proper redress, and ASIC had been slow to act. In

Macquarie's case there were also concerns that financial advisers were deliberately misclassifying retail clients as sophisticated investors – a move that involved less paperwork for the adviser and made it easier to channel the investors into high-fee-paying, complex financial products, some of which were Macquarie's.

The other big reveal was that Macquarie advisers were habitually cheating on their mandatory online training exams, known as 'continuous professional development' – part of the relatively light professional accreditation requirements faced by financial advisers. According to the whistleblower, it was common practice for advisers to hand around cheat sheets during open-book exams. The cheat sheets were known as 'the Penske File' – a name any *Seinfeld* fan would immediately recognise.

I worked with senior Fairfax business journalist Ben Butler on the investigation. At the time, we agreed not to quote directly from the confidential document in our articles, or even refer to it, to protect the source. But four years on, I revisited the file and was given permission by my source to quote it for this book.

Macquarie Private Wealth had been having problems since 2008. ASIC had launched surveillance on the group in December 2011, uncovering serious compliance issues with the files of a 'significant' number of advisers. Macquarie had entered into a two-year enforceable undertaking in January 2013 requiring remediation for customers affected by compliance failures. Despite this, the confidential document showed that Macquarie still had much to do to clean up its act. A sample of fifteen advisers and 143 files had found that sixty files had insufficient client information, ninety-three had no record of research carried out by the adviser, 110 had no record that the adviser suggested alternative products for their client, and in 114 cases the advice or situation couldn't be assessed.

Less than two weeks after our story was published,[1] on 15 August 2014, ASIC held a press conference announcing that Macquarie would set up a remediation scheme and write to 160,000 customers who may have been receiving poor financial advice since 2004. The articles Ben and I had written also blew the lid on the lax standards and lack of professionalism that had been allowed to proliferate in a sector entrusted with people's life savings. As Wacka Williams said in Senate estimates, 'You can walk out of the shearing shed, do an eight-day, I repeat, eight-day – not eight-week – crash course, then you've qualified under the *Corporations Act* to be a financial planner.'[2] It was extraordinary to consider that the banking and financial sector was now facing a situation where two banks were embroiled in compensation schemes potentially involving hundreds of thousands of people who, it seemed likely, had been given inappropriate advice by planners who had possibly less than two weeks' training and only secondary education.

*

Around this time in mid-2014, a group of people financially devastated by yet another corporate scandal decided it was their turn to speak up. They varied in age, background and education, but they all had one thing in common: they had been convinced to put money into an ill-fated managed investment scheme, or MIS, called Timbercorp, and had been left with massive debts on near-worthless investments.

Timbercorp, one of the most notorious of the GFC-era collapses, had toppled in April 2009. It had been one of the country's biggest MISs, with 18,500 people putting money into $2 billion worth of supposedly tax effective olive, mango and timber projects over seventeen years. The precise structures varied, but essentially investors bought a portion of a plantation or olive grove. They would in theory reap the harvest proceeds in years to come and would also be given an upfront tax deduction for their investment. As well as being tax-effective, the products were enthusiastically supported by various Howard government ministers, who viewed the agribusiness MIS sector as a job-generator for regional Australia. Almost overnight, it seemed, small towns in Tasmania and south-west Western Australia found themselves surrounded by blue-gum plantations, and vast almond and olive projects were planted in irrigated parts of Victoria. It was an investment craze that was literally changing the landscape of parts of rural Australia.

The MIS products were sold, for the most part, by accountants and financial advisers, who earned big commissions, of at least 10 per cent, on the products. In many cases, investors borrowed to buy their MIS products, using specially tailored and marketed loans. ANZ Bank was a key provider of these investor loans through the financing arm of Timbercorp.

But things started to unravel in February 2007 when the Australian Taxation Office changed its tax ruling and banned upfront tax deductions on certain MISs. Timbercorp's chief executive, Sol Rabinowicz, wrote to his board, warning that the tax ruling could delay crucial financing deals, causing 'significant pressure on the short-term cash flow'.[3]

He was right. The flow of new money dried up. Profits started to dive, and in November 2008 the company flagged asset sales to pay down debts. In April 2009, crippled by a cash-flow crisis and secured debts of $750 million, Timbercorp called in administrators. When the company went under, 7511 investor-borrowers owed $478 million in grower loans.

On legal advice, some investors stopped repaying their loans and pinned their hopes on a class action. When that failed, their debts more than doubled, thanks to high penalty interest rates imposed on those who didn't keep up their loan repayments.

Now the investors wanted to be heard. One group called itself the Holt Norman Ashman Baker Action Group (HNAB-AG), after the financial advisers who'd given them bad advice. Many were former clients of the ex-financial adviser and accountant Peter Holt, who was one of the biggest sellers of Timbercorp's MIS products. Holt would later be described in Federal Parliament by Senator Sam Dastyari as a 'crook, a criminal and a fraudster', and was eventually banned as a financial adviser by ASIC in September 2012 for three years after failing to comply with numerous financial services laws. He was still allowed to practise in his accounting firm, though.

Members of HNAB-AG had been speaking with staff of Industry Super Australia, the peak lobby group for industry funds, and had met its deputy managing director, Robbie Campo. Campo wanted to give them a platform to have their stories heard. She and her associate Matt Linden had been aggressively lobbying to stop the wind-back of FoFA – in fact, most of the industry funds were doggedly opposing the wind-back of FoFA believing it to be detrimental to consumers. Industry funds philosophically disagreed with commissions, on the basis that they encouraged advisers to place clients in the products that paid the biggest commissions, which weren't always the ones that best suited their needs. Campo and Linden decided to bring some victims to Canberra to demonstrate to politicians and the media the potentially traumatic impact of conflicted remuneration.

I was working at *Four Corners* on the 'Banking Bad' episode when Campo introduced me to Naomi Halpern, an HNAB-AG member who was one of Holt's victims. He'd been her accountant for six years before he started to give her financial advice. Holt suggested Halpern put money into government-backed agricultural investment schemes that offered tax deductions. The schemes were designed to encourage people to look at other forms of investment aside from super which would not only fund their retirement but also help the environment and farmers. He pitched it as a conservative investment when it was really high risk; it also paid him large, undisclosed commissions. Holt placed Halpern in two margin loans but didn't tell her that her home was being used as security for the second one. When Timbercorp collapsed, she was left owing a fortune to finance companies. Halpern said she had made it clear to Holt that she was a low-risk investor; he had reassured her that his strategy was safe and conservative.

In September 2014, I was introduced to a whistleblower from Timbercorp who was willing to expose ANZ's role as its financier. The whistleblower requested anonymity because he was still working in the banking industry. I discussed the story with my colleague Ruth Williams, who at that time was Saturday business editor at the *Sydney Morning Herald* and *The Age*. She was ideally placed to work with me on it because she had a forensic investigative style and had covered Timbercorp and Great Southern from their rapid expansion in the early 2000s to their spectacular collapses, as well as the messy aftermath.

The whistleblower gave us an old laptop brimming with confidential emails, spreadsheets of broker sales and secret commissions, and internal documents, all of which vividly brought to life the final months and weeks of Timbercorp. Long before the company collapsed, its executives knew it was in trouble. A May 2007 email from a senior executive in the company's horticulture operations reported that a number of Timbercorp projects were not delivering on forecasts. The 2006 olive harvest was expected to achieve just 44 per cent of the original forecast; the 2007 mango harvest would achieve just 52 per cent of forecasts. 'Please treat this email as strictly confidential,' the email said.

Both Timbercorp and ANZ were aware of these issues, yet they didn't notify the market or investors. Timbercorp kept selling its products harder than ever and, although it was struggling to refinance its high levels of debt, ANZ kept approving loans to new investors in the schemes. The internal documents showed that ANZ lifted its 'grower loan facility' for Timbercorp by $6 million to $26 million in February 2007, to $45 million in April 2007, then to $60 million in November 2007. Eventually, in February 2008, it raised it to $150 million. Some of the 2008 projects signed up for by investors would never be planted. But the debts still had to be repaid to the banks.

The mess raised questions about the role of banks in such schemes. It also raised alarm bells about ASIC, which had known the Timbercorp schemes were flawed but had done nothing. The research houses that had given a positive rating to the products in return for a payment from Timbercorp were also complicit, along with the financial planners who flogged Timbercorp investments to people based on those positive ratings. Many of the investors who bought the products didn't understand what they were buying.

Based on the documents, the whistleblower's evidence and the compelling stories of the victims, we knew we had a story that had the potential to make a real difference. And it wasn't just about Timbercorp, it was about the way the entire financial advice industry operated – and how too often the modest financial ambitions of ordinary people were trashed by advisers chasing fat commissions.

The first of our Timbercorp articles appeared in *The Age* and the *Sydney Morning Herald* on 8 November 2014.[4] It opened by quoting an email from Timbercorp boss, Sol Rabinowicz, to his chief financial officer, John Murray, referring to a meeting they'd attended earlier that day with executives from ANZ during the final weeks leading up to Timbercorp's collapse. The email said, 'Hmmn! At least this hasn't shaken my view as to the extent to which banks can f*ck you over and why bank debt should always be the least preferred option.'

Murray emailed Rabinowicz back saying, 'Summary is that they will vary the facilities to achieve what they want, but expect it to be very expensive, many roles for ANZ going forward and very tight controls on how much toilet paper you use when you have to have a crap.'

The point that ANZ had made loud and clear to Murray and Rabinowicz during that 8 October 2008 meeting was, according to Murray's email: 'Some stakeholders will need to get burnt.'

Our articles also quoted Sam Dastyari, who had met with ANZ's most senior officeholders and come away with a feeling that they had 'obfuscated, denied and tried to minimise their own involvement'. He added: 'The bank has a corporate, moral and social responsibility that it isn't meeting.'

Meanwhile, Timbercorp's liquidator, KordaMentha, was quietly working behind the scenes on behalf of creditors, including ANZ, issuing seventy writs a week to Timbercorp investors who still owed hundreds of millions of dollars in debts to the bank.

Timbercorp was a compelling reminder of the inherent danger of watering down the new protections proposed by the FoFA reforms, and our articles added momentum to a call for a new Senate inquiry hearing, scheduled for 12 November 2014 at Melbourne Town Hall, which would be attended by Senators Sam Dastyari (Labor), Peter Whish-Wilson (Greens) and Nick Xenophon (independent). Dozens of Timbercorp victims, including Naomi Halpern, organised to get there early with placards, before moving inside to watch the action. Some victims had already emailed or spoken to crossbench senators Jacqui Lambie and Ricky Muir, outlining their stories.

At the hearing, a former Timbercorp executive called Andrew Peterson reinforced the findings in our article, alleging that ANZ had continued to lend to Timbercorp Finance despite the company's problems. 'They would have had to see how the projects were going, the default loan book, how Timbercorp was going forward,' Peterson told the inquiry.[5]

Peter Whish-Wilson issued a press release after the hearing saying, 'Never before have I seen so many people turn up and watch a Senate inquiry public hearing. Today alone justifies the efforts by the Greens to instigate this inquiry. I want to thank all the victims of the Timbercorp collapse who braved the inquiry to give their heart-wrenching evidence. Today is just the beginning. We have only just begun to lift the lid on the systemic failures and misconduct evident in the collapse of dodgy MIS schemes.'[6]

*

It was at this point that Dastyari, Xenophon and Whish-Wilson decided to mount a last-ditch effort to sink Cormann's financial advice regulations. With just two additional votes still needed, Dastyari and Xenophon focussed their efforts on two crossbench senators who had shown sympathy for the Timbercorp victims, Jacqui Lambie of the Palmer United Party (PUP), which had done a backroom deal with the government in July 2014 to support its wind-back of the FoFA reforms, and Ricky Muir, who had won a seat for the Australian Motoring Enthusiast Party.

On the weekend of 15–16 November 2014, while all eyes were on the G20 in Brisbane, Dastyari caught the red-eye flight to Burnie in Tasmania to spend the day with Jacqui Lambie. Since the PUP had made its July 2014 pact with the Coalition, Lambie's relationship with Palmer had deteriorated and she had made a few comments in parliament indicating she regretted her decision to support the deal. Dastyari recalls: 'Nick was saying to me privately, "There's something there … She's almost there." So I felt like I had to go over [to Tasmania] and basically bring her in from the cold. Her big fear at that point was being alone. She hadn't been in the Senate long, and she was afraid.'

Dastyari and Lambie spent the day discussing various issues, including why it was so important to stop the regulations to wind back FoFA going through. 'I treated [Lambie] like I would treat a soft delegate at an ALP conference,' Dastyari recalls, 'and gave her the emotional assurance that she was going to be okay. The commitment we gave her was we would only get her to come across if we knew we were going to win.' By late Sunday afternoon, Dastyari had convinced Lambie to vote against the Coalition's regulations.

By Monday, Xenophon had also managed to get Muir on side. After a series of victims had contacted him, including Naomi Halpern, Muir also regretted his initial decision to side with the government. He was a former forestry worker from Gippsland with firsthand knowledge of the impact of Timbercorp and had a few constitutents who had lost everything.

With the two senators on board, Dastyari's team, who called themselves the Coalition of Commonsense, now had enough votes to stop the regulations in the Senate on 19 November, as long as there were no last-minute changes of mind. Xenophon's plan was not to let Muir out of his sights the night before the vote.

He and Dastyari took Muir out to dinner at a Chinese restaurant in Canberra and plied him with alcohol. 'It was the classic ALP strategy of get him pissed off his face so he couldn't do any other deals,' Dastyari recalls.

At 8 pm Xenophon called Cormann to give him a heads-up about what was to play out the next day. Cormann listened as Xenophon told him there would be a vote to disallow the regulations, meaning that Labor's original FoFA laws would retain their full power. Dastyari remembers, 'We're sitting there and Ricky's phone starts ringing, and it's Cormann. [Ricky] had thirty missed calls from Mathias Cormann. Then Clive [Palmer]'s calling him. The whole time, I'm trying to get Nick to distract him, so I can turn his phone over so he can't see who is calling and his phone is just ringing and ringing and I'm saying, "Have another drink."'

The Coalition of Commonsense agreed to meet early the next morning at Xenophon's office and wait until it was time to front the media in a press conference and then vote. When Muir walked into Xenophon's office he looked frazzled. Xenophon was sitting behind his desk, papers piled everywhere, but he was hyped up, aware that history was about to be made and he was the chief architect. They were about to make headlines.

Until the vote took place, however, everything was on a knife's edge. Cormann had been completely flatfooted and politically outmanoeuvred but he was still working the phones. He rang and reminded Lambie and Muir of their obligation to honour the agreement they'd made in conjunction with Clive Palmer and the government in July to support the changes to FoFA. Muir had signed the motion in the Senate a day earlier, which signals that a decision has been made and a vote will be cast, but reality was starting to hit. He asked if he could stay in Xenophon's office instead of fronting the media. 'He's saying, "I'll vote for you guys", then all of a sudden he says, "Can't I abstain?"' Dastyari recalls.

'You are going to be dragged kicking and screaming,' Dastyari told Muir half-jokingly.

They knew if Muir didn't do the press conference they would lose him in the vote. They needed to lock him in. 'It was like a scene from *Reservoir Dogs*,' Dastyari says. 'We planned to go the long way and catch the cameras as a "Fuck you" to Mathias ... It was the world's best presser [press conference].'

Later that morning the vote took place, with Lambie and Muir citing the human stories stemming from Timbercorp's demise as the reason for their change of heart. 'I will not allow the Liberal Party and their supporters to wind back consumer protection at a time when the financial advice industry has been shown to act in a scandalous manner,' said Lambie.

The high fives were now coming from Industry Super Australia, the Coalition of Commonsense and the many victims of financial abuse. The regulations had been scrubbed out and the original FoFA reforms would remain in force.

The wealth management mouthpiece, the Financial Services Council, hit the media with predictions of chaos and a 'legal quagmire' which would lead to disruption and unnecessary costs and reduce the affordability and accessibility of financial advice. But the headlines focussed on the ambush of Cormann's proposed regulations by Labor and the Greens. It was a watershed moment: not only had FoFA caused the PUP's Tasmanian senator to break with Clive Palmer, forever altering parliament, but financial advice and bank misconduct had made it into the mainstream. Momentum for change was building.

Chapter 10

Trouble on the Death Star

NAB's dirty secrets

'HI ADELE, MY NAME is "John". I work at NAB in the Wealth/MLC division.'

So began a fresh scandal, revealed by an insider at NAB who felt compelled to contact me after seeing wrongdoing and a culture of cover-up inside the bank. It was February 2015, three months after FoFA had been saved, and I had effectively become the go-to person for whistleblowers in the financial services industry after the attention the CBA, Macquarie and Timbercorp scandals had received. In addition, the bravery of Jeff Morris had triggered a chain reaction, encouraging other whistleblowers to contact me with further stories of wrongdoing. It was a terrible indictment on the corporate regulator whose job it is to investigate misconduct.

The NAB insider said he didn't trust the bank's internal whistleblower hotline, as a couple of colleagues had used it and had ended up losing their jobs. Nor did he trust ASIC. He said he had seen what had happened to Morris, as well as too many staff moving between the financial services sector and ASIC. He considered me a safer option because I had no vested interest. He'd also been impressed by the way I'd stood up to Gina Rinehart's attempts to obtain the identities of my sources after I'd written her unauthorised biography.

The NAB whistleblower wrote, 'John isn't my real name. I can't reveal my identity and require maximum discretion. I have a wife and children. The cultural atmosphere at NAB at large is "toxic" and "volatile". All I hear about are ... psychopathic behaviours – "winning is everything" type of behaviours.' He went on: 'This is a CBA disaster waiting to happen and [I] am amazed how and why the regulator isn't all over this ... I'm providing this information because a lot of us are frustrated with the "motherhood" statements and lack of commitment by management to take these issues seriously – as is evidenced by the contents of reports I'm going to provide [to] you.'

It was no coincidence that the email was sent on 10 February 2015, just days after NAB's relatively new chief executive, the New Zealand–born career banker Andrew Thorburn, had been hailed as NAB's new messiah, for apparently turning around a decade of poor shareholder returns. The bank, under the effervescent Thorburn, had posted a strong quarterly profit of $1.65 billion while unveiling a series of asset sales, including spinning off and listing the Great Western Bank and selling £1.2 billion of higher-risk loans from its British commercial real estate portfolio. But the whistleblower was unimpressed by Thorburn and senior management at NAB.'

Some of the issues John raised related to long-term problems within the bank's credit risk department, which was supposed to monitor such things as systemic inadequacies in loan documentation and charging fees for no service, and ensure they were properly flagged and managed.

According to John, NAB had a culture of burying bad news, which dated back to at least 2002, when it had been rocked by a foreign exchange traders scandal. Four members of NAB's forex trading desk, on the hunt for big bonuses and bragging rights, had lost $360 million and then falsified records to cover their tracks. The scandal had snowballed into a crisis that had claimed the chief executive Frank Cicutto's job and sparked a bitter board split, which subsequently felled NAB's then chairman, Charles Allen.

The bank, its reputation in tatters, had promised to clean up its act. It seemed that it would be forced to do so under close supervision by APRA, after APRA published a scathing report into the forex disaster, noting that within NAB 'risk management controls were seen as trip-wires to be negotiated'.[1] Yet in the decade-plus since, John claimed, little had changed. Serious issues were toned down in NAB reports sent to various committees at the bank, such as the Wealth Operational Risk and Compliance Committee and the Group Chief Risk Officer Office.

After I agreed to protect his identity, John sent me a series of internal NAB documents that supported everything he'd claimed – and revealed much more. I could see that what John was exposing had the potential to be a big story, one that, yet again, would vividly illustrate the extent of the rot in Australia's banking system.

My first port of call was Ruth Williams. She was about to go on maternity leave but, like me, immediately recognised the importance of this new lead. We were still on a high after our Timbercorp articles had helped stop the wind-back of FoFA. This exposé promised to help push for a royal commission.

The trove of documents John had sent was so vast that Ruth and I had to devise our own filing system for it. We worked out a timeline setting out when the key documents were written and what they contained, as well as important events in the banking and political worlds that had influenced or were mentioned in the leaked material. While we had no reason to doubt John's motivations, we needed to independently verify the authenticity of his documents, first by crosschecking every fact, name and event mentioned against publicly available records and by running them past other contacts in the banking sector.

The documents were, at times, dense and highly technical, and many of them had been heavily 'word-smithed' to downplay problems, just as John had described. But not even this internal spin could cover up the evidence of a dysfunctional culture. One internal NAB document from August 2014, with the lengthy and lofty title of 'Memorandum for group risk return management committee: NAB Wealth advice review', had been commissioned by NAB in response to the June 2014 report of the Senate inquiry into ASIC. Andrew Hagger, who was running NAB's wealth division at the time, had authored the memorandum which, despite containing some troubling revelations about the state of NAB's advice division, had been heavily spun by him to suggest that while NAB had detected a few issues in its advice arm – with a few rogue planners – the bank had dealt with them swiftly. Hagger's memorandum suggested that compliance was strong and customers were the epicentre of everything NAB did.

Hagger had written: 'The differences between NAB Wealth's operations and CBA's as described in the Senate inquiry are significant. In contrast, NAB Wealth had and continues to have a strong culture and compliance framework with no bias toward higher revenue earners with regard to audits conducted and consequence management. We use experienced industry-leading non-executive directors to differentiate our governance processes. With their independence they assist in addressing any conflicts of interest that are escalated to their attention including compliance related issues, sales practices and approved products (including NAB Group products).'[2]

In cases of 'inappropriate advice', Hagger claimed NAB had terminated the employment of the wrongdoers and extended its reviews 'beyond the initial issue identification and findings to identify related cases'. In reality, some had been allowed to leave – and pick up a reference on the way out.

Hagger's report even managed to put a positive spin on the fact that NAB had identified and quietly dismissed thirty-seven financial planners, for reasons including that they had provided their clients with inappropriate advice, had committed forgery or fraud or had committed repeated compliance breaches.

The report stated that one of the bank's star planners, Graeme Cowper, had been terminated in 2010 for 'file reconstruction' – in other words, retrospectively altering records to cover up mistakes or misconduct – and compliance breaches. A more familiar name mentioned was that of Emmanuel Cassimatis, who had quit as an agent of NAB's MLC arm in the 1990s after being caught applying a 'cookie-cutter' approach to his job – giving all of his clients the same financial advice regardless of their age, financial background or risk profile.

According to Hagger's report, NAB had everything under control and there was nothing to worry about. But the documents spoke for themselves. Of the financial planners removed for misconduct, only eight had been reported to ASIC. Cassimatis had not been the subject of a breach report to ASIC. None of the planners accused of forgery or fraud had been reported to the police. At least thirty-three planners NAB had pushed out received no black marks against their names, so they were able to move to similar jobs elsewhere and repeat the same poor behaviour. Some of them did, with catastrophic results.

Graeme Cowper had been the subject of a breach report to ASIC, but NAB hadn't terminated him, contrary to what had been stated in Hagger's internal report. In fact, NAB had allowed him to resign and given him a glowing letter wishing him 'every success in the future', as well as a payout of $185,000. He'd then moved from firm to firm before ending up at AMP.

The sackings and the compensation payments made by NAB Wealth – to seven hundred customers totalling between $10 million and $15 million – had been kept quiet by NAB and were unknown to ASIC or the public. That meant there had been no oversight or transparency regarding how customers were being compensated.

In the absence of any outside scrutiny, Ruth and I suspected NAB hadn't treated customers fairly. Cowper had had hundreds of clients, yet NAB had compensated only fifty-three. I called CBA whistleblower Jeff Morris to inform him there was another scandal ready to blow. Morris wasn't surprised. One of the Ferrets who'd left CBA in disgust had gone on to work at NAB financial planning, only to discover the culture there was as bad or, possibly, worse than CBA's.

Morris, it turned out, had also helped a former colleague, single mother Veronica Coulston, battle NAB for compensation after Cowper's inappropriate advice had left her financially devastated. Morris had happened to bump into Coulston and been shocked by her appearance: her face was drawn, her eyes were hollow and she hadn't been sleeping. She told him how her life had been destroyed after she had made the fateful decision to use an inheritance to pay down her mortgage with NAB. When she went into a NAB branch to do so, a bank employee had insisted she see Cowper (no doubt thereby earning a referral fee). Instead of recommending Coulston pay down her mortgage, Cowper plunged her inheritance into high-fee-paying NAB funds and pushed her to borrow to invest more.

By 2009, after her investments had plummeted in value, Coulston owed $350,000, including the debt on a maxed-out credit card. Yet Cowper's advice was to increase her line of credit, even though she was only earning $45,000 a year as a secretary at the time.

It soon became clear to Morris that Coulston's problems had arisen as a result of another bonus-incentivised financial planner determined to flog more product to vulnerable, low-income clients. Just like Storm Financial. Just like 'Dodgy Don' Nguyen at CBA. NAB couldn't lose. If Coulston defaulted, the bank could sell her home and recoup all the funds.

As Morris and Coulston tried to build a case for compensation with NAB, they were confronted with a wall of silence and obfuscation. The bank refused to hand over key documents, such as the original signed loan application forms and assessments, claiming they'd been lost.

Eventually Morris found a key loan document in Coulston's files which had been filled out by Cowper and was riddled with errors and, crucially, overstated Coulston's asset position. Morris wrote a blistering letter to NAB chairman Michael Chaney, asking him to investigate the 'predatory lending' and the conduct of 'bonus incentivised employees of NAB'. The bank paid Coulston a small amount in compensation, and hoped she would go away.

During a meeting with ASIC staff in February 2011, Morris raised Cowper's conduct at NAB. Morris was still working at CBA, and it was more than two years since he had blown the whistle on CBA and Don Nguyen. He pointed out the parallels with CBA and Nguyen, including NAB's unwillingness to discipline a planner who wrote them a lot of business. Morris was assured that somebody at ASIC would investigate his allegations. Four years had passed since then and nothing had been done.

*

Ruth and I compiled a detailed set of questions to send to NAB days ahead of the deadline for our article. NAB responded with an invitation to interview Andrew Hagger at the bank's headquarters in Melbourne's Docklands, with the only slot available just hours before we were due to file our article. When we arrived, Hagger – smooth, polished, confident – sported a big smile. As we turned on our recorders, he launched into a contrite spiel. But he made it clear that he believed NAB had no 'systemic issues'.

Hagger put a positive spin on the documents we'd obtained. Rather than them being evidence of deep-seated issues, he pitched them as a healthy sign that the bank was confronting its (limited) problems. He was emphatic that NAB wasn't like CBA, no matter how much we referred to the leaked documents and the specific problems they revealed – such as cost and time overruns on multiple critical projects, a recent spike in internal breaches reported to regulators, and the numerous highly rated internal risks.

It wasn't just Hagger we had to contend with as our deadline for filing loomed. Cowper had responded to a list of questions we'd asked him about his time at NAB with a threat to sue us for defamation if we went ahead and published our article. We decided to press on, believing it was too important a story not to run.

The article appeared on the front page of the *Sydney Morning Herald* on 21 February 2015.[3] It was accompanied by a photo of an angry Cowper getting into his car, and it made a wider point: 'The revelations that NAB's financial advice arm has been infected with some of the same contagions as CBA's – including forged client signatures, file reconstructions, and poor advice leading to compensation payouts for some clients – underscores the problems festering in Australia's financial advice industry. They are likely to re-energise calls for a royal commission, which the Abbott government has so far resisted.'

After the article went to print – as with the previous scandals we had exposed – Ruth and I received a torrent of emails from other victims of Graeme Cowper, outlining their stories. Some had never received compensation, others had received a pittance. We also received some emails from former NAB staff who identified other rogue advisers and lax compliance systems.

NAB apologised and opened up a compensation scheme. Senators Sam Dastyari and Wacka Williams held an inquiry into NAB, which required senior bank executives along with NAB victims to come to parliament to give evidence. Veronica Coulston attended, accompanied by Jeff Morris. The NAB whistleblower, John, listened to evidence and sent questions to me to pass to various senators grilling the executives.

Meanwhile Graeme Cowper's lawyers sent Fairfax a letter requesting tens of thousands of dollars for defaming him. The letter said if we paid up, he would go away. If we didn't, he would issue legal proceedings for defamation. Fairfax's lawyers sent a politely written letter back telling Cowper to go his hardest.

Our exposé had prompted AMP – Cowper's employer at the time – to suspend him while it examined his client files. What AMP uncovered in the files resulted in Cowper's dismissal. Cowper fought AMP for unfair dismissal and filed a defamation claim against Ruth, myself, Jeff Morris and Fairfax. The defamation action took more than a year to go to trial. Some would-be defamation plaintiffs give up along the way, but Cowper was determined to press on. The case was eventually scheduled for a four-week jury trial at the NSW Supreme Court in late 2016.

Cowper would soon come to regret his decision to proceed with his action. The court evidence painted a disturbing picture of what had gone on at NAB. 'Who do you think you f***ing are? ... If you try to get me, I'm going to throw you under the f***ing bus,' Cowper had told a NAB compliance manager while he was conducting a random compliance check of Cowper's files, according to evidence given by the compliance manager in court.

On the eve of his cross-examination, Cowper capitulated. He had to pay $200,000 in legal costs and agreed that judgement should be entered in our favour. All up Cowper's 'inappropriate' advice forced NAB to pay more than two hundred clients $13.4 million in compensation. In June 2018, ASIC finally issued a four-year banning order preventing Cowper working as a financial adviser. But by that time he had already left the industry.

As we were compiling our NAB investigation in 2015, the failings of ASIC again emerged as a significant theme. One of the documents sent by the NAB whistleblower revealed a shocking fact about ASIC that had not yet been exposed. The document referred to a draft media release ASIC had sent to NAB for 'review'. It turned out that the year before, ASIC had offered NAB – an institution that it regulated – the opportunity to check and suggest changes to ASIC's own media release about wrongdoing by the bank before it was sent out to the media and made public. The media release related to a four-year-long system error that affected tens of thousands of customers. In the release, ASIC acknowledged the 'co-operative approach taken by NAB Wealth in this matter'.[4] That raised a lot of eyebrows, as it suggested that the regulator was rather too chummy with those it regulated. As the whistleblower pointed out, the strategy conveniently resulted in minimal media coverage and public reaction. A month later, the ASIC chairman, Greg Medcraft, having been hauled in front of a parliamentary hearing, tried to justify the practice but conceded that ASIC had since reviewed its policies and would now allow only a short window of up to twenty-four hours for an institution to review a press release, and that would only be to check accuracy, not amend the wording.

The cosy relationship between NAB and ASIC was highlighted in other documents too, one of which smugly described the bank's relationship as 'open and trusting'. What was even more shocking was that the cooperation between ASIC and NAB had occurred around the time Greg Medcraft had been lamenting in parliament how ASIC had been too trusting of CBA.

*

In 2004 banking analyst Brett Le Mesurier (who would later be interrogated by ASIC about his Macquarie Bank analysis) had mischievously referred to NAB's UK banking arm as the 'Death Star', a play on NAB's red star logo. More than a decade later, the phrase was revived when NAB subsidiaries Clydesdale Bank and Yorkshire Bank were caught up in a scandal.

NAB had entered the UK market in the late 1980s and early 1990s, purchasing banks including Clydesdale Bank and Yorkshire Bank. Then, as part of a sales drive, these NAB subsidiaries had started aggressively selling complex business loans to small-business owners, who usually believed they were signing up for standard business loans. Called tailored business loans (TBLs), these loans incorporated embedded hedging products, which meant they were unregulated and risky.

When interest rates plunged during the GFC, thousands of customers of these loans went to the bank to change their contracts to take advantage of the lower rates. It was then they realised what they had signed up for. Buried in the contract was a prohibitively large break fee – up to 40 per cent of the loan in some cases. Many customers had no idea they had signed a contract laced with derivatives, which left them saddled with interest repayments as much as three times their bank's variable rate. The products, and the resulting devastation they caused, prompted an investigation in 2014 by the UK financial regulator and a parliamentary inquiry into nine banks, including Clydesdale. At that inquiry, David Thorburn, who had resigned as chief executive of Clydesdale in January 2015, admitted that the relevant terms and conditions letters of TBLs would not pass a plain-English test. He also conceded that TBL customers could not reasonably have anticipated the costs to which they had exposed themselves.[5]

A Yorkshire Bank customer, David Farndon, who had read about the NAB financial planning scandal, tipped me off about this situation, saying, 'You should look at the damage NAB has done in the UK. It has destroyed families, businesses. These bank people need to go to prison. It's a disgrace. If you need case studies please contact me as there are hundreds.' He went on to say that his family had suffered terrible treatment from the Yorkshire Bank. 'Currently they're trying to take my home of ten years. They are also trying to take the home of my eighty-three-year-old mother, who has Alzheimer's. Normally businesses reward their loyal customers. But not NAB, they destroy them.' Farndon said he had been with Yorkshire Bank for ten years and never missed a payment.

The more stories I listened to, the more I could see parallels with the 1980s foreign currency loans scandal, which had caught out Wacka and others, and, more recently, the debacle at Bankwest, which had pulled the rug out from numerous small businesses after CBA became its new owner. One of the worst stories I heard – and wrote about – was that of John Glare, who had bought a majestic four-hundred-year-old country manor house in Dorset in 2002 for £4.5 million to use as his home and business premises. He converted it into a Christian resource centre and a reception house for weddings. The business was financed by a TBL of £3.95 million with Clydesdale.

When the GFC hit and interest rates plunged, Glare wondered why his interest rates were soaring to the point where his loan repayments were becoming unaffordable. When he realised he'd signed a TBL, he tried to break the contract but was told by Clydesdale staff that doing so would cost him £783,383. 'I was stunned,' Glare said, noting that the break fee represented 20 per cent of the principal of the original £3.95 million loan. Glare was evicted from his Dorset manor house in June 2010 and became homeless. He lodged a complaint with the UK's Financial Ombudsman Service to get a copy of his file. In 2012 he received a box of documents, possibly from the ombudsman's office, which included bombshell internal emails between Clydesdale Bank and NAB that put everything into perspective. 'The emails made me realise that it was the bank's wrongdoing that caused my ruin, not the economic downturn,' Glare said. 'When I think back to the year before my eviction, it was a daily battlefield. One month I had to explain to staff that their pay would be paid a week late, the next month it was two weeks late. Some staff left, others failed to turn up to work saying they couldn't afford to pay for the petrol. I had to explain to couples that their receptions were cancelled. I had to explain to churches and Christian groups that their conferences were cancelled.'

In 2014 – four years after Glare started battling with Clydesdale – the bank finally admitted it had mis-sold Glare the loan and agreed to settle all the damages he could prove. However, it offered no compensation for the business he had lost. Glare fought the bank and lost, but is now planning further legal action.

In March 2015, the Treasury Committee of the UK Parliament released a damning report into mis-selling by nine banks, including NAB's Clydesdale Bank. It found that NAB had behaved badly by mis-selling the TBLs tailored to small-business owners and that this had 'led to considerable consumer detriment'. It said that customers were kept in the dark about the risks and that the bank structured the products to deliberately avoid regulation. That ensured less paperwork, and little or no recourse for the customer when things went pear-shaped. As a result, the authorities were left 'powerless to enforce compensation for customers to whom products were mis-sold'. The Clydesdale Bank alone had sold 11,271 TBLs in the decade up to mid-2012, of which 8372 were unregulated, meaning borrowers had no protection. The loans on average ranged between hundreds of thousands of pounds and £3 million.

After years of investor pressure following poor performance and reputational damage, NAB finally decided to get out of the UK in 2016 and hived off its local banks to a holding company, CYBG. In allowing this, the UK Prudential Regulation Authority requested that NAB enter a conduct indemnity agreement with CYBG to cover potential losses related to legacy conduct costs not covered by existing provisions it had made. Those legacy costs included the TBLs as well as payment protection insurance (PPI) – insurance that enables customers to keep repaying debts if they get sick or lose their job, which was sold as add-on insurance when customers took out a car loan, credit card or mortgage. NAB's agreement with CYBG included a capped indemnity of more than £1 billion, but that has been exhausted – so far PPIs have cost the British banking industry, including Clydesdale and Yorkshire banks, £40 billion in remediation.

For those who missed out and believe they are entitled to compensation for NAB's TBLs, the fight is far from over. UK claims management group RGL, led by Australian expatriate banker James Hayward, launched a class action in May 2019 that alleges Clydesdale and NAB mis-sold these complex loans between 2001 and 2012. It is funded by the UK's biggest litigation funder, Augusta Venture, and it alleges deceit, misrepresentation, negligent misstatement, breach of contract and unjust enrichment. So far 140 claimants have signed up and the cases of another two thousand potential claimants, estimated to be owed hundreds of millions of pounds, are being evaluated. If consequential damages are included, the overall costs could exceed £1 billion.

A separate legal action is also being prepared by the CYBG Remediation Support Group for a probable launch in June 2019, on behalf of hundreds of claimants. NAB and CYBG plan to fight the action in the courts, but are inviting some complainants to discuss their concerns directly. NAB also reportedly backs a proposal for a business ombudsman to examine certain cases. One relates to John Guidi, a sixty-three-year-old small-business operator who was bankrupted by mis-sold loans and faced the loss of his home of thirty years. He attracted publicity when he started a hunger strike in March and slept in a tent outside the Glasgow head office of CYBG. When I rang him in early May, he had just suspended his protest after CYBG had invited him to discuss a resolution. 'I need to get a solution for me and my family, failing which I will resume my hunger strike,' he said. 'What does a drowning man do? Grabs on to anything he can.' As of June 2019, he was still waiting and said, 'This is troubling as the prospect of resuming my hunger strike is not one that I face without grave trepidation.'

Chapter 11
Shooting the messenger

IOOF's smear campaign

By LATE FEBRUARY 2015, a crisis of confidence was building in the community about the financial services sector and the safety of retirement savings. The NAB scandal, which had erupted on 20 February, had reinforced the need for reform and tougher regulation. After failing to wind back FoFA, the government had installed a new financial services minister, Josh Frydenberg, to restore trust in the industry He promised by March there would be a public financial adviser register so that customers could look up the name of their adviser to check their education standards, work history and any previous sanctions or banning orders. He also promised to look at a code of ethics for the sector and give ASIC powers to intervene and ban products.

The measures were welcome, but given the mounting scandals – first CBA, then Macquarie, ANZ and Timbercorp, and now NAB – many saw them as Band-Aid solutions. And another big revelation of financial misconduct was about to be made. This time the scoundrel was financial services giant, IOOF, the once venerable friendly society that had been founded in 1846 as the Independent Order of Odd Fellows and, through numerous acquisitions, had transformed itself into a financial behemoth with $150 billion of Australians' retirement savings under its watch. I received an email on 10 February 2015 from an insider wanting to expose wrongdoing. I had met him previously when he worked for another financial institution. He said he had followed the various scandals I had exposed, had been inspired by CBA whistleblower Jeff Morris and felt it was his duty to let the country know what was going on inside IOOF.

He told me he had proof of insider trading, the deliberate misrepresentation of performance figures on funds, rampant cheating in exams by staff, and other serious breaches of the law. He also had evidence that the head of the research department had been investigated by the company for frontrunning, but this had been covered up. Frontrunning is when someone buys a stock knowing a research report is coming that will send the share price up and thus benefit the buyer of the stock. It is illegal.

My contact's only request was that I keep his name out of my reports. IOOF knew he was the whistleblower, but he didn't want his photo or identity splashed across the media because he was still young and didn't want to rule himself out of getting another job in the financial services industry. He suggested the pseudonym Guy Fawkes.

Guy said he had initially told IOOF's compliance officer what he had uncovered. He was then advised by human resources (HR) that the compliance officer and his boss had beat him to it and lodged an 'unofficial' complaint about Guy to HR. From that point on, he was bullied and ostracised in the office. He went on stress leave and on the second day he was notified by HR that his email had been switched off. A couple of weeks later, on Christmas Eve 2014, IOOF's company secretary looked at the allegations Guy had lodged and decided 'no further action was warranted' and the 'matter will be considered closed'. In early January 2015, Guy went to the Fair Work Commission and lodged a bullying and harassment claim, which outlined some of the misconduct he had uncovered. During the Fair Work process, IOOF terminated his employment, claiming Guy's allegations were 'vexatious' and that he had used confidential information, in breach of his workplace obligations. His termination letter cited a report by PricewaterhouseCoopers, which had carried out an independent investigation, paid for by IOOF, into his allegations and found them to be unsubstantiated.

This looked like another red-hot scandal. I asked a colleague, Sarah Danckert, who'd recently moved to *The Age* from *The Australian*, to work on the investigation with me, and she agreed. I then flew to Sydney to meet up with Guy and collect a USB containing thousands of IOOF documents. Some of them showed that one senior officer had been investigated internally on suspicion of insider trading. The company didn't report it to ASIC. Instead, internal emails showed the staff member had been given a warning and told to donate the profits made on the illegal activity to a charity of IOOF's choice.

Other documents revealed that Guy's boss had been investigated for frontrunning on a relative's account, which had resulted in a final warning. Yet other documents showed that the same executive had been given a further final warning in 2014 and stripped of his responsible manager status for getting staff to cheat on his behalf in exams. Emails discussed breaches and errors in the unit pricing of some of IOOF's cash management trusts. One exchange between two compliance officers tasked with compiling a list of breaches in a handful of IOOF's cash management trusts contained the bombshell comment: 'There seems to be just as many unit pricing incidents as there were breaches.'

When our story was published in *The Age* and the *Sydney Morning Herald* on 20 June 2015, it provoked a huge reaction.[1] IOOF's share price fell more than 20 per cent, ASIC launched an investigation into the company, and Greens senator Peter Whish-Wilson introduced a motion for a royal commission into the finance sector.[2] Wacka crossed the floor to support the motion. It was defeated 39 to 14 after Labor sided with the government. But the drums were getting louder.

Nine days after our article appeared, I received a curious email from one of the most senior IOOF officials in the company, saying: '[The source of your articles about IOOF] is not a "whistleblower", Adele. He is a blackmailer who has done this before to another major financial institution. They paid up. We refused (as we should) … and have paid the consequences via your sensationalist articles.' The email said IOOF had reported the blackmail to NSW Police at the time, along with other related matters, and said of the whistleblower, 'He sent intimidatory emails to several staff members implying via innuendo that their children could be under threat of kidnapping or worse at the schools they attended.' He had also demanded the job of his boss, the email said. 'You have been sucked in by a person who has known mental problems and in doing so you and the newspaper have grossly abused the privileges given to journalists to report fairly.'

He continued: 'For you to conclude that IOOF is "dodgy" based on the information you have been given (which neither myself nor the board has seen) is beyond belief … I am also concerned at the gross abuse of parliamentary privilege that occurred during the week … If you were in receipt of stolen information or files relating to a company, you should have handed them and/or the information over to IOOF and not simply pass [*sic*] them on to Senator Williams so you could use Parliament to extend your ill-founded and sensationalist campaign … Parliament should not be used as some sort of kangaroo court … and certainly not to suit the revenge objectives of a blackmailer who didn't get his way.'

The email shocked me. I had experienced companies trying to smear whistleblowers to diminish their credibility and divert attention from the main game, but this was in another league. Here was a senior official alleging blackmail, theft and mental health issues. Over the next few days I received a number of anonymous calls from industry insiders warning me to be careful because the whistleblower was a known shyster. I tried not to feel rattled but believed it was my duty to let Guy know what was being said about him. He too was shaken and began to worry for his safety.

I agreed to meet the IOOF official and requested he bring along proof of his allegations, including the blackmailing emails. We agreed to meet at the Grand Hyatt on Collins Street in Melbourne's CBD on the morning of 30 June. Sarah Danckert came with me. When we arrived I was surprised by the behaviour of the bald, bespectacled middle-aged man, who had brought along an external public relations (PR) person for support. The PR person became visibly uncomfortable as we sat and listened to what was simply a character assassination of the whistleblower. There was nothing to back up the allegations: no 'blackmail' emails, no police report, no evidence that the whistleblower had mental health issues or had blackmailed his previous employer.

It was disturbing to think that a Top 100 company in Australia could operate in such a manner. Instead of trying to get to the bottom of the allegations about IOOF, the company was attempting to smear the messenger.

*

Meanwhile our story had prompted Senator Sam Dastyari to use the senate to try and get to the bottom of the scandal. On 8 July 2015, IOOF boss, Chris Kelaher, was called before a senate hearing in Sydney. Kelaher repeatedly claimed a company had no obligation to report a suspicion of frontrunning or insider trading, in contradiction of ASIC regulatory guide RG 238, which stated that a company that is a market participant, such as IOOF's Bridges Financial, where the manager worked, had to report any suspicion of either frontrunning or insider trading.

On 8 July 2016, Chris Kelaher was grinning from ear to ear when ASIC completed its investigation into IOOF and issued a one-page media release.[3] It found issues with IOOF's compliance arrangements, breach reporting, management of conflicts of interest, the staff trading policy, disclosure, whistleblower management and protection, and cybersecurity. Yet ASIC failed to fine, sanction or ban IOOF, instigate legal action against the company, amend its licence conditions or even enter an enforceable undertaking with it.

Kelaher gave an interview to *The Australian* where he crowed that he had always maintained that there was 'no truth' in the allegations, and that the closing of the probe cleared the way for IOOF to build its business. 'You can say it a hundred times, but now the regulator has come out and said it and it's very pleasing,' he said. 'The company is on the cusp of a fairly bright future.'[4]

In disgust, I wrote a column highlighting the fact that the core function of any financial services company is to ensure proper compliance and disclosure. According to ASIC's findings, IOOF had fallen well short of this. Yet the best ASIC could say was it had 'reached an agreement' that IOOF would appoint an external compliance consultant to 'conduct an expanded, broader and more comprehensive review of compliance arrangements within all IOOF business units'.[5] ASIC preferred to outsource its job to an 'independent expert' who would be paid for by IOOF, with IOOF setting the terms of reference – with ASIC's oversight.

ASIC had taken twelve months to conclude its investigation, and although the whistleblower had contacted the regulator on numerous occasions and handed over 52,000 documents, he had received little response. Apart from a few emails and a thirty-five-minute meeting organised after he complained about inaction to ASIC's chairman, Greg Medcraft, there was silence from the regulator.

ASIC's do-nothing approach after its investigation sent a signal to IOOF that it was business as usual – for now.

Chapter 12
Claims denied

CommInsure's unscrupulous tactics

For weeks, Dr Ben Koh, Commonwealth Bank's chief medical officer had been trying to find the courage to call me. Koh had become a whistleblower at CBA's life insurance arm, CommInsure, and things had turned nasty. He knew he had weeks, if not days, before he would be dismissed by CommInsure and marched off the premises. Finally, desperate to speak to someone who understood the machinations of the bank, he reached out to me by email on 8 July 2015, on the very day Chris Kelaher appeared in front of the Senate hearing in Sydney. 'Is there a tel no. I can call to speak to you in confidence?' he wrote. He also called Jeff Morris and asked if they could meet urgently.

When I spoke to Koh on the phone, he sounded desperate. He told me he had joined the insurer in 2013 to run a team of medical professionals tasked with assessing insurance claims – CommInsure had even issued a press release touting his arrival. But a year later he had turned whistleblower and taken allegations to its highest executives and the CommInsure board. They included claims that the life insurer regularly 'lost' files; spied on customers for the purpose of knocking back claims; used outdated medical definitions to avoid payouts; leaned on doctors to knock back claims; and asked Koh to overrule colleagues' medical opinions without sound evidence for doing so.

Koh pointed out to me that life insurance is a contract of faith. Most Australians have life insurance policies, either directly or through their super fund. They are purchased on trust. CBA was breaching that trust.

I compared notes with Jeff Morris and realised that what Koh was saying, if it stacked up, had the potential to undermine confidence in the $44 billion life insurance industry. The public was getting used to financial advice scandals and breaches of lending laws that led to customers having to sell farms, houses and businesses even when payments hadn't been missed. But knocking back legitimate insurance claims of sick and dying people showed how far the tentacles of malpractice had spread in CBA's financial services departments.

In August, Koh's employment was terminated. He told me the bank had offered him money to sign a gag order and resign. 'These people do not understand that you can't buy integrity,' he said. When he'd refused, his boss, CommInsure chief executive Helen Troup had summoned him to a meeting, where he was sacked. Troup's reason for his dismissal was that he'd breached the bank's IT policies by forwarding work files to his personal email account – an action he'd taken because he was concerned the files would go missing. He said he had been given approval to do so by his then boss and that everyone did it.

It was to no avail. 'I walked away and told myself, I don't need your money. I'm not going to be silenced by your gag order. And you can choose to say whatever you want to my colleagues. I have no control over that. But damn if I'm going to be silenced.' Yet Koh wasn't quite ready to go public and convincing him to speak out wasn't easy. Even after talking to Jeff Morris, he preferred to be anonymous. I knew it would be more powerful if he revealed his identity, so I kept on at him, pointing out that he didn't plan to go back into the industry.

I knew Koh was toying with the idea of suing the bank, so I introduced him to John Berrill, a lawyer who'd recently resigned from class-action law firm Maurice Blackburn. I also brought in Wacka, who was outraged that CBA didn't appear to have learned any lessons since the Senate inquiry and was more than ever convinced it was time for a royal commission.

Fortuitously, I received a cache of internal CommInsure documents and emails at this point, some from a fake email address, some in an envelope, that backed up what Koh was saying about the culture and antics inside the claims department at CommInsure. They included heated emails between doctors and CBA claims managers over customer claims; reports of files going missing; and written complaints that doctors were being pressured to change opinions to avoid payouts. Other documents confirmed that outdated medical definitions were still being used, including those of heart attacks, cancer, strokes and rheumatoid arthritis. Following a report of a rise in bladder cancer claims, a team was asked to tighten its definition of the illness, but in such a way that it would not attract the attention of the ratings agencies (which use formulas to compare benefits with premiums and work out a value-for-money measure), who might lower CommInsure's ratings.

The overwhelming message of the documents was that CommInsure would generally do all it could to delay, deny and, if all else failed, litigate claims. It reminded me of CBA's treatment of Noel Stevens, who died fighting the bank. It was a clear case of valuing profit before people. What became apparent was the role senior executives had given to claims managers. Despite limited training and lack of medical degrees, they were the ones who decided when to ask a medical officer for an opinion and what medical information should be provided to that officer. And there was evidence in the documents that the remuneration of some claims staff was linked to key performance indicators such as net loss ratios – the ratio of paid insurance claims to premiums earned (for instance, $80 in claims for every $160 in collected premiums produces a loss ratio of 50 per cent). Between the documents and Koh's testimony, CBA had a lot of explaining to do.

I read through the documents and pored over numerous cases showing terrible treatment of customers by the insurer. One case that choked me up – and did so again when I re-read it – was a middle-aged man who made a total and permanent disability (TPD) claim following a diagnosis of motor neurone disease. This terminal illness affects the nerve cells controlling the muscles that enable us to move, speak, breathe and swallow, and leads to a horrific and painful death. The treatment of the man by CommInsure was ghastly.

The man lodged a claim and was given the runaround as he was trying to grapple with his health. Eight months after his diagnosis, one of his doctors sent a letter to CommInsure describing his condition as rapidly deteriorating. The patient's arms and hands were paralysed, he couldn't walk and he might not survive the next few months. The response from CommInsure was unconscionable: 'We are unable to do this calculation at present. We would first need to receive and assess the TPD claim and ensure he meets the criteria to receive TPD before we can look at a possible calculation.' A relative of the man then hired a lawyer, who fired off an email to the senior claims manager saying, 'Your behaviour towards our client is inappropriate and appears even malicious.' But four months later the lawyer was still trying to get a payment from CommInsure, which continued to drag its heels.

By this stage the man was bed bound, couldn't swallow, speak or move his head. A letter sent by a doctor to the man's lawyer said, 'Psychologically he is distressed, depressed and naturally frightened by his condition. He is ventilated … His prognosis is extremely poor. I believe that sadly, it is unlikely that he will live for more than a few months.' Yet still CommInsure delayed the payment. It was only after he died that the bank finally paid out.

Another case that resonated with me was that of James Kessel, a forty-six-year-old diesel mechanic, who had lived all his life in the tiny northern NSW town of Wee Waa. Kessel had had a heart attack in September 2014 that was so severe that his heart stopped and nurses had to restart it using a defibrillator. Yet, the bank denied his claim because he didn't have a high enough level of a protein called troponin I in his blood. (A particular level of troponin I indicates that a heart attack has occurred.)

Kessel was dirt poor, living in a tin shed and trying to scrape together a living when I went to meet him. He'd taken out a life insurance policy with CommInsure more than twenty-five years earlier and had faithfully paid premiums for a trauma policy which should have covered him if he had a life-threatening illness such as a heart attack.

What James didn't know when I met him was that the troponin I level accepted as indicative of a heart attack had changed more than a decade before, yet, as evidenced in the documents I had received, CommInsure had continued to use the old, higher measure as its benchmark – which resulted in legitimate claims like Kessel's being denied. Indeed, Ben Koh had conducted an internal audit of heart attack claims and found that more than half of legitimate claims were being knocked back due to the bank's use of the outdated definition.

The Age and the *Sydney Morning Herald* gave me the green light to cover the story. I also pitched it to *Four Corners*, suggesting I work on the program with researcher Mario Christodoulou and Klaus Toft, the producer who'd worked with me on a wage fraud exposé of convenience store giant 7-Eleven. At this stage Koh was still deciding whether to go public, but I had enough to proceed while waiting to see if he would change his mind. I was also hoping that a high-profile television report might bolster the case for a royal commission. With Malcolm Turnbull having recently taken over from Tony Abbott as Prime Minister, I thought there was a chance the Coalition might change its stance on this issue.

After *Four Corners* gave me the go-ahead, James Kessel was one of the first people who agreed to be interviewed. We flew to Wee Waa in January 2016. As the camera rolled, I showed Kessel internal bank documents reporting that his case had been escalated to an internal CommInsure committee meeting in December 2014, days before his claim had been rejected. The committee trawled through four years of his medical records trying to find a reason to reject his claim, but decided he had disclosed everything. 'The sole reason the insured does not satisfy the policy terms is due to him not reaching the troponin I threshold, which is not in line with current medical practice,' an email said. The email also warned that if the decision was disputed it would attract negative attention from the Financial Ombudsman Service. 'We recommend that the committee consider this claim for ex gratia payment and that the committee also discuss the amount to be paid.'

But CommInsure didn't make that payment. Instead, as Kessel told me, 'They sent me a letter, which ... simply states, that,

"Your troponin levels were not at the right level so you don't get it." Goodbye. Have another heart attack. Better luck next time.'

It was less than two years since Narev had apologised for the financial planning scandal at CBA, and here we were again. The bank was on track to generate a $10 billion profit, and was the most profitable company in Australia, but it was doing it at the expense of its most vulnerable customers.

*

It seemed CBA didn't discriminate in its treatment of policyholders – even if they were employees. Another person we tracked down for an interview on *Four Corners* was thirty-two-year-old Matthew Attwater, who had been handpicked from the bank's 44,000 workers to be named CBA's employee of the year in November 2010. Ralph Norris, then CEO, personally praised Attwater's abilities.

It was all downhill from there. A close relative with a history of violence savagely attacked Attwater and cut off his dog's head. Attwater showed up for work covered in bruises, but although the physical abrasions healed, his mental state deteriorated and he spiralled into a deep depression.

The bank organised a meeting for Attwater with a forensic psychiatrist. The psychiatrist found that Attwater's symptoms were 'severe' and he presented 'as a severely disabled person who is markedly affected by a cluster of psychiatric symptoms which would fall under the broad heading of PTSD [post-traumatic stress disorder]. In addition, there were strong elements of social phobia.' The psychiatrist advised that Attwater should be medically retired from the bank and 'the workforce in general'. Attwater was told to lodge a TPD claim. He was insured with CommInsure through a

CBA superannuation fund. But his claim was rejected on the basis he could work.

'My world stopped that day,' said Attwater. 'How can one department say, "No, sorry, you're so disabled that you can no longer work for us and that you'll never, ever be able to work in any industry," and then for an insurance assessor to look at that and say, "Well, no, not really. You can ... there's more things that you can do"?'

Given that Attwater had been 'ill-health retired' from the bank, his lawyers arranged for nine different psychiatric and other medical reports. They all supported his claim, but CommInsure continued to refuse to pay out.

A similar case involved Helen Polydoropoulos, a CBA employee I interviewed who was diagnosed with multiple sclerosis (MS) and was 'ill-health retired' by the bank in late 2011. MS affects the central nervous system and is a painful, debilitating and chronic disease, which is currently incurable. Like Attwater, Polydoropoulos had a life insurance policy with CommInsure, so when she was 'retired' by the bank she lodged a TPD claim. It was rejected. Over the next four years, she lodged multiple claims and each one was turned down by the same medical officer who had retired her from the bank.

The penultimate person to be interviewed for the joint Fairfax/*Four Corners* investigation was Ben Koh, who was still running hot and cold on whether to appear. He'd been speaking to Jeff Morris and John Berrill, but he was still having trouble deciding. Koh finally agreed to appear and let us use his full name and position, but asked that we film only the back of his head.

As we were finalising the story, a CBA representative rang and said that Ian Narev, who had repeatedly declined to be interviewed, now wanted to talk, with the unusual proviso that the interview be run in full on the websites of both the ABC and Fairfax. Fairfax agreed, but the ABC declined as that was contrary to its policy.

The interview with Narev was bizarre. I had twenty minutes and a lot of questions to cover. Narev had clearly rehearsed his talking points and been fully briefed on all the case studies, including Evan Pashalis, but he wasn't expecting me to show him part of a video interview with Pashalis, whose insurance claim had been rejected twice despite him being diagnosed by two specialists as terminally ill with acute myeloid leukaemia. In the interview with Pashalis, I asked him how he felt about his treatment by CommInsure. He replied, 'Unfortunately, I'm not surprised at all. It's just so frustrating. Why would you torment a dying person and their family? What do they gain out of this? A few hundred thousand dollars? I would have put funds aside for my daughter's future ... I could [have planned] for her schools, place[d] deposits, [done] what I needed to do for my family once I'm gone. This is just outrageous. I don't know ... what we need to do. But I'll tell you one thing: before I leave this planet, I'll fight with every [bit of] energy I can muster.'

I asked Narev if he had anything to say to Evan Pashalis. Narev replied, 'Well, first of all, that is an extremely distressing video to see in relation to any customer of the Commonwealth Bank. So the first thing I will say to him is how sorry I personally feel. And I will be conveying my apologies to him personally and inviting him to have the opportunity to come to speak to me ... so I can make sure I understand at a human level exactly what he's gone through.' Narev went on to apologise to all the victims, saying CommInsure staff were already reviewing and updating medical claims.

In relation to the bank's treatment of Koh, and in response to Koh's allegations, he fudged every question. When I asked

Narev whether he'd responded to Koh after receiving an email Koh had written to him the previous August outlining some of his concerns, Narev said, 'I need to emphasise again what I said before, which is: when specific complaints are raised anywhere from inside the insurance business, there are certain prescribed procedures in terms of how to deal with those sorts of concerns.'

I asked Narev what CBA sacking Koh after he'd become a whistleblower told us about the bank's attitude to speaking up about the truth. Narev replied, 'As part of the, ah, emphasis that our board has put, I have put, ah, over a period of time on ethics and values, we are emphasising the importance of people speaking up when they see something wrong, but actually also when they've got good ideas, because that's a big part of being in an innovative culture.'

Narev stumbled through the interview, doing his best to ignore the questions I put to him. It was the same old story: apologies and hand-wringing and promises that big changes were underway. In fact, like Narev's responses, little had changed at CBA.

*

Hours before the *Four Corners* program, 'Money for Nothing',[1] aired, Wacka Williams called me in a panic to say someone from CBA's PR team (who still works there today and who had tried to smear Jeff Morris years before) had phoned him to say that one of our case studies, James Kessel, was a con man and had faked his heart attack and that his brother had also faked a heart attack to lodge fraudulent insurance claims. The PR person said the Kessels were a family of crooks and James Kessel was pushing drugs in Wee Waa.

Wacka was worried. I was angry, but I knew the PR person was wrong and trying to undermine the story: I had seen how poor Kessel was and knew he had never pursued a claim against the bank. My blood boiled at the dirty tactics CBA was using in an attempt to disparage and undermine our witness. I told Wacka to watch the program, as it included an interview with the cardiologist who'd saved Kessel's life. I told him Kessel's brother had actually died of heart failure caused by an undiagnosed heart condition that had taken the family by surprise. As for drug pushing, that seemed implausible, given the poverty Kessel was living in when we met him.

The next day Wacka rang the PR person and said, 'Did you watch the show? Some fake heart attack. [James Kesssel] was dead and got brought back. And his brother died.' Wacka said the PR person took it in his stride, claiming the allegations had come from an anonymous tip and that he would still call the police about the drugs in case the story was true.

*

In response to the program, Narev apologised publicly, but he also began punishing the messenger. Within days, CBA pulled millions of dollars of advertising across the entire Fairfax group, indefinitely. This was around the time Fairfax had announced it was axing 120 jobs as part of a cost-cutting exercise, and I felt sick to the stomach about the further loss of revenue.

Then David Cohen, CBA's chief legal counsel, wrote a letter to the ABC and Fairfax in which he said: 'We understand from Adele Ferguson, the journalist featured in the *Four Corners* program on 7 March 2016, that she has received personal information about CommInsure customers from Dr Ben Koh, a former employee of Commonwealth Bank.' But I had never told anyone how I'd received the internal documents or who had sent them, and I had certainly never told CBA or David Cohen they had come from Dr Koh. Cohen went on to say that the information included highly confidential and sensitive medical, financial and private information and that, 'If Fairfax or the ABC has held or currently holds personal information of CommInsure customers without the express consent of each affected customer, it will be necessary for CommInsure to notify the Privacy Commissioner of a privacy breach and to inform the Australian Prudential Regulation Authority.'[2] He requested that by the following morning we confirm we'd had the express consent of each affected customer to be in possession of their personal information. Fairfax and the ABC sent a polite response denying I had revealed who was the source of the documents.

A few days later I received a phone call from a PR person at Maurice Blackburn asking if I'd spoken to one of their clients, who was also a claimant of CommInsure. They told me the woman's name, but I hadn't heard of her. They alleged she'd said that 'Adele from *Four Corners*' had called her and recited her medical history chapter and verse, including that she suffered from depression and had been a victim of domestic violence. The PR person told me the woman said 'Adele' had then suggested she meet with lawyer Michael Bates to discuss her claim and that all her airfares, accommodation and expenses would be paid for. The woman claimed to be shaken that somebody knew all her personal details and had rung up Maurice Blackburn and CommInsure as a result.

Apparently 'Adele' was moonlighting as a spruiker for a law firm. The problem was, whoever had stolen my identity hadn't done their research properly. Ben Koh had a lawyer called Michael Bates, who worked with John Berrill, but he was based in Melbourne, whereas the Michael Bates that fake Adele was spruiking was a patent lawyer based in Sydney. Whoever was behind it was clearly trying to discredit me by suggesting I was a client thief, a spruiker, on the take, and illegally using personal records.

Despite that clumsy mistake, the allegation shook me because whoever had done this clearly wanted to damage my reputation. I rang the Melbourne Michael Bates and he said a CommInsure lawyer he'd been dealing with had told him that 'Adele from *Four Corners*' had been ringing a claims manager with twenty years' experience and threatening to subpoena her if she didn't hand over information. I asked Michael to go back to the lawyer and ask the claims manager to put that in writing. When Michael spoke to the lawyer again, he was told it was a customer rather than a claims manager 'Adele from *Four Corners*' had called. When a Fairfax lawyer then wrote to CBA to let the bank know somebody was impersonating me, he didn't receive a response.

Around the same time, my husband and I noticed a van parked outside our house. It had been there a couple of days. It eventually dawned on me it might be surveillance. We went outside and stared at it for a few moments then walked back inside the house. By the time we looked out the window again, which would have been less than forty seconds later, the van had sped off. Coincidence or paranoia?

Chapter 13

Battle lines

Labor gets onboard

AFTER 'MONEY FOR NOTHING' was broadcast and published in *The Age* and the *Sydney Morning Herald*, I received a fresh flood of emails. Meanwhile Assistant Treasurer Kelly O'Dwyer took to the airwaves saying the story was, 'very, very, very troubling and shocking'. But then, just as the Coalition government was attempting to keep a lid on the CommInsure scandal by getting ASIC to investigate it, it became the catalyst that put a royal commission firmly on Labor's agenda. Sam Dastyari, who was close to Bill Shorten at the time, recalls, 'There was a strong narrative inside the [Labor] Party: do it for the election, do it for the election.' Trade unions had also become increasingly vocal about the need for a royal commission into the top end of town, after the Coalition had established one into trade unions.

Shadow Federal Treasurer Chris Bowen asked Dastyari's former staffer Cameron Sinclair to write a short paper on why a royal commission into the financial sector was needed. In early April 2016, Sinclair's report was circulated among Labor's federal leadership group. But before taking any radical steps Bowen wanted to exhaust all avenues. Calling a royal commission was a dramatic step because the banking sector was the lifeblood of the economy and Labor didn't want to antagonise such a powerful group if it could avoid it.

Bowen spoke to banking CEOs one on one, telling them that if there were any more scandals they needed to understand how thin the ice was getting. But the CEOs believed their own spin. According to Dastyari, they said to Bowen, 'We have had twenty-seven years of growth in the banking sector. You can't rip it apart.'

Bowen then gave Dastyari the authority to sound out the CEOs of banks on financially backing a compensation scheme of last resort, a scheme that would be available to victims of misconduct who were ineligible for compensation because their financial adviser or financial services provider had refused to pay or had collapsed. The idea for such a scheme had come about after the Financial Ombudsman Service revealed that 18 per cent of its rulings against financial advisers and financial services providers, totalling more than $13 million, remained unpaid, with many more consumers unable to proceed because their advisers had disappeared.

'I was told to go fuck myself,' Dastyari says, describing how the bankers he spoke to kept using phrases like 'moral hazard' and warning that such a compensation scheme would only encourage small licensees to behave recklessly in the expectation that if something went wrong the scheme would pick up the tab. The bank CEOs also asked why they should have to pay for bad planners who hadn't been part of their banks. The Labor Party argument that Dastyari conveyed to the banks was that the banks benefited more than anyone else from the health of the economic ecosystem and the compensation they'd be paying would only cost about $50 million a year. Dastyari was astonished by the CEOs' responses. 'The arrogance [of the CEOs] was incredible. That was when Bill [Shorten] and Bowen came on board about a banking royal commission.'

*

On 5 April 2016, the banks were back in the headlines when ASIC took Westpac to the Federal Court over alleged bank bill swap rate rigging. Bank bill swap rates (BBSWs) are benchmarks used to set interest rates on most business loans and on loans between banks. Before September 2013, when the alleged manipulation occurred, BBSWs were set daily by the Australian Financial Markets Association, the industry's professional body, on the basis of interest rates quoted by up to fourteen banks. The process relied on the banks providing accurate, independent figures. The day after the news of the legal action against Westpac for manipulating its figures, Turnbull's adviser rang me to tell me his boss was about to give the banks a spray at Westpac's 199th birthday party. The speech was akin to a school principal admonishing naughty children without imposing any punishment. 'Have our bankers … lived up to the standards we expect, not just the laws we enact?' he asked the audience of bankers at a glitzy lunch in Sydney's Walsh Bay. 'We have to acknowledge that there have been too many troubling incidents over recent times for them simply to be dismissed.'[1]

Turnbull's lack of action, particularly after the CommInsure scandal, marked a turning point for Labor. On 8 April, Bill Shorten called me in the morning to thank me for my work and to let me know he was holding a press conference to announce Labor would call for a banking royal commission if the party won government. Bowen, meanwhile, rang the CEOs of each of the big four banks and told them about the decision.

The battle lines were now clearly drawn.

The Coalition had a bad track record when it came to protecting consumers. It had tried to water down the Future of

Financial Advice (FoFA) reforms at the height of CBA's financial planning scandal; it had taken the financial knife to ASIC's budget despite the Senate's damning 2014 report that ASIC was failing to regulate effectively; and it had gone soft on the misdeeds of Australia's $44 billion life insurance industry. The government had also had a revolving door of assistant Treasurers and financial services ministers – from Arthur Sinodinos to Mathias Cormann (acting role) to Josh Frydenberg and Kelly O'Dwyer. This had done little for industry stability and continuity.

To make matters worse, the Coalition was trying to push a multi-billion-dollar tax break for big business through parliament. It had tried to hose down public outrage by suggesting the banks front up to parliament once a year and be grilled by the Standing Committee on Economics. But that the banks should be given a massive tax break was a bridge too far for many Australians.

*

As Turnbull moved into pre-election mode in the middle of 2016, he peddled the line that Labor's push for a royal commission was nothing more than a 'populist campaign' and a waste of time and money. Turnbull claimed a royal commission would 'enrich the legal profession, cost hundreds of millions of dollars, take many years and end up, no doubt, recommending the types of measures that are already in this year's budget'.[2]

Scott Morrison, who was then Federal Treasurer, echoed his political master, saying, 'It's a well-regulated sector', and '[the call for a royal commission] is nothing more than a populist whinge'. He accused Bill Shorten of 'playing reckless political games with one of the core pillars of our economy', which could 'undermine confidence in the banking and finance system'. Morrison also claimed that the talk of a royal commission was doing irreparable economic damage abroad.[3]

The government tried to present ASIC as a regulator that would come down hard on the banks. Realising nobody was buying that line, it decided to move ahead with a plan to release a package of measures to beef up the regulator's powers and resources. The plan, which was the result of a capability review of ASIC the previous year, had been gathering dust on the desk of Kelly O'Dwyer, the Minister for Revenue and Financial Services, as the government worked out what to do with it. The final report included ASIC's response to the review, but didn't include an eight-page 'aide memoire' that the review panel had written after reading ASIC's response.[4] O'Dwyer had received the aide memoire on 10 December 2015, but it had never been released publicly, although it had been widely circulated by the minister and by Treasury, with the recipients then passing it on to others. It was common knowledge the contents were damning of ASIC.

I lodged a Freedom of Information request for a copy of the aide memoire but received a heavily redacted version from Treasury on the basis that handing over the information would not be in the public interest. When I compared the redacted version with the unredacted copy I was quietly shown, I was shocked. The aide memoire didn't put ASIC in a very good light. It challenged ASIC's response to the report, particularly the part where ASIC said it agreed with most of the panel's recommendations but that almost half were unnecessary, either because they were already ASIC's current practice or were in the process of being implemented. The aide memoire rejected this response as 'superficial' and 'disarmingly misleading' and said, 'The panel considers its recommendations to be necessary, as ASIC's actions in such areas are mostly "too little too late" and more work is needed to lift ASIC to the required standard.' It also noted that ASIC's misapprehension was so great as to suggest it was possibly deliberate and pointed out that 'the current [ASIC] leadership can't understand, acknowledge or take responsibility for current shortcomings. As such it is unlikely they will make substantive changes.' It was damning stuff.

Yet on 20 April, just under a fortnight after Bill Shorten's promise to initiate a royal commission, Scott Morrison called a press conference in Canberra where he described ASIC as a tough cop on the beat. He also extended ASIC chairman Greg Medcraft's contract by eighteen months. 'There is nothing that ASIC can't do that a royal commission can do,' Morrison said. 'I mean, ASIC can do it all now and I think that's the clear message to those who are proposing this [royal commission] arrangement: ASIC can do the job right now.'[5]

In lock step, the Australian Bankers' Association outlined a suite of reforms, including a review of products and commissions paid to sales staff, the standardising of whistleblower protection, and the improvement of complaints handling and dispute resolution.[6] Mistakenly, they hoped these would be enough to reverse the growing public appetite for a royal commission.

Retired Nationals senator John 'Wacka' Williams at his sheep farm and home in Inverell, NSW, where he spent most of his time when he wasn't helping battlers fight bank misconduct. *(Nancy Capel)*

A former chairman of the Trade Practices Commission and the Australian Competition and Consumer Commission, Professor Allan Fels called out misconduct in the life insurance industry in 1991 and worked tirelessly to protect consumers. *(Arsineh Houspian/Fairfax Media)*

On 13 March 2000, Commonwealth Bank (CBA) boss David Murray and Colonial Mutual CEO Peter Smedley held a joint press conference to announce the merger of CBA and Colonial to create the country's biggest wealth management institution. *(Peter Rae/Fairfax Media)*

After stockbroking firm Opes Prime collapsed in 2008, Mick Gatto (centre) and his colleagues John Khoury (left) and Matt Tomas travelled to Singapore to attempt to retrieve money lost by investors. *(Aaron Francis/ Newspix)*

Left: Storm Financial founders Emmanuel Cassimatis and his wife, Julie, at their Townsville mansion before the demise of the financial advice company, also in 2008. *(Mark Cranitch/Newspix)*
Below: Visibly distressed victims of Storm Financial gathered at a parliamentary inquiry into the company's collapse, in Brisbane, September 2009. *(Paul Harris/Fairfax Media)*

A former star financial planner at CBA who brought financial ruin to many of the bank's clients, 'Dodgy' Don Nguyen was caught on film during the shooting of the *Four Corners* 'Banking Bad' program in 2014. *(Fairfax Media)*

In conversation with Adele Ferguson at a Walkley Foundation lunch in Sydney in October 2014, ASIC chairman Greg Medcraft admitted Australia had become a paradise for white-collar crime. *(Ben Rushton/Fairfax Media)*

Campaigner Merilyn Swan outside the CBA branch in Chatswood, Sydney, where her parents were misadvised by Don Nguyen. Swan has spent years seeking compensation on their behalf. *(James Brickwood/Fairfax Media)*

After suffering a heart attack and being resuscitated with a defibrillator, James Kessel had his trauma claim denied by CommInsure – on the basis of an outdated medical definition. *(Matt Miegel/Fairfax Media)*

Whistleblower Jeff Morris (left) helped his former colleague Veronica Coulston (right) battle NAB for compensation after she ran up hundreds of thousands of dollars of debt by following advice from adviser Graeme Cowper. *(Nick Moir/Fairfax Media)*

Senators Mark Bishop and Doug Cameron attended a Senate hearing on 6 June 2013 as part of the Senate Economics References Committee inquiry into the performance of ASIC, Australia's corporate regulator. *(Alex Ellinghausen/Fairfax Media)*

Led by Naomi Halpern (dressed in red), victims of the collapse of the Timbercorp managed-investment scheme rallied in Melbourne on 12 November 2014, ahead of a Senate hearing into the scheme and the role of banks. Many had lost their life savings and were left owing large debts to ANZ. *(Josh Robenstone/Fairfax Media)*

Sam Dastyari (with the red tie) and the 'Coalition of Commonsense' organised a press conference on 19 November 2014 to announce they had the numbers to scrap proposed dilutions to the Future of Financial Advice laws. To the right of Dastyari are Ricky Muir, Nick Xenophon and Jacqui Lambie; at left are John Madigan and Peter Whish-Wilson. *(Andrew Meares/Fairfax Media)*

IOOF boss Chris Kelaher appeared before a parliamentary inquiry into the company in July 2015. CBA whistleblower Jeff Morris can be seen in the background, at right. *(Peter Rae/Fairfax Media)*

Prime Minister Malcolm Turnbull (right) and Treasurer Scott Morrison (left) at a press conference at Parliament House on 30 November 2017 to reluctantly announce a royal commission into banking. The Coalition imposed a time limit on the commission of twelve months. *(Alex Ellinghausen/Fairfax Media)*

Kenneth Hayne QC, a former High Court judge, was selected to preside over the Royal Commission into Misconduct in the Banking, Superannuation and Financial Services Industry. Not only was the time limited, so were the commission's terms. One area of inquiry the government did include was union-backed industry super funds. *(Eddie Jim/Fairfax Media)*

Senior Counsel Assisting Rowena Orr QC, flanked by junior barristers Albert Dinelli and Eloise Dias. Orr swiftly earned a reputation for demolishing witnesses and for her mastery of the detailed and complex evidence. *(Eddie Jim/Fairfax Media)*

AMP senior executive Jack Regan on his way to appear before the royal commission on 17 April 2018. Under intense questioning from Michael Hodge QC, Regan was unable to recall exactly how many times AMP had lied to ASIC. *(Joe Castro/AAP)*

NAB executive Andrew Hagger (left) and Senior Counsel Assisting Michael Hodge QC (right). On 13 August, Hodge took Hagger to task over NAB's disregard for the law and ASIC. Hagger resigned a month later. *(Darrian Traynor/ Fairfax Media; David Geraghty/AAP, The Australian Pool)*

NAB boss Andrew Thorburn leaving the royal commission on 26 November 2018 after a gruelling day in the witness box. He had admitted that NAB had become more focused on profits and short-term gains than the interests of its customers. *(David Geraghty/Newspix)*

During the seventh round of public hearings, the chair of CBA, Catherine Livingstone, was grilled about a range of scandals affecting the bank, as well as the CBA board's decision to allow senior executives to receive their full bonuses. *(Louise Kennerley/Fairfax Media)*

Stern-faced Kenneth Hayne delivered his final report to nervous-looking Treasurer Josh Frydenberg on 1 February 2019. The photo opportunity became excruciating when Hayne refused to shake hands with Frydenberg. *(Kym Smith/AAP, Fairfax Media Pool)*

Ken Henry gave an extraordinary performance at the royal commission, scoffing at questions and muttering under his breath. Days after the publication of Hayne's scathing final report, he agreed to resign. *(Dominic Lorimer/Fairfax Media)*

Chapter 14

Banksters

Money laundering with CBA

In September 2016, Wacka Williams fulfilled a promise he had made to James Kessel during the CommInsure scandal to bring about a parliamentary inquiry into the $44 billion life insurance industry. It was conducted by the Parliamentary Joint Committee on Corporations and Financial Services. The terms of reference were broad, and the aim was to examine whether all insurers, not just CBA, were engaging in unethical practices to avoid paying claims. As the inquiry kicked off in early 2017, it became obvious the problems were industry-wide. Each hearing, which exposed misleading advice, mis-selling and the poor treatment of customers with mental health problems, strengthened Labor's case for a royal commission – and made the government more resolute not to have one.

Then out of the blue came an announcement that sparked a social media frenzy and caused a collective wail from the banking industry. At 12.26 pm on Thursday 3 August 2017, the country's financial intelligence agency, the Australian Transaction Reports and Analysis Centre (AUSTRAC), tweeted: '@AUSTRAC today initiated civil penalty proceedings against CBA for serious non-compliance with AML/CTF [*Anti-Money Laundering and Counter-Terrorism Financing Act*].'[1] It included a hyperlink to a press release with more juicy details.[2]

Journalists around the country, including myself, were staggered to read that CBA was embroiled in yet another financial scandal. This time the bank was being accused of failing to report serious breaches in the use of its network of more than 500 intelligent deposit machines (IDMs). These had been rolled out in 2012 and accepted deposits of $20,000, with no limit on the number of transactions that could be made each day.

Under the federal *Anti-Money Laundering and Counter-Terrorism Financing Act 2006*, banks must report all transactions in excess of $10,000 to AUSTRAC. In CBA's case, AUSTRAC alleged there had been no fewer than 53,700 instances since 2012 when this threshold had been breached on its IDMs. What's more, six of the breaches related to customers identified by the bank as having links to terrorism or terrorism financing. CBA had also failed in its obligations to monitor 778,370 accounts known as 'affected accounts' between 2012 and 2016. As AUSTRAC subsequently noted, 'It is essential to the integrity of the Australian financial system that a major bank such as CommBank has compliant and appropriate risk-based systems and controls in place to deter money laundering and terrorism finance.'[3]

These were astounding allegations. Essentially, AUSTRAC was saying CBA had let crime syndicates, drug dealers and terrorists wash hundreds of millions of dollars through IDMs, despite there being strict federal compliance rules in place to prevent such activities.

Given the seriousness of the allegations, Treasury, ASIC and APRA organised a series of meetings to discuss the implications of the legal action. Bank PR departments across the country ran into crisis talks. I called CBA's media team at about 4 pm and was told that the bank had been fully cooperating with AUSTRAC and didn't understand why AUSTRAC had rushed off to court without warning. The conversation turned to the breaches, which the media person claimed had been caused by an innocent software-coding error that resulted in reports that should have automatically been sent to AUSTRAC on cash transactions of more than $10,000 not being sent. The upshot, according to CBA, was that it was only one breach, not the 53,000-plus breaches alleged by AUSTRAC. One breach of failing to report on cash transactions over $10,000 can incur a penalty of up to $18 million. For 53,000-plus breaches, the penalty was potentially billions of dollars.

Talkback radio lit up with extraordinary stories about how the biggest bank in the country, which was about to report a record $9.8 billion profit, had facilitated the movement of illegal money. Callers reported bank tellers having told their superiors about suspicious-looking customers stuffing thousands of dollars in machines, and nothing being done. At CBA's Leichhardt MarketPlace branch in Sydney's inner west, the manager received an alert on his computer and rushed outside to find a middle-aged man shoving money into the IDM. When he questioned him, the man sped off in his car, later turning up at the Mascot branch to deposit his money.

It was widely known that criminals liked IDMs because the cash could be deposited anonymously, automatically counted and instantly credited to a CBA account, from where the funds could be immediately transferred, even overseas. Gangs used this system to move illicit money right under the noses of law enforcement authorities.

It became apparent from the number of breaches and the length of time it had gone on that CBA had set up its IDM system without proper risk assessments or controls. AUSTRAC estimated that $8.9 billion had been deposited through the machines before any risk assessment was made. This was despite a recent exponential rise in cash deposits through IDMs, in one month reaching almost $2 billion, and alerts from internal transaction monitoring services and the Australian Federal Police (AFP). One key flaw in the system was that CBA gave customers thirty days' notice before closing their accounts, which gave criminals plenty of time to set up a new criminal account or transfer the money offshore before any action could be taken.

AUSTRAC's statement of claim and amended statement of claim were littered with shocking case studies. In one example, the AFP issued an order of notice to the bank on 18 May 2015, requesting information in relation to a specific suspicious account it had been investigating. No customer due diligence was carried out in response to this request. Another case related to Strike Force Bugam, a joint investigation between the AFP and the Australian Criminal Intelligence Commission into a drug- and gun-running operation based in Sydney. Ringleader Thi Lan Phuong Pham, who was arrested at Sydney airport in January 2017, had used CBA's IDMs since 2012 to launder millions of dollars, including $42 million laundered on behalf of other organised crime groups between March and August 2016. NSW Police alleged that Pham directed Australian nationals (the money mules) to collect large sums of cash from the organised crime groups and then feed them into the IDMs.

CBA knew of the investigation because the Organised Crime Squad of the NSW Police had served the bank with a Notice to Produce Documents on 24 April 2017, to form part of a brief of evidence against one of the mules charged with money laundering. CBA produced the documents on 2 May. At that time, CBA should have sent suspicious matter reports (SMRs) to AUSTRAC – under the law, it had three days to do so. Yet, as the regulator noted, 'At no time has CommBank given the AUSTRAC CEO an SMR in relation to the matters pleaded.'[4]

Investors reacted to the scandal by dumping CBA shares, wiping $6 billion off the bank's market value as speculation mounted that fines could cost the bank anywhere between $1 billion and $3 billion, not to mention reputational damage and possible overseas regulatory fines. In response to the falling share price, CBA issued an ASX announcement on Friday 4 August saying that it had noted 'the media coverage of the civil penalty proceedings initiated yesterday by AUSTRAC for alleged non-compliance with the *Anti-Money Laundering and Counter-Terrorism Financing Act 2006*. The matter is subject to court proceedings. We are currently reviewing AUSTRAC's claim and will file a statement of defence. We will keep the market informed of any updates.'

A decision had been made at CBA to keep CEO Ian Narev out of the spotlight, but by Saturday some commentators were calling for his head. So Narev's minders changed tack and decided to offer a select few journalists a one-on-one interview with the CEO on the following Sunday. The invitation didn't extend to me or any of my colleagues at the *Sydney Morning Herald* and *The Age*. Narev's messages relayed to journalists from the *Financial Review* and *The Australian* were aimed at the investment community, regulators and politicians. He made it clear he had no intention of quitting his role. 'I am really committed,' he told the *Financial Review*, adding, 'I am really enjoying the job. The board has made its view clear and I am going to keep going until I can't give it 100 per cent or the board decides there is a better option.'[5]

On Tuesday 8 August, Catherine Livingstone, chair of the CBA board, was called to Canberra to see Treasurer Scott Morrison.

Morrison later reported to parliament, saying he'd told Livingstone he'd taken advice from Treasury, APRA and ASIC. 'The matter that AUSTRAC is pursuing in the courts with the Commonwealth Bank of Australia is very, very serious, and that matter should be properly pursued through the courts,' he said.[6] Turnbull told parliament that to call a royal commission would see legal action against CBA delayed or stayed, saying, 'AUSTRAC is on the case, doing its job. It's uncovered the wrongdoing and it's pursuing it.'[7]

In a PR strategy to win media and community support, Livingstone issued a media release on 8 August, saying the short-term variable bonuses of all senior executives, including Narev, had been scrubbed for 2017 and the board had cut its fees by 20 per cent. It was an attempt to demonstrate shared responsibility for the damage done to the bank's reputation and defuse some of the anger ahead of the release of the bank's annual results, scheduled for the following day. Livingstone also threw her weight behind Narev, saying he 'has the full support of the Board'.[8]

But it was too late. The cutting of short-term bonuses for executives was seen by the public as a hollow gesture, given that senior executives earned millions of dollars a year. Heads needed to roll. Matt Comyn, who until the AUSTRAC affair had been considered Narev's heir apparent, was clearly vulnerable, as the scandal had happened in his retail bank under his watch.

*

As the doors were flung open for CBA's profit announcement at the bank's head office in Sydney, TV crews, photographers and journalists flooded in. Narev entered soon after, trying to project calmness as he greeted the media circus. I dialled into the press conference from Melbourne and noted Narev's demeanour. It was a tough juggling act trying to navigate the AUSTRAC scandal at the same time as announcing a record profit of almost $10 billion. 'Obviously, the Commonwealth Bank's had a lot of attention over the last few days for not great reasons, for reasons that don't reflect well on the bank, or on me,' he began. His attempt at contrition faded as he started to rattle off improvements in customer satisfaction surveys, people and culture surveys, and the success of the bank's new Speak Up policy for whistleblowers.

Narev's speech smacked of hubris and a disconnect with reality. For the previous year CBA had been batting off the scandal at CommInsure and the continued fallout from the financial planning debacle. During the press conference he revealed that the bank was selling CommInsure; yet at the same time he assured the media the decision to sell had nothing to do with the scandal.

His response prompted widespread criticism. There was hardly a senior figure in Australia who didn't then put the boot into CBA and the banking sector as a whole. The Reserve Bank governor, Philip Lowe, used a Senate Economics Committee hearing in Melbourne to make a critical speech about the banks and their short-term profit mindset and cultural collapse, saying, 'The desire for short-term profit has meant not enough attention is being paid to risk management, trust has been strained, banks know that.'[9]

Even ASIC seemed to have had enough. In a separate parliamentary committee hearing held in Sydney, ASIC's chairman, Greg Medcraft, announced he would be launching an ASIC investigation into whether officers and directors at CBA had complied with their duties under the *Corporations Act*, and whether CBA had complied with its continuous disclosure obligations, its licensing obligations and its financial reporting obligations. The board of a company is responsible for overseeing the tone and culture of a company. It is also responsible for ensuring the company meets all compliance and risk management requirements, has the right senior management in place and oversees the company's remuneration policies. The CBA board's handling of the bank's various scandals, including the financial planning scandal, the life insurance scandal and the AUSTRAC scandal had been a disgrace.

*

On Monday 14 August 2017, at 8.21 am, eleven days after AUSTRAC had launched legal action, seven days after Narev had said he wasn't going anywhere, and less than a week after the CBA board had expressed its 'full support' for him, the bank issued an ASX announcement saying that Narev would be gone by June the following year. On the same day, the PR department organised a teleconference fronted by Catherine Livingstone. I was keen to hear how the bank planned to spin this one.

Livingstone denied outright that Narev's retirement plans had anything to do with the AUSTRAC scandal. She also confirmed Narev still retained the full support of the board. Her message was that Narev was approaching six years in the role, there'd been organisational discussions and decisions made, and that CBA was just being transparent by telling the ASX, given all the speculation about his tenure.

When asked if Narev had offered his resignation, Livingstone ignored the question and said, 'Ian has done a remarkable job and the board has full confidence in his continuing as chief executive right up until the day that he leaves.' During Narev's tenure, which had begun on 1 December 2011, CBA's share price had soared from $48.39 to $81.49, so his focus on profit had been rewarded. However, with scandals mounting, it was time for him to go.

Chapter 15

About-turn

The reluctant royal commission

THE ATMOSPHERE WAS ELECTRIFYING. Minutes before 10 am on 15 November 2017, millions of Australians stopped and tuned in to hear David Kalisch, head of the Australian Bureau of Statistics, deliver the verdict on a national postal vote on same-sex marriage. Crowds gathered in the streets, at special events, and in hotels, pumping the air as Kalisch declared that a majority of Australians had voted yes. The applause was deafening and some burst into the song, 'I am, you are, we are Australian.'

Prime Minister Malcolm Turnbull, who had flown back to Australia that morning, declared history had been made. 'They voted yes for fairness, yes for commitment, yes for love.'[1] People rallied, calling on the Coalition government to act on the verdict and pass the necessary legislation to make it law.

But not everyone was jubilant. In the days before the official count of the postal vote, a small group of social conservatives in the right wing of the Liberal and National parties had become concerned that a private member's bill drafted by moderate West Australian Liberal Senator Dean Smith to enable same-sex marriage would wind back religious freedoms and human rights.

'In the event of a "yes" vote, the Dean Smith bill is an insufficient basis to start the conversation,' Liberal senator Eric Abetz told the *Sydney Morning Herald* on 10 November.[2] Abetz, who'd been part of the conservative 'no' campaign, was backing an alternative bill by Liberal Senator James Paterson, which called for greater religious guarantees than Smith had proposed in his bill.

In defiance of Abetz and others and as pressure mounted on Turnbull to act decisively, Smith introduced his private member's bill to amend the *Marriage Act* to the Senate on 15 November. He had the backing of the Greens, Labor and a few independents.

Sections of the National Party saw Smith's move as treacherous. Tensions had been brewing inside the Liberal and National parties for some time and they were about to blow wide open. Ex-Queensland police detective, grazier, property developer and Nationals Senator Barry O'Sullivan had taken particular umbrage at Smith's ploy to push his bill through the Senate. O'Sullivan told Wacka Williams, 'Two can play that game.'

O'Sullivan's idea was that if the progressive Liberals could use a private member's bill and get cross-party support for their cause, why not do the same for a commission of inquiry into the banks. O'Sullivan had a number of constituents who were farmers and was well aware of their poor treatment by the banks. As a member of the Coalition he had fallen into line with the party's position on a royal commission, but privately he believed one was warranted.

The advantage of a commission of inquiry was that it would have similar powers to a royal commission but didn't need to be established by the government, and would report to parliament, not the government. O'Sullivan was also of the view that the Nationals had to start differentiating themselves from the Liberal Party.

O'Sullivan's logic was persuasive. A number of Nationals, including Wacka, had long wanted a royal commission into the banks, and the polls were showing Australians wanted one, so why not? The Greens had already introduced a private member's bill for a royal commission in the Senate on 21 March 2017, with the support of the ALP, some crossbenchers and One Nation, so cross-party support was already there. 'Australians want their day in the sun,' O'Sullivan said. 'If it's good enough for conservative governments to have royal commissions into trade unions, Pink Batts and detention centres, then it is good enough to have one for the banks, as they are more corrupt than the unions and on a scale much bigger.'[3]

O'Sullivan discussed his plan with Wacka and said the new bill would incorporate the intentions of the Greens' private member's bill as well as a Banking Commission of Inquiry Bill independent MP Bob Katter had proposed in late 2016 after seeing how farmers had been treated by the banks. That way he would have ready-made cross-party support, just as Smith had received for the same-sex marriage bill. On 19 November, I called O'Sullivan to assess how serious he was. His message to me was clear: he had cross-party support in the Senate and he believed he had it in the House of Representatives. With Barnaby Joyce and John Alexander out of the House fighting by-elections caused by the dual citizenship fiasco, O'Sullivan only needed two backbenchers to cross the floor, and he was confident he had between two and five. I wrote up the story for the *Financial Review* on 20 November.[4]

As speculation swirled around Canberra, bank lobbyists descended like swat teams trying to gauge the temperature on O'Sullivan's bill. The banks still had the direct ear of government through the powerful Financial Sector Advisory Council (FSAC), a body Kelly O'Dwyer had set up in May 2016 in response to David Murray's 2014 Financial System Inquiry, which included a recommendation to set up such a council to provide the government with advice on the performance of the regulators – ASIC, APRA and the Reserve Bank – and on policies relating to the financial system, including potential areas for regulatory reform. Its nine-member board included Westpac CEO Brian Hartzer, AMP CEO Craig Meller and Suncorp CEO Michael Cameron. But there was only so much influence the FSAC could wield in an environment where support was growing rapidly for a commission of inquiry or a royal commission, either now or when Labor came to power. Some banks had already started preparing for that day by booking law firms and QCs and planning their PR strategies, bank insiders confirmed.

O'Sullivan and Wacka hit the phones hard. Wacka rang Queensland Nationals MP Llew O'Brien, a relative newcomer to politics, having won the blue-ribbon conservative Queensland seat of Wide Bay in July 2016 after Warren Truss retired. 'Llew, I want you to muscle up. I want you to come out and publicly support a royal commission,' Wacka told me later.

O'Brien had been a country policeman working out of a two-man police station before becoming a politician. He knew nothing about the cut and thrust of high finance, but he'd seen the human misery caused by bank misconduct. He also had firsthand experience of the games life insurers played when it came to discriminating against customers with a mental illness, having been diagnosed with post-traumatic stress disorder while he was a policeman. O'Brien saw a royal commission or commission of inquiry as a chance to get life insurance and mental illness on the agenda. He had made his views clear to Barnaby Joyce a few months after winning his seat, but Joyce had told him to keep his head down. 'Barnaby spoke about the risks involved with a royal commission and some of the things that they were doing that would help small regional businesses. I decided not to come out publicly at that time, but I was certainly a sleeper on a royal commission,' he says.

O'Brien's vote would be significant, since lower house National MP George Christensen, another Queenslander, had already made it clear months earlier that he supported a royal commission and was willing to cross the floor to get one. Christensen was conscious that One Nation was a danger to his seat and that Pauline Hanson had earned a lot of brownie points among farmers by voicing her support for a royal commission in July 2016; he had since been working behind the scenes with Bob Katter, who continued to be a strong supporter of a royal commission. All at once, O'Brien became the key to turning a banking commission of inquiry into reality. If he went public, it was now almost a certainty.

*

The next ten days would make history.

On Monday 20 November, a contact in parliament tweeted me, saying, 'Just heard a whisper that Turnbull is cancelling a week of sitting to avoid O'Sullivan's private member's bill for a commission of inquiry into the banks. If true, the Nats will go nuclear.'

It was true. Turnbull had been spooked by the media speculation that O'Sullivan was working the numbers in the lower house. O'Sullivan already had Christensen's vote, now there was talk that O'Brien had turned. The government took the unprecedented step of postponing a sitting of the House of Representatives to avoid a showdown.

On Wednesday 22 November, the *Daily Telegraph* reported a leak in Cabinet about a discussion regarding O'Sullivan and his banking commission of inquiry.[5] The article said that Immigration Minister Peter Dutton had suggested the government drop its opposition to a banking inquiry, but Treasurer Scott Morrison had argued it was best to hold the line. The leak of Cabinet discussions was the best illustration yet that the Coalition was in trouble. It was so serious that Julie Bishop called for an investigation to find the source of the leak.

Former Prime Minister John Howard, a long-time supporter of the banks, said, 'I would be staggered if the Coalition proposes a bank royal commission, that is rank socialism.' Howard urged the banks to hold the line and predicted disaster if a royal commission was held. He said the banks had 'demonstrated in 2009 that they were amongst the best run, the most prudentially supervised and the most well capitalised in the world'.[6] Howard's glowing endorsement would come back to haunt him and the many, many others who'd argued an inquiry into banks was a waste of time.

It was a hectic period for the Coalition government, which was already in strife. It was polling badly, members were threatening to cross the floor, backbenchers were uneasy, and now there were leaks in Cabinet. The Queensland state election campaign was in full swing and the Federal Government was worried that a bad result in Queensland would spread further gloom in the party. But the number crunchers didn't think O'Sullivan could muster enough votes in the lower house, and even if he did, they thought they could win them back – as they always had.

Just as Labor had attempted, but failed to do earlier, Scott Morrison decided to try to get the banks to support a compensation scheme of last resort, which he believed would pacify O'Sullivan and other National Party rebels. Morrison organised an urgent meeting with the chairs of the big four banks to discuss the idea. Again, they rejected it. Morrison had already hit them up for a

$6.2 billion bank levy in the May Budget, which they weren't happy about.

The business sector was also concerned at the language Morrison was increasingly using against the banks. In an interview with the *Daily Telegraph* he'd employed the term 'voodoo' to describe the setting of rate rises by the banks and warned that the competition watchdog, the Australian Competition and Consumer Commission (ACCC), would monitor the rises carefully.

It was death by a thousand cuts.

The bank meeting with Morrison had another effect. It prompted the bank chairs to reach out to each other and discuss the best way to handle the situation and win back community trust. ANZ chairman David Gonski, who was renowned for his diplomacy, had long held the view that ANZ had to go soft and not antagonise the government or the community. ANZ and the bank's chief executive, Shayne Elliott, had always been the first to offer mea culpas for bad bank behaviour. As well as being a friend of Turnbull, Gonski had headed the government's education review. He had taken a more conciliatory stand than other bank heads in May when the government had hit the banks with the multi-billion-dollar levy for poor behaviour. Though he didn't like the levy, he hadn't agreed with the shrill response of the Australian Banking Association and some of the other banks. He held the view that you don't build bridges by launching a street war. Along with NAB's chairman, Ken Henry, Gonski reached the conclusion that the banks needed to take back control of the agenda regarding a commission of inquiry into the financial sector, and find the best path forward as quickly as possible, before events overtook them.

On 25 November, following poor results for the Coalition in the Queensland state election, O'Sullivan was certain the time to act had come. 'Since the Liberals and Nationals in Queensland merged in 2008 we have become homogenous, and One Nation and others were filling the third-party vacuum the merger created,' he told the *Financial Review*. 'There's been a clear message sent to us. We have to differentiate ourselves, and behaviour and policy are the two ways.'[7]

Turnbull was now in very real danger of being defeated in the lower house. By the time he called O'Brien on 27 November, it was too late. 'Malcolm pointed out how significant a move it was, particularly for a first-term MP,' O'Brien recalls with a laugh. But O'Brien had heard all the arguments about the risks to the economy, how it would undermine the country internationally and how expensive it would be. When Turnbull asked O'Brien how much he thought a royal commission might cost, O'Brien pointed out that the government had already spent $122 million on the same-sex-marriage postal vote. O'Brien also drew a parallel between the cost of a royal commission and the $100 million Turnbull had pledged towards the building of the Townsville Football Stadium, which O'Brien thought was a waste of money.

Turnbull, Kelly O'Dwyer and Morrison started to put contingency plans in place. Investors were getting jittery. The same day Turnbull spoke to O'Brien, the bank chairs met. They decided they needed to get Turnbull to call a royal commission immediately so that the government could set the terms of reference, rather than leaving it to O'Sullivan, whose terms of reference would be much more wide ranging.

Morrison and O'Dwyer pulled out all stops to get O'Sullivan and O'Brien to change their minds. A 9.30 am meeting for Wednesday 29 November was organised, at which O'Dwyer spoke to O'Sullivan. He refused to budge. Thirty minutes later, at 10 am, when O'Brien walked into Morrison's office, he sensed an air of resignation in the room and assumed that Turnbull had told Morrison he wasn't going to change his position. 'By that time,' O'Brien says, 'I believe the letter from the banks calling for a royal commission was already in train.'

Morrison rattled off the various risks associated with a royal commission to O'Brien and asked him what he thought it would achieve. O'Brien was aware of the profound impact of the Fitzgerald Inquiry into police misconduct in Queensland, which had resulted in the premier being deposed and the jailing of three former Cabinet ministers, a police commissioner and corrupt police. He told Morrison that 'there needed to be a cultural change in the sector and a royal commission was the most powerful way to affect a real cultural change'. The meeting ended with a handshake.

That afternoon, the CEOs and chairs of the big four banks sent a joint letter to Morrison, which they indicated would go to the ASX the next morning. It said: 'In light of the latest wave of speculation about a parliamentary commission of inquiry into the banking and finance sector, we believe it is now imperative for the Australian Government to act decisively to deliver certainty to Australia's financial services sector, our customers and the community.' Despite the banks having consistently argued against a royal commission, the letter went on to say it was now in the national interest for the political uncertainty to end: 'It is hurting confidence in our financial services system, including in offshore markets, and has diminished trust and respect for our sector and people. It also risks undermining the critical perception that our banks are unquestionably strong. In our view, a properly constituted inquiry must have several significant characteristics. It should be led by an eminent and respected ex-judicial officer. Its terms of reference should be thoughtfully drafted and free of political influence. Its scope should be sufficient to cover the community's core concerns which include banking, insurance, superannuation and non-ADI [authorised deposit-taking institutions] finance providers. Further to avoid confusion and inconsistency, the inquiry must to the most practical extent replace other ongoing inquiries.'[8]

An emergency meeting of the government's Cabinet was called for 8.30 am to sign off on the royal commission and its terms of reference.

*

At 8.31 am on 30 November, NAB's chief executive, Andrew Thorburn, called Wacka to tell him the news. Wacka and Thorburn had met many times over the previous few years and had built up a respect for each other. When Wacka got off the phone, he called me. Though I'd known it was only a matter of time before a royal commission took place, I hadn't anticipated it would be at the behest of the banks.

At 9 am Turnbull and Morrison appeared in the Prime Minister's Courtyard for a press conference. Both men were wearing dark suits, white shirts and matching blue ties. They were also wearing similarly pained expressions. Through the large open double doors behind them was an eye-catching heavily decorated Christmas tree, its lights flickering on and off. But there was little Christmas cheer as the Prime Minister, standing impassively next to Morrison, declared that a royal commission was 'regrettable but necessary'. 'This will not be an open-ended commission, it will not put capitalism on trial, as some people in the parliament prefer,' Turnbull said.[9]

In lock step, Morrison said the royal commission was 'regrettable but necessary to take control given the uncertainty, disruption and damage caused by the political events'. It was hard for Morrison to spin it any other way given he had voted against a royal commission twenty-six times.

The government stipulated that the royal commission would have a budget of $75 million, would be headed by one commissioner and would be completed within twelve months. It would also include an investigation of union-backed industry funds. It would not, however, have the power to award compensation to individuals or be allowed to cover matters that might prejudice, compromise or duplicate other inquiries or criminal or civil proceedings – which ruled out a lot of areas of questionable activity, including bank bill swap rates, the allegations raised by Dr Koh in his legal case against CBA, and the AUSTRAC scandal.

The announcement was a huge political backdown for Turnbull and a major blow to his leadership. He looked weak and indecisive. His backflip had just guaranteed the party and himself another negative monthly Newspoll, and he would later have to concede that it was a 'political mistake' not to have called a royal commission sooner.[10]

O'Sullivan, the man who had led the revolt, was jubilant: 'It's a great win for millions of Australians who are now going to see a serious inquiry looking into the culture of banking.' Christensen agreed, saying, 'I'm hoping that this is going to be a thorough root-and-branch review of the banking sector, it's going to weed out these systemic cases of misconduct, and perhaps criminal actions by big banks, and we'll get some justice for the victims of banking misconduct.'[11]

After Turnbull and Morrison's press conference, I called Jeff Morris, whose phone had been running hot. He was overjoyed that a royal commission had been called but worried that it might be a whitewash. 'The turgid and dishonest conduct of the banks will take many years to uncover fully,' he said. 'One year is too short. Does it mean the banks have written the terms of reference too?' Opposition leader Bill Shorten made the withering comment: 'Only when the four big banks give a permission slip for Mr Turnbull does he give in and hold a banking royal commission.'[12]

Regardless of the compromises, the people of Australia had been heard and a royal commission had finally been called.

Part Two

A blast of sunlight

The royal commission names and shames

Chapter 16

Round 1: Consumer lending

The mortgage-broking rort

ON 14 DECEMBER 2017 Kenneth Madison Hayne AC, a former High Court judge, was appointed as the commissioner for the Royal Commission into Misconduct in the Banking, Superannuation and Financial Services Industry. Hayne made it abundantly clear from the start that he had been given a strict timetable of twelve months to examine documents and listen to testimony before delivering a final report with recommendations on 1 February 2019.

There was nothing about Hayne's legalistic, black-letter approach and his conservative leanings that would have challenged the banks' expectation that they could 'manage' the commission. After all, they had asked for the inquiry and Turnbull had handpicked Hayne; some bankers even foolishly hoped Hayne would be sympathetic, given his father had been a banker.

With infinite resources – and a matching dose of hubris – the banks were confident they would be able to outwit Hayne by starving the proceedings of documents, supplying superficial submissions, requesting confidentiality on documents and, if all else failed, presenting voluminous quantities they thought would swamp the resources of the commission.

*

On 15 December 2017, Hayne wrote to sixty-one financial institutions, regulators and industry associations, asking them to describe any misconduct they had become aware of over the preceding decade and say what steps had been taken to fix the problems. The institutions were given six weeks to file their responses. But Hayne felt the replies weren't comprehensive enough, so on 2 February 2018 he wrote to a number of the institutions asking for more detailed responses. It was a request that let the industry and regulators know that he meant business.

ANZ CEO Shayne Elliott went on the front foot with ANZ's list, writing an accompanying two-thousand-word heartfelt reflection on the need for a royal commission, conceding that ANZ's submission 'shows we've had some significant failures over the last decade'. His letter gave off a sense of foreboding that misconduct previously unknown to the public would surface. 'It would be easy to lay the blame on a few bad apples or to say that these are largely historical technical glitches resulting from large complex IT systems. That would be wrong.'[1]

Elliott added: 'For me, it's completely unacceptable that we have caused some of our customers financial harm and emotional stress.'

He also noted: 'It's often cited that not one bank depositor lost money during the GFC, but as [David Murray's 2014] Financial System Inquiry found we know more than 80,000 Australians lost billions of dollars as a result of the collapse of managed investment schemes, poor financial planning advice and other misconduct.'

It was one of the few times the boss of a bank would publicly acknowledge what had happened in a sincere manner, before and during the royal commission.

Westpac showed either ineptitude or disrespect when it submitted its misconduct list then had to quickly amend it a few days later after realising it had failed to include some crucial episodes. Hayne noted his displeasure, later writing, 'This course of events points towards a disjointed, piecemeal approach to monitoring compliance with applicable laws.'[2]

CBA and NAB complained to the commission that the task of compiling a list of misconduct was too large and too complex and the deadline too tight.

Hayne treated their excuses with contempt. 'Taken together, the course of events and the explanations proffered can lead only to the conclusion that neither CBA nor NAB could readily identify how or to what extent [they] had been failing to comply with the law,' he said. In other words, the banks didn't have systems in place that could give senior executives and directors of the board an overall picture and timeline of the extent of misconduct or compliance failures. Instead, information was presented in a disjointed way which could be explained away as, in Hayne's words, 'a small number of people choosing to behave unethically'.

Hayne's comments were a timely reminder of the shabby risk management systems in our biggest banks. All banks struggled to compile a thorough list of wrongdoing, due to disparate or old systems. Indeed, Rowena Orr, senior counsel assisting the inquiry, described CBA's submission as 'not in a form that made it possible to understand the type and the scale of the misconduct'.

In the week leading up to the first round of hearings, CBA's freshly minted boss, Matt Comyn, who'd succeeded Ian Narev, announced that CBA would stop selling the much-criticised insurance automatically included with some credit cards and personal loans. It was a clever attempt to neutralise the impact of some shocking behaviour likely to be revealed during round one of the royal commission, which would examine misconduct in consumer lending, including home loans, car loans and consumer-credit loans. CBA's personal-loan insurance was the same junk insurance that had run afoul of ASIC, resulting in a multi-million-dollar fine on the same day Narev had announced his resignation. It was the very product Comyn would tell the royal commission months later had been raised with Narev as being problematic and opaque at a meeting on 28 May 2015.

*

Among the people there to watch the first day's hearings at the Owen Dixon Commonwealth Law Courts building in Melbourne, on Tuesday, 13 March 2018, were spin doctors, lawyers, bankers and victims. After walking through security, many struggled to find free seats. The journalists meanwhile headed downstairs to a dank media room in the basement to watch two large screens, one showing extracts of documents and subtitles for the hearing-impaired, and the other showing a live stream of the commission itself.

From the moment Commissioner Hayne walked into the crowded hearing room, bowed to all in attendance, and sat down in a big leather chair, with the witness box to his right, the royal commission became compulsive – and for me addictive – viewing. Hayne made it clear he was not a man to trifle with. His long, jagged face and dour demeanour conveyed that he didn't suffer fools. He warned financial institutions and witnesses that they needed to follow his instructions to the letter. If a deadline to supply documents was missed, they would be shamed. If a question wasn't answered, it would be repeated until it was. He would be running a tight ship and woe betide anyone who didn't fall into line.

He also laid out the topics to be dealt with by the royal commission and said they would be divided into seven rounds of two-week hearings over sixty-eight days. The first round would cover consumer lending, the second would be about financial advice, the third would deal with loans to small and medium enterprises, the fourth would examine people's experiences with financial services entities in regional and remote communities, the fifth would be about superannuation, the sixth would be about insurance, and the final round would call the CEOs and examine the causes of misconduct in the financial sector and possible regulatory reform.

Counsel assisting the royal commission included the formidable QCs Rowena Orr and Michael Hodge, along with barristers Albert Dinelli, Eloise Dias, Mark Costello, Claire Schneider, Mark Hosking, Sarah Zeleznikow and Tim Farhall, and a team of lawyers from the Australian Government Solicitor's office led by Simon Daley and Simon Sherwood.

The royal commission would use the latest computer software to identify particular phrases or combinations of words, and then search through the mountains of evidence for related material that might prove invaluable to the investigation. Between the software and the battalion of lawyers, the mission was to piece together documents and emails from various departments of the banks to find misconduct, patterns of behaviour and inconsistencies. When witnesses took the stand, their well-rehearsed excuses would be seen for what they were.

*

Round one got underway with its examination of consumer lending. Home lending is the backbone of banking, representing 60 per cent of banks' overall loan books. It is also where most banks' profits are made and where many abuses had occurred, particularly the selling of home loans to customers who couldn't afford them. Irresponsible lending has played a massive role in the property bubble in Australian cities and in the country's addiction to debt, putting our economy in a precarious situation should there be a sudden downturn when the time comes for interest rates to rise. We may still be sitting on a ticking time bomb, thanks to profligate lending by the banks.

In March 2017, APRA had imposed restrictions on lenders limiting new interest-only lending to 30 per cent of home loans written. A month later, the Reserve Bank's April 2017 Financial Stability Review warned that the rising threats to Australia's financial stability included a surge in interest-only loans and a rise in household debt. It said that if the property bubble burst or interest rates rose, the fallout could be catastrophic because one-third of borrowers – generally borrowers who'd recently signed up for a loan or were on low incomes – had 'either no accrued buffer or a buffer of less than one month's repayments'.[3] If anything went wrong, these borrowers would be in serious trouble. The practice of quick twenty-four-hour approval for a home loan has come at a cost. So too has the relentless pressure from investors for banks to keep breaking record profits. It created a situation where banks increasingly relied on not just their own staff to sell loans but the growing army of mortgage brokers whose business model was based on getting a commission each time they sold a home loan. In her opening remarks at the royal commission, Rowena Orr commented on the power of the mortgage-broking industry, citing figures from the Mortgage and Finance Association of

Australia showing that mortgage brokers were responsible for 55.7 per cent of all residential home loans. In the September quarter of 2017 mortgage brokers had settled $52 billion of all residential home loans, and across the whole of 2017 NAB had approved more than 89,000 home loans submitted by brokers, resulting in total lending of $30 billion. Forty-one per cent of CBA's home loan portfolio was offered through mortgage brokers; for ANZ the figure was 58 per cent.

The way mortgage broking works is that brokers tie themselves to mortgage aggregators who have a list of home-loan products and banks to choose from. Each bank pays the aggregator an upfront commission and a trailing commission, which is then passed on to the broker when a loan is written. This business model leaves the banks open to misconduct and home loan fraud, as some mortgage brokers are tempted to put clients into loans bigger than they can afford in order to earn a larger commission. As we have seen, in some cases, they have fraudulently signed loan documents to make a sale. In September and October 2017 UBS banking analyst Jonathan Mott headed a series of investigations that examined so-called 'liar loans' – cases where borrowers or their brokers overstated their repayment capacity in order to obtain bigger loans. Mott estimated that $500 billion worth of 'liar loans' had been issued – equivalent to almost one-third of mortgages in the system.[4]

What the royal commission subsequently revealed about mortgage broking was horrifying. For example, the country's biggest mortgage broker, Aussie Home Loans, owned by CBA, was grilled over its handling of fraudulent brokers. In one case, the royal commission was told, broker Shiv Sahay was sacked after Aussie was alerted to fraud, but his customers were never informed as to why he was no longer representing them. Nor did

Aussie tell the banks whose loans it brokered, because to do so would have stopped it collecting his trailing commission. It also decided against notifying ASIC.

One of Sahay's customers was accused of providing inconsistent documents to the bank and was threatened with being charged and possibly jailed. Distressed, the customer rang Aussie, believing there had been a mistake in her paperwork. Instead of telling her the truth, the mortgage broker now handling her case was more concerned about whether it would affect her trailing commission. In email correspondence, the broker told another broker, 'I know it isn't the best timing, with what has happened, but will this affect the commissions paid on the file?'

Orr quizzed Lynda Harris, an Aussie Home Loans general manager, on why the customer hadn't been told Sahay was responsible for the fraud and was instead led to believe it was a bank error. 'That was the process then,' Harris said, adding that she disagreed with it now. Harris was then asked if it was still the case that customers weren't contacted if their broker had engaged in fraud. 'I can't tell you one way or the other, I'm sorry,' Harris said.

In 2015, Sahay had pleaded guilty in the Downing Centre Local Court to three charges of fraud after an ASIC investigation found that he created false bank statements for seventeen of his clients to obtain home loans totalling $7 million. For each loan he received $5500 in upfront commissions plus a trailing commission. He was sentenced to community service.[5]

Orr then referred to an internal audit of CBA's mortgage-broking business in August 2017, which showed loose compliance systems and inadequate oversight of the loans being referred by mortgage brokers to the bank's home-lending division. The audit found there were 13,000 active brokers submitting over 12,000 loan applications per month, but management didn't have the mechanisms or tools to 'proactively identify broker behaviours' to ensure they were doing the right thing by their customers, including collecting the appropriate documents to verify whether the loans were affordable. The audit also discovered anomalies in loan documentation. As the commission made clear, such oversights and misconduct were rife across the entire mortgage-broking sector.

The royal commission then heard how, in 2017, as part of a plan to stave off a royal commission and rebuild community trust, the Australian Bankers' Association had commissioned retired senior Australian public servant Stephen Sedgwick to conduct a review into product-sales commissions in retail banking, including mortgage broking. Sedgwick recommended banning commissions and moving to a fee-for-service system. His report said this form of remuneration was in customers' best interests.[6]

In fact, as Sedgwick noted, CBA's Ian Narev had filed a confidential submission in early 2017 to Sedgwick that suggested moving away from commissions towards a flat-fee payment. Narev highlighted the conflicts attached to commissions and noted that mortgage brokers were not covered by laws regulating financial advice, 'even though buying a home and taking out a mortgage is one of the most important financial decisions an Australian consumer will make'.

Against that backdrop, CBA's general manager of home buying Daniel Huggins was called to give testimony on mortgage broking and the CBA. Rowena Orr asked Huggins why CBA hadn't changed the business model in light of Narev's letter to Sedgwick. Huggins replied, 'Well, I think as Mr Narev mentions in his note that these changes would need to be done on a uniform basis. Otherwise, what is a very important business to the Commonwealth Bank could be substantially damaged.'

Essentially what Huggins was saying was that the model for mortgage broking might be unethical, it might lead to adverse consequences for customers, but being the first to change its approach would negatively impact the bank. It was another case of profit before people.

Orr said it was 'open to the commissioner to find that [fraudulent behaviour] arose not merely because of rogue conduct by individual brokers but because the systems, processes and culture at [CBA's mortgage-broking business] Aussie Home Loans permitted such misconduct to occur … Aussie Home Loans' risk management systems did not adequately prevent, detect or respond to the fraud; they did not create clear accountabilities for risk or prioritise ownership of risk, and they did not require reports to be made to law enforcement authorities, regulators or disciplinary bodies.'

*

Besides mortgage broking, some banks use introducer programs, where commissions, or a spotter's fee, are paid in exchange for referrals from financial planners, accountants, property developers, solicitors and builders. The royal commission examined NAB's introducer program, which accounted for $24 billion of loans the bank had written over a period of three years.

In its 31 January 2018 submission to the royal commission, NAB had admitted its introducer program had problems. It described 'inappropriate conduct by a cohort of bankers and/or third parties, resulting in loans not being established in accordance with the group's policies and responsible lending obligations'.

Rowena Orr put it more bluntly when she cross-examined NAB's executive general manager of broker partnerships,

Anthony Waldron. 'Let's be frank, Mr Waldron,' she said, 'there was fraudulent conduct engaged in by NAB bankers and by introducers. Do you agree with that? ... We see no reference [in NAB's submission] to any fraudulent conduct. In fact, the language is very qualified in the description of the conduct here ... Now, what I want to put to you is that NAB knows and you know that there were unsuitable loans, there was false documentation, there was dishonest application of customers' signatures on consent forms and there was the misstatement of some loans in loan documentation. All of those things occurred, did they not?'

Waldron replied, 'Yes, we can now say that they have occurred.'

The brutal reality was that the misconduct included forgery, fraud and a bribery ring whereby staff across five branches took cash bribes to activate home loans based on fake documents. It involved branch managers, introducers and branch staff. Orr said it had taken a whistleblower's disclosures to NAB to highlight the problem. According to the whistleblower's email, read by Orr, 'One customer recently said they told him that he could borrow $800,000 when his property was valued at $400,000. The money exchanges hands in white envelopes over the counter of the bank.' The scam included supplying fake pay-slips, fake identification documents and fake Medicare cards to secure loans. The fake documentation was allegedly used by the bankers to obtain loans for customers who otherwise would not qualify for them but also to artificially inflate their sales figures so they might be promoted, Orr told the commission. 'They charged $2800 for each customer for home loans mainly and also personal loans,' she said.

Waldron's excuse for NAB's downplaying of the misconduct in its submission was that the bank was 'still going through the process of reviewing files'. But Orr had too many documents about the bribery at her fingertips to be duped. Referring to emails and internal documents, she showed that the bank had known about the problem since at least November 2015 but had taken until February 2016 to report it to ASIC. (The law requires banks to tell ASIC about any significant breaches within ten days, so NAB was months overdue.) Other internal NAB documents presented at the commission listed further oversights in the bank's home loan department, including a lack of proper checks and balances to identify emerging problems, such as fraud.

As the three days of hearings on the lending sector showed, the issues raised about NAB were equally relevant to the rest of the banking sector, including Westpac, ANZ and CBA. Target-based incentives, which drove a sales-at-any-cost mentality, were at the heart of what went wrong inside the banks. They created distortions and encouraged poor behaviour which the banks failed to detect in a timely manner; when they did, it took them too long to deal with the issues, to the detriment of customers. The banks had tolerated forgery, fraud, bribery, slow remediation and questionable compliance, and treated the regulators and the law with utter contempt.

NAB tried to suggest that it had changed its remuneration and incentive schemes to reduce such conflicts. But the royal commission looked behind the spin and found that NAB and other banks continued to award bonuses to staff for achieving targets for the sale of home loans.

It seemed that the banks were happy to continue to support a flawed business model until change was imposed on it. When Orr asked CBA CEO Matt Comyn whether he had any plans to stop commission payments to mortgage brokers, he replied, 'Not – not that I can – no, there is not.'

When Orr asked him, 'Why is that, Mr Comyn?' he replied, 'Well, we're wondering what might be recommended from the commission.'

'You're waiting for us?' asked Orr.

'You seem to be probing in the … in the right areas, yes.'

Orr and everyone else at the hearing were staggered by Comyn's response. Hayne raised his eyebrows. He must have thought to himself: what the hell is going on here?

Chapter 17

Round 2: Financial advice

Theft, lies, and fees for no service

THERE WAS A GROWING sense of excitement at the opening on 16 April 2018 of the second round of hearings, which would deal with malfeasance in financial planning. Financial planning is a substantial industry. The top five financial institutions – CBA, Westpac, ANZ, NAB and AMP – control about 50 per cent by revenue, estimated at $4.6 billion, and there are around 25,000 financial advisers acting as a distribution channel for financial products to more than 2.3 million Australians, many of them retirees. It's an area, as we have seen, that has had more than its fair share of scandals, and putting the sector on trial was always going to be a showstopper.

The royal commission had decided to focus on a little-publicised scandal: fees for no service – or 'money for nothing' – whereby customers paid their hard-earned cash for financial advice but received nothing in return. The big four banks and AMP, as noted, had raked in at least $1 billion in fees for services they hadn't provided. A nice little earner, if you can get away with it.

The gouging had been uncovered as a direct result of the Future of Financial Advice (FoFA) legislation demanding financial advisers write to customers every two years and let them know what they'd done for them during that period, including listing their fees, services and returns – if the customer was happy, the contract would continue, if not the customer could end the contract. The details had been set out by ASIC in an October 2016 report that looked into practices at AMP, ANZ, CBA, NAB, Westpac and the Macquarie Group. It revealed at that time that 200,000 customers had been systemically robbed of an estimated $178 million for financial advice they had never received.[1]

In typical ASIC style, the report underplayed the significance of the issue, suggesting the problems had arisen due to poor systems and that the institutions were doing all they could to repay the customers they had gouged. The report said, 'After determining that there were systemic fee-for-service failures, the licensees designed and implemented processes to identify the customers affected. Most of the licensees ... have engaged external consultancy firms ... to identify and compensate affected customers, or to provide some level of assurance in relation to those activities. In general, the banking and financial services institutions and their external advisers have used ... high-level processes to identify potentially affected customers.'

But after delving into what had occurred at AMP and CBA, the royal commission painted a much more alarming picture, and again demonstrated how ineffective and weak ASIC had been. As early as 2006, AMP financial advisers had been caught inappropriately switching customers into AMP superannuation funds to earn fat commissions and generate profits for the company, then under the leadership of Chief Executive Andrew Mohl. ASIC had found problems in almost half of the files it reviewed, and

AMP had entered into an enforceable undertaking with ASIC, which included a commitment from AMP to remediate up to 7000 customers and fix the mess. The assumption was AMP had cleaned up its act and kept its nose clean. That was until the royal commission showed otherwise.

*

It was like something out of a Monty Python sketch when Anthony 'Jack' Regan, AMP's head of advice, stepped into the witness box to be grilled by Michael Hodge QC. Under intense questioning, Regan admitted that the insurance giant had made misleading statements to ASIC on at least twenty occasions. The exchanges bordered on the farcical as Hodge tried to work out which part of the company's toxic culture Regan was apologising for.

'When you say, Mr Regan, "On behalf of AMP I apologise unreservedly – for the regulatory breaches which are discussed below",' asked Hodge, 'what are you apologising for?'

Regan replied, 'I will have to take that on notice.'

'That's not really how it works. Is the answer you just don't know?' Hodge countered.

'Yes, I'm uncertain,' said Regan.

'I'm uncertain,' was Regan's constant refrain while he was in the witness box. Ironically, he'd been hired as head of advice in 2017 to improve AMP's governance. Before that he had run AMP's New Zealand financial services department.

Later in the questioning Hodge said to Regan, 'I want to take you through the false and misleading statements that AMP made to ASIC.' Everyone leaned forward to hear more.

Hodge asked Regan to confirm that the initial breach notice given to ASIC by AMP on 27 May 2015 had stated that none of the customers affected by the breach had paid for periodic reviews of their financial position.

'Yes,' Regan replied.

'And that was untrue, wasn't it?' asked Hodge.

'Yes, I believe it was,' Regan replied.

Hodge then revealed that back in 2009 AMP had filed a breach report with ASIC that it was charging clients a fee for no service as a result of inadequate monitoring controls. It had agreed to fix the system.

But in 2011 the issue had resurfaced again when an AMP manager told her boss, Michael Guggenheimer, the managing director of financial planning, that ASIC should be alerted to fees-for-no-service breaches. Guggenheimer thought otherwise, saying, 'I'd like to challenge the notion of this being a breach, it's not an AFSL [Australian Financial Services Licence] requirement, it's a business rule.'

Hodge asked Regan: 'No breach notice was ever given to ASIC in 2011 in relation to this?'

Regan replied, 'That's correct.'

It wasn't until 2015 that AMP launched an internal investigation, after ANZ had publicly announced it had been charging customers fees for no service. Hodge said, 'What we seem to be seeing is that a conscious decision is made to protect the profitability of AMP at the expense of complying with AMP's licence. Do you agree?'

Regan replied, 'Yes.'

Hodge returned to the 2015 breach report, in which AMP had told ASIC that the fees-for-no-service issue had been caused by an administrative error. Hodge said, 'The processes didn't fail, did they, Mr Regan? There was a deliberate decision made by AMP to retain fees on some of these clients?'

Regan replied, 'As I recall, I think it's both.'

Hodge said, 'By my count this was the fourteenth false or misleading statement by AMP to ASIC. You're losing count?'

Hodge counted another six lies before moving on to his next target, AMP chair Catherine Brenner. She had commissioned law firm Clayton Utz to investigate the issues, writing in an email to the law firm, 'This investigation will be entirely independent of the business and is commissioned exclusively by the board through me and the CEO.' Yet, as demonstrated in emails between AMP and Clayton Utz produced at the royal commission, the board, including Brenner, had made a series of changes to the report before the final version was presented to ASIC. All up, Hodge, who had by now earned himself the nickname 'the baby-faced assassin', outlined twenty-five different draft versions of the Clayton Utz report that had been workshopped with AMP before the final report was submitted to ASIC. In one version Brenner wanted to ensure the Clayton Utz document included a statement that CEO Craig Meller had no knowledge of the fees-for-no-service scandal.

The Clayton Utz report was presented by Brenner and legal counsel Brian Salter in a meeting in October 2017 with ASIC's then chairman, Greg Medcraft, and deputy chair, Peter Kell. Hodge asked Regan, 'Do you feel any discomfort at having met with ASIC and said to them, "This is an independent report", in light of what you've now seen?'

Regan replied, 'There is a level of discomfort, yes.'

'And that's because, from your perspective, looking at it, the report appears far less than independent of the company. Do you agree?' asked Hodge.

'That's correct,' Regan replied.

Just before Regan left the witness box, Hodge got him to admit what had been clear to many for some time. 'It's clear that we preference the interest of shareholders ... at the expense of clients,' Regan said.

As Regan walked out, head bowed, a momentary silence engulfed the courtroom. By the end of the day, $600 million had been wiped from the value of AMP's stock, and the heads of AMP boss Craig Meller and Catherine Brenner were on the block. Meller resigned a week later, and soon Brenner's position became untenable. Nothing could save her from the wrath of investors as class-action law firms circled. On 30 April, two weeks after Regan had given evidence, Brenner fell on her sword after an emergency board meeting failed to back her.

When the commission handed down its preliminary findings at the end of the two-week hearing into financial planning, saying it was open to finding AMP had committed criminal offences in four of the twenty instances in which it misled ASIC over the fees-for-no-service scandal, there was panic. Clayton Utz rushed to protect its battered reputation, denying it had done anything wrong and releasing a statement saying that it hadn't misled ASIC and that the investigation had been 'undertaken according to the terms of reference set by AMP'. AMP's legal counsel, Brian Salter, also denied any wrongdoing, saying he was just doing his job. Like Meller and Brenner, he lost his position.

Following its testimony, AMP lodged a submission with the royal commission in May, attempting to downplay some of the allegations that had been raised. It stated that, based on the company's own records, AMP had misled ASIC only seven times, not the twenty tallied up at the royal commission.

*

Regan's royal commission appearance became legendary and left a lasting legacy, in that bank lawyers would subsequently work intensively with witnesses, briefing them on how to frame their responses to protect their brands and prevent incrimination.

Hodge's next target was the hard-nosed senior CBA executive Marianne Perkovic, who had previously worked in the bank's wealth management advice business. She was to begin her testimony on 19 April and talk about her role in the bank's own fees-for-no-service fiasco.

As Perkovic settled into the witness box, Jeff Morris and Merilyn Swan tuned in to watch, confident more dirty linen would be aired. Swan had met Perkovic on a number of occasions as she sought proper compensation for her parents, and considered her part of the CBA cabal that regarded the evidence of victims and whistleblowers as little more than an inconvenience.

Perkovic had a long history in financial planning, having worked at Count Financial for eleven years before moving to CBA in January 2010, a month before whistleblower Jeff Morris went in person to ASIC, forcing it to launch an investigation.

Hodge's focus in his questioning of Perkovic was a breach report from 2014. In July of that year, two years after first discovering customers were paying for a service they weren't receiving, CBA had given ASIC an 'early warning', then issued a breach report on 13 August.

After half an hour of Perkovic ducking and weaving in response to questions, Hodge lost patience: 'Ms Perkovic, is the reason that you are dissembling in answering my question in order to attempt to pre-emptively explain why it is that CFPL [Commonwealth Financial Planning Limited] took more than two years to notify ASIC of its breach?'

'So, at the point in time in 2012 there was no known breach,' Perkovic replied vaguely.

Hayne then intervened. 'It will be safer for you if you attend to counsel's questions,' he advised.

The tension in the courtroom rose. The more Perkovic tried to answer questions using 'context', the more it looked like she was prevaricating. The more Hodge referred to documents to prove his point that CBA knew about the problem but had failed to file a breach report with ASIC, the more convoluted Perkovic's responses became.

Merilyn Swan summed up the mood when she muttered to Jeff Morris: 'Just answer the bloody question. It's yes or no. It's not that hard!' She sent me an email saying, 'I think I have heard this argument before. We didn't know what we didn't know even if we knew it and we knew we didn't know it.'

Hodge turned to a memo written by risk management executive Jaime Henderson, in April 2012 which mentioned a 'brief analysis' of 257 clients paying ongoing fees for no service, then Hodge took Perkovic forensically through a series of reports that had confirmed there were problems. In one report in June 2012, Deloitte had written, 'Systems to identify clients that have signed up to and/or receive ongoing service arrangements are inadequate.' Deloitte also said, 'The process to identify and communicate with customers in a timely manner is ineffective.'

'Do you say, having received this report, that you still weren't sure whether you had an issue about the provision of ongoing service to clients?' Hodge asked Perkovic.

The gallery craned to hear her response, thinking this might be the one to nail her, but Perkovic was too clever by half. 'The report told us what we knew,' she replied, 'which was that we didn't have effective systems and monitoring to be able to identify

227

had the service not been delivered. It didn't tell us that we weren't delivering ongoing service.'

Hodge was frustrated, 'Is the explanation that you want to offer as to why it is that it took CBA more than two years to notify ASIC of its ongoing service fee problems that CBA systems were so hopeless that it had no idea what was going on in its business?'

Perkovic's answer was yes.

'Do you agree that CFPL habitually charged clients for services that were not provided?'

'We didn't know whether the services were provided or not,' Perkovic replied.

'Well, you knew that at least in the case of 1050 clients it was by Deloitte's consideration at least highly likely, if not certain, that these clients were not being provided with services because they were allocated to fifty inactive planners. You agree?'

'Yes,' Perkovic conceded.

'So I will ask my question again: do you agree that as at the date of this report, CFPL knew that it habitually charged clients for services that were not provided?' Hodge asked.

Perkovic replied, 'We knew that we didn't have the supervision and monitoring to determine whether the services were being provided or not.'

Hodge had failed to trap Perkovic into admitting a breach report should have been filed two years earlier, but her performance didn't win her any fans. It was obvious that CBA's culture was such that it had known there were serious problems with its systems, and there was enough evidence from internal reports and the Deloitte review to indicate customers were paying for a service they weren't receiving, but it had continued to charge fees for another two years. If CBA was serious about abiding by the law, as soon as it saw Jaime Henderson's memo it should have suspended payments until a proper investigation had been completed.

As Jeff Morris listened to Perkovic fail to answer the questions, he got angrier and angrier. It gave him flashbacks of what he had gone through at CBA when he had tried to highlight misconduct and the bank's executives had refused to admit it was happening. At 3.04 pm, Morris sent a submission to the royal commission (which anyone could do) and forwarded a copy to me. In his text he underlined the fact that fees for no service had been the bedrock not just of CBA financial planning but of the entire industry. Advisers made most of their money on upfront commissions and trailing commissions. If an adviser wasn't directly employed by the bank but owned their own business and operated under a bank licence, the number of clients on the books and the amount of commissions they generated each year were seen as an asset that could be included in any eventual sale of the company. The usual yardstick for valuing the business was to add up the annual trailing commissions earned and multiply them by four. 'The reason these income streams were so valuable,' Morris said, 'was because, like real estate agents' rent rolls, they were essentially unearned ... By contrast, revenues from, say, accounting practices trade on much lower multiples because they actually have to be earned each year.'

It was this abject failure of culture that resulted in a new twist in the fees-for-no-service scandal: charging dead people for advice. With Perkovic still in the hot seat, Hodge referred to a report by CBA subsidiary Count, dated 2015, called 'Count Financial Risk & Compliance Forum', which found a deceased client was charged fees on an account that hadn't been finalised from 2003 to at least November 2015, despite the planner knowing the client had passed away in 2004. There were audible gasps in the room. The report noted, 'Adviser provided advice to a client in 2003 who passed away in 2004, adviser is aware that the client is dead but the ASF [adviser service fee] ... continues to be charged. When asked, he said he didn't know what to do and had contacted the public trustee but didn't hear back. Depending on outcome, recommend possible warning to adviser.'

Nor was this an isolated case. Hodge revealed how numerous reports about the practice had been made to the bank. Two reviews included the comments, 'One client dies in 2007. Contact made with deceased's wife in 2013 but no action taken,' and 'The last three reviews conducted have indicated that this adviser has provided no advice to any client' – yet the bank had sat on the reports for years before informing the regulator.

It was atrocious behaviour. There had been no concern about consequences or customers, and it made a mockery of CBA advertisements and lofty statements about putting customers' interests first and how the banks fixed problems as soon as they arose.

If there was any lingering doubt where customers ranked in the priority list of our biggest banks and AMP, the testimony from Regan and Perkovic said it all.

*

I had hoped the royal commission would drill into some of the CBA executives who had left the bank – and moved elsewhere in the industry – after having presided over some of the illegal behaviour, the cover-ups Morris had pointed out (including forgery and fraud) and a compliance team that was ignored. This wasn't to be because of the commission's tight deadline. It did, however, shine a light into the dark recesses of financial planning in other organisations, including NAB.

One widespread practice uncovered there involved getting staff to falsely witness the documents of customers, including insurance policy documents. A NAB planner, Bradley Meyn, forged the initials of a married couple without the clients' knowledge or consent after failing to properly fill in their death benefit nomination forms. He put the husband's initials on the wife's form and the wife's initials on the husband's form and asked a bank customer service officer to witness the forms, even though that officer hadn't been there when the clients signed the forms. Meyn's employment was terminated in 2016 but he was not reported to ASIC for another six months.

A review by NAB in early 2017 found that 353 employees, including planners and customer service officers, had been involved in incorrectly witnessing binding client documents. NAB executive Andrew Hagger told the commission he believed the conduct of falsely witnessing statements was attributable to employee indifference and a desire to engage in shortcuts, and blamed it on 'a failure of discipline'. Rowena Orr described it as 'a failure of culture', and pointed out that it could result in estate trustees invalidating the form and making decisions about a client's estate against their wishes. Even after it became aware of the practice, NAB took six months to lodge a breach notice with ASIC. To discipline the wrongdoers, NAB docked 25 per cent off their bonuses, while the executives in the division lost 10 per cent of their bonuses. Hagger had $60,000 shaved from his bonus that year.

'Which left you with the variable component – the bonus for that year – of $960,000?' Orr asked.

'Correct,' replied Hagger.

*

It was fitting that the royal commission's tumultuous two-week hearing into the financial planning industry, which had revealed so much wrongdoing, closed with a review of the industry's watchdog, ASIC, to assess whether it had done its job chasing the wrongdoers and protecting the public.

ASIC chose Louise Macaulay, the senior executive leader of the team responsible for the financial advice industry, for the task of defending ASIC. Macaulay didn't cover herself or ASIC in glory when her answers revealed a slow, hesitant, reluctant regulator that chose compromise rather than wielding the big stick.

The statistics presented at the hearing were damning of ASIC. In the previous five years the regulator had not instigated any civil penalty proceedings against a financial adviser; in the previous decade it had criminally prosecuted just one holder of an Australian Financial Services Licence (AFSL); and it had never prosecuted a licensee for failing to comply with the ten-day time limit for reporting a breach. Even more shocking were the revelations that ASIC investigated less than half of 'significant' breach reports filed by licensees, and the average time that elapsed between a member of the public making a complaint about poor financial advice and ASIC reaching a decision about how to act on the complaint was almost two years.

Then there were the enforceable undertakings that were entered into with licensees. Rowena Orr asked Macaulay about enforceable undertakings ASIC had entered into with ANZ and CBA in respect of the fees-for-no-service issue. '$3 million from each [ANZ and CBA] to mark the level of misconduct. How did ASIC determine that $3 million was an appropriate figure for those community benefit payments?'

Macaulay replied, 'I can't say how that figure was fixed and reached.'

Orr asked, 'Do you think those figures were adequate, given the size of those two organisations and the seriousness of the conduct that was the subject of the enforceable undertaking?'

Macaulay responded, 'Well, certainly when you look at the balance sheet of those institutions it's enormous. So $3 million is not a large amount of money at all.'

She was right. In 2018, CBA earned just under $10 billion and ANZ raked in $6.4 billion in profits over the same period.

*

The royal commission had laid bare the entrails of the financial planning industry and shown that a weak regulator had allowed it to flourish. By this time the Coalition government was looking for positive ways to share in the headlines. The best way to do that was to talk about jail terms for the blue bloods.

Treasurer Scott Morrison announced new criminal penalties of up to ten years' jail and maximum fines of $945,000 for individuals breaching the *Corporations Act 2001*. Civil penalties would increase tenfold, with maximum fines of either $1.05 million for individuals or $10.5 million for corporations, or three times the benefit gained or loss avoided, or 10 per cent of annual turnover – again, whichever was largest. In reference to AMP's revelations, including lying to the regulator, Morrison warned 'this type of despicable behaviour does carry jail sentences under the *Corporations Act*'.[2]

The Coalition was forced to eat humble pie. Turnbull said he was shocked by the revelations and admitted it was a 'clear political error' not to call the royal commission earlier.[3]

Barnaby Joyce, speaking from the backbench after his extra-marital affair, joined the chorus and tweeted, 'In the past

I argued against a royal commission into banking. I was wrong. What I have heard so far is beyond disturbing.'4 Former Prime Minister Tony Abbott chose to shift the blame to ASIC. One Nation leader, Pauline Hanson, demanded the banks be forced to repay the costs of the royal commission, 'no questions asked'. Labor's Bill Shorten went a step further and said the royal commission needed to be extended. In a letter to Prime Minister Turnbull, he said, 'In just fourteen days of hearings the public had heard shocking and shameful evidence about systemic wrongdoing and a culture of cover-up in the banking industry ... Consideration of extending the Royal Commission's reporting time, of an associated compensation scheme for victims, and giving an apology to victims is the least the Government can do given it dragged its feet for so long in acting on the scandals plaguing the banking and financial services sector.'5 Not surprisingly, given the thousands of victims lodging submissions and the complexity and size of the industry, questions about the timing of the royal commission would become a recurring theme.

Chapter 18

Round 3: Small-business loans

The banks dodge a bullet

'I'M AS BLIND AS a bat, I had cancer and I have been used.'

So announced Carolyn Flanagan, a sixty-seven-year-old woman on a disability pension, who appeared as a witness during the third round of the royal commission's hearings in Melbourne. Beginning on 21 May 2018, these hearings would deal with loans to small and medium enterprises.

Everyone watching had a good idea of what would emerge when Flanagan entered the witness box to testify about a risky guarantor bank loan she'd taken out on behalf of her daughter. A pattern had already emerged in the first two hearings of bank customers being regularly shafted and always coming a distant second to profits.

Flanagan's story would be a variation on an old theme and would raise fears that the royal commission might recommend regulation that made it harder for guarantors, including parents, to underwrite business loans for family members. Westpac, in particular, argued that such a move would cut off a key supply of small-business credit to the detriment of the economy.

Small businesses are big business for the banks. Around the country, 2.2 million small businesses employ about five million people. A portion of small businesses are farms, which face the additional challenges of the weather and big supermarkets squeezing them. The big four banks are their main source of credit. Farms are the economic lifeblood of the nation and each year the banks lend them billions of dollars. Investors and bankers were very concerned about this round of the royal commission because of the amounts of money involved and the potential impact on profit – and shares – if laws were changed to make it more difficult to lend to small businesses.

Michael Hodge had a shopping list of complaints against the banks in relation to small business. It included some familiar items: the sale of fraudulent loans, the sale of inappropriate loans for financial incentives, failure to notify ASIC of breaches, charging fees for services not provided, accepting incorrect and incomplete loan applications, double-charging interest on business overdrafts, and overcharging interest.

In its submission to the royal commission, ANZ had admitted that two business bankers had colluded with third parties to write forty-seven fraudulent loans. CBA had charged thousands of businesses double the interest they were supposed to be paying on business transactions and overdraft accounts then failed to report the breach to ASIC or its clients – and it was two and a half years before customers were notified about the breach and repaid the money. NAB had confessed to incorrect disclosure of interest rates and incorrect calculation of interest, resulting in incidents where clients were being overcharged.

With the scene set, Flanagan was beamed into the courtroom via a videolink from Sydney, after her doctor had said she was too sick to travel to Melbourne. Flanagan explained that she had agreed to help her daughter to obtain a loan of $160,000 from Westpac to buy a pool-maintenance franchise in western Sydney, and had offered her house as security.

But Flanagan had glaucoma and couldn't see, her memory was foggy as a result of an operation for cancer, and she suffered from osteoporosis and other medical problems, including the effects of multiple strokes. So when it came to completing the appropriate application forms, she was unable to read the details, write answers or even sign her name. To get around this and enable the loan to go through, the Westpac officer pre-filled the guarantor document with false information. He also wrote 'yes' in answer to a question on an acknowledgement form asking Flanagan if she had 'read the guarantee and indemnity ... carefully'. (Westpac later claimed Flanagan had received independent legal advice before signing the loan documents, something Flanagan denied.)

Hodge went through the loan application for Flanagan's daughter and showed it to be riddled with errors, inconsistencies and contradictions. This prompted Commissioner Hayne to suggest that getting a small-business loan was more about process than substance, box-ticking rather than checking facts.

'Yes, I think that's a correct assessment,' Westpac general manager of commercial banking Alastair Welsh told the commission. 'It was more form, and the substance was more anchored in the security position and not anchored in [the] understanding of Ms Flanagan's income or potential to pay back the debt.'

Flanagan's case identified serious defects in Westpac's procedures for issuing small-business guarantor loans. For example, the bank hadn't checked other discrepancies, such as the loan being for $160,000 when the pool-maintenance franchise her daughter was buying cost $85,000, which was a serious problem in itself.

When the pool-franchise business failed, Westpac called in the loan. With Flanagan unable to pay, the bank attempted to evict her from her home. If Flanagan hadn't received help from Legal Aid NSW, which brokered a deal for her to stay in her home until she died, she would have been out on the street, homeless.

Flanagan's case highlighted the dangers of elderly parents acting as guarantors for their children's loans, and of banks allowing incapacitated and possibly ill-informed customers to sign highly complex legal documents – a particularly damaging practice since loans to small businesses aren't covered by the strong consumer-protection laws that apply to individuals borrowing money.

Concerned by the message Flanagan's story might send, Alastair Welsh repeated the banking industry's mantra that the practice of parents acting as guarantors should be allowed to continue nevertheless, saying, 'Many parents want to back their children. The reality is in Australian society, we're often asset rich and cashflow poor … The support of a guarantee for many small businesses is critical.' It was a message banks desperately wanted to convey to politicians: everything was fine and guarantor loans should be left alone.

*

Another part of the round-three testimony into small- and medium-business loans that grabbed attention was CBA's shabby treatment of customers when a technology 'glitch' had resulted in the bank overcharging thousands of small-business owners millions of dollars on two overdraft products, one of which was a simple business overdraft. Slow remediation, an attempt to cover up the matter, and failure to make a breach report to ASIC were just some of the revelations.

The issue had emerged in 2013 when a customer alerted CBA to the overcharging of interest on their overdrafts. Instead of charging 16 per cent, it was charging a nose-bleeding 32 per cent or more. The bank implemented a manual fix in late 2013 until a system solution was implemented in May 2015. The 'system fix' worked in 95-plus per cent of cases but more than 2500 customers continued to be overcharged. Yet CBA didn't believe it needed to notify ASIC of the breach.

When Clive van Horen, CBA's executive general manager of retail products, was questioned at the royal commission on 24 May 2018, he responded with a cavalier attitude and tried to defend the scandal as a 'technical' problem. It may have started out as a glitch in their computer systems or a coding error, but it snowballed into another example of misconduct at CBA caused by a culture focussed on profit and image rather than doing the right thing.

Counsel assisting, Albert Dinelli, described the devastating impact of the 'technical' problem on one customer who had been overcharged: 'I went to the bank and was quite directly and abruptly told that a bank is a business and that is the price you pay for borrowing money,' the small-business owner, whose name was withheld, said. 'On three separate occasions, I had broken down in the bank asking them to help me understand why it didn't matter much that I was trying to pay back my overdraft and high interest charges and I could not get ahead.'

After the woman's third visit CBA realised the mistake was not hers, but that it had been charging her the interest rate of 32 per cent. Instead of taking the issue further to see how many other customers were being overcharged, the bank tried to isolate it to one case. 'Due to some system error, we have been charging a customer 32 per cent interest instead of 16 per cent,' an email from a staff member of the bank said. 'To resolve the matter, I recommend to early charge off and approve a payment arrangement of $50 a week. If not, the matter will escalate and might be raised as systemic, because it could be happening with more customers, too.'

The revelations were sickening, as was van Horen's attitude. Dinelli asked him, 'Do I understand that email to be a suggestion that it be settled so that the issue isn't raised and thus becomes a systemic issue?'

'Yes ... I think the person was clearly trying to resolve the complaint for the customer,' van Horen replied.

The bank offered the customer $2750 in compensation, but when she threatened to go to the media it upped its offer to $3494 'as a commercial decision to resolve the matter'.

Inside the courtroom, onlookers looked on aghast as van Horen continued to downplay the bank's actions. When Dinelli said to him, 'And there were two reasons for CBA wishing to have this dealt with speedily. One was the bad PR?' van Horen replied simply, 'Fair to say.'

Dinelli then said, 'One was also the fear of it being identified as a systemic issue?' to which van Horen replied, 'I wouldn't be comfortable saying that that was a CBA view.'

Unhappy with the offer, the customer lodged a claim with the Financial Ombudsman Service. It was this decision that forced CBA to broaden its investigation. As Dinelli pointed out, if the customer had left the matter alone and not gone to the FOS, the bank might never have looked into the problem and thousands of others would have continued to be overcharged.

Yet still CBA played the game. Dinelli read out another email van Horen had written requesting a ten-day delay in remediation payments – which CBA had already taken two and a half years to move towards – to avoid poor PR: 'Can we make all this happen, letters and actual refunds, after House of Reps hearing on 7 March? Eliminates the chance of this being brought up in the hearings and a delay of ten days is immaterial.' He was referring to a scheduled appearance by CBA's then chief executive Ian Narev and Matt Comyn, who was running CBA's retail bank, in Federal Parliament on 7 March 2017.

It was typical of the practice already highlighted at previous inquiries into banks cosying up with regulators. Hayne asked van Horen to explain his actions.

'At the time, we did not believe there was any reportable breach,' van Horen responded. 'In terms of materiality … it was less than 1500 customers out of 10 million. It was, you know, I think, .002 per cent of our total earnings. So it was a very small issue in the scheme of things … A judgement call I made in the moment … And I accept it was the wrong decision, but that was the decision I made.'

It was an answer that encapsulated the bank's culture of denial.

Dinelli pursued the issue of CBA's delay in reporting the breach to ASIC, asking if it was true that it wasn't until 15 May, with the royal commission approaching, that CBA made a disclosure to ASIC and conceded its conduct was misleading or deceptive.

Van Horen replied, 'Yes. I believe so.'

That meant that from the time CBA realised there was an issue of overcharging until the completion of remediation – 960 days – it sent out ten statements to its customers. Dinelli pointed out that ten statements to 2500 customers meant there were '25,000 instances of those false or misleading representations'. 'Is that right?' he asked van Horen.

'Look, I think this feels to me like a very legal interpretation of the legislation. I absolutely couldn't agree – you know, I don't know enough about that to say yes.'

'Well, your letter did say, "The issue may also give rise to other breaches of financial services law,"' said Dinelli.

'Yes,' van Horen replied.

Dinelli then tried to get van Horen to admit there had been an actual breach of the law.

'I don't understand that,' van Horen replied. 'So you're asking me quite a legal question. I'm not going to be able to give you an answer to that.

Here was another banker who'd been briefed by his lawyers to concede as little as possible, even when the evidence was in front of him.

*

Another disturbing case study in this round of hearings involved Marion Messih, whose experience as a Pie Face franchisee illustrated a frequent lack of due diligence on the part of banks and small-business owners when it came to loans for franchised businesses.

I'd developed a keen interest in Australia's $170 billion franchise industry after a series of exposés into Domino's Pizza, 7-Eleven, Caltex and the Retail Food Group, which has brands including Gloria Jean's Coffees, Michel's Pattiserie and Brumby's Bakery. The owners of numerous franchises – small businesses – across the sector had suffered financial devastation and mental health issues after watching their dream of owning a small business turn into a personal and financial nightmare. The common theme was abuse of power by the big franchisors, with fee gouging, excessive rebates, an imbalance of power and unconscionable contracts, all of which made the business model unworkable for many franchisees.

Banks had played a role in the financial ruin of thousands of franchisees across the country. They did this by accrediting franchise operators, which the franchisors marketed as an endorsement of their business model, and by their willingness to lend money to franchisees wanting to purchase a franchise. In return for the accreditation, franchisors steered franchisees to borrow from the accrediting bank. This goes a long way to explaining the rapid growth of the franchise sector and the havoc it has wreaked on some franchisees' lives.

Westpac had accredited Pie Face, a franchise network renowned for selling both pies and coffee. Pie Face steered Messih and her brother and sister-in-law to borrow $360,000 from Westpac to buy a Pie Face store. Soon after, she realised the previous owner had 'exaggerated' the financial figures. To try and make their franchise profitable, Messih worked fourteen-hour days, opening at 5 am and knocking off at 7 pm. 'If we made $500 a week it was a miracle,' Messih told the royal commission.

Eighteen months after investing in the store, Messih and her brother and sister-in-law called it quits. That same year the entire Pie Face network collapsed, leaving many franchisees stranded and paying off bank loans. It would later emerge Pie Face hadn't made a profit in ten years, which makes you wonder what sort of checks banks do before accrediting franchise networks.

Messih said that after giving up the franchise, 'I had the business loan, I had a credit card with Commonwealth Bank that I was paying off and also another Westpac credit card that I was paying off … It was just too much.' Although Messih received rental income from an investment property she owned, it didn't cover all the expenses she had.

Messih and a group of other Pie Face franchisees lodged a claim with the Financial Ombudsman Service, saying Westpac should never have given them a business loan and should refund the interest and bank charges. Meanwhile, the letters and phone calls from Westpac to Messih demanding payment ramped up. Messih recalled to the commission how she'd told Westpac, 'Well, you're going to let me starve to death, even though I have got no money.'

She decided to sell her investment property 'just to breathe'. Of the $750,000 she received for it, Messih planned to clear her debts by paying off $165,000 she owed on the investment property and $330,000 she owed on her home loan. She also planned to repay her half of the business loan with Westpac (the other half was still with her brother and sister-in-law).

But the day before the settlement occurred, instead of accepting her half of the loan repayment and coming to an arrangement with her brother and sister-in-law, Westpac decided to take 100 per cent of the loan from Messih. Her sister-in-law was now paying her back $120 a week, the royal commission heard.

'It was the worst time of my life,' Messih said. 'I don't want to ever go through that again. I had my kids paying my bills for me – paying my loans for me … I worked hard to get where I was. It's gone. All of it has gone. I still owe money, when I should be retired by now. But I still owe money.'

Despite this shocking evidence, the royal commission failed to investigate the ramifications of banks accrediting franchisors, the level of comfort bank accreditation of a franchisor gives to franchisees signing up for life-changing business loans, or the extent of due diligence undertaken by the banks. This was a lost opportunity.

As the curtains closed on the third round of hearing, there was a sense of relief among bankers and investors. Despite some uncomfortable moments, no scalps had been taken and there was no expectation of government intervention in tightening restrictions on lending to small businesses or banning guarantors. Numerous breaches of the banking code of conduct and the *Corporations Act* had been revealed, and there'd been yet more examples of a culture that put profit before people and of the banks' questionable accreditation of franchise models. Clearly there was an obvious imbalance of power between banks and small businesses. But the commission made it clear it wasn't prepared to touch that area.

The banks had dodged a bullet in another part of their business, but there were many more bullets to come.

Chapter 19

Round 4: Services in regional and remote communities

Preying on rural battlers

THE FOURTH ROUND OF hearings began on 25 June in Brisbane then moved to Darwin to ensure the 6.9 million Australians living in remote and regional communities didn't feel they'd been forgotten. It opened like any other hearing, with Rowena Orr laying out a detailed summary of the issues, then grilling the first witness, but on day two it turned political when crossbencher Bob Katter, sitting in the gallery, became frustrated and shouted, 'Are we going to address why these things happened and what we can do about it to improve it in the future? Is the commission going to address those issues?'

Katter was referring to the treatment of farmers experiencing financial stress and hardship. He was concerned that the royal commission had allocated too little time to deal with their specific problems.

To everyone's surprise, Hayne responded to Katter's impassioned plea: 'Mr Katter, I've indicated the course I will follow ... We're looking at these things at the moment through the lens of particular case studies,' he said. 'I understand your concern, you're not the only one who's concerned, Mr Katter. There's a lot of people out there concerned and I know that.'

Hayne didn't have to look too far as a group of aggrieved farmers had assembled outside the commission to protest. He had also seen the sheer volume of submissions from farmers outlining harrowing stories. So he acquiesced and announced he would reschedule the hearings for the rest of the week to allocate more time to these issues. It wasn't enough to appease the farmers – Katter, the National Farmers' Federation and some National Party members including Wacka Williams – but it defused what could have become a much bigger political issue.

Getting back to business, Orr outlined a series of farm cases where ANZ had played hardball with customers after acquiring the loan book of the Landmark rural bank in 2010. In one case, a third-generation farming family from Western Australia, was issued with a default notice in 2013, a month after the patriarch, Stephen Harley, had suffered a heart attack and his wife, Janine, had asked ANZ for more time to make repayments. The bank granted an extension on the condition the family vacate the property within twenty-four hours if they failed to make a payment by the deadline.

'Was one day a reasonable period?' Hayne asked ANZ executive Ben Steinberg.

'In an environment where we've executed an agreement with a customer who's been advised of the ramifications of the agreement, I believe it is reasonable,' Steinberg replied.

After hearing a string of stories about forced farm sales, mental anguish inflicted on communities, and the role of the banks, it became apparent that this was another area where the banks had failed their communities.

*

By the time the commission reached Darwin, the topic had switched from the treatment of farmers to funeral insurers exploiting the cultural significance of Indigenous mourning ceremonies in order to persuade Aboriginal and Torres Strait Islander people to buy insurance they couldn't afford and didn't understand. The hearing became emotionally charged when Aboriginal woman Tracey Walsh broke down as she recounted how she had signed up with Aboriginal Community Benefits Fund (which is not connected with any Indigenous organisation) and paid $10,000 in premiums for a policy that would only ever pay a maximum of $8000 in the event of her death. She had believed that if she paid more than $8000, the extra money would go to her family.

The royal commission also heard recordings of phone calls made by a sales agent at Select AFSL, which trades under the name Let's Insure, to a sixty-year-old Aboriginal woman, Kathy Marika, for whom English is her second language. The agent was aggressively pushing Marika to buy funeral insurance, despite being told she already had insurance through her superannuation. The policies were underwritten by St Andrews Insurance, owned by Bank of Queensland until the bank announced its sale in April 2018, just ahead of the hearing.

Marika gave evidence that she didn't know what she was being sold. During one call in August 2015, which lasted thirty-eight minutes, Marika was told her existing policy in her super fund had an 'expiry date' and 'you can't actually cover the whole family'. By the end of the call, the agent had signed her up for a funeral insurance policy for herself, her three children and five grandchildren. On another occasion he called her back for names and contact details of her friends and work colleagues. 'He was offering me the vouchers. He told me about the vouchers before, then he said he was going to give me vouchers from Coles and Myers, which I didn't get,' she said.

On 16 September 2015, struggling to pay her bills, she tried to cancel her policy, but Let's Insure continued to deduct the premiums. Marika described how Let's Insure called her, sometimes daily, for more names and leads. Concerned the insurer would hound others as they had done to her, she warned her friends not to take any calls from a private number. In March 2016, unemployed and finding it hard to pay her electricity bills, she asked Legal Aid NSW for help. On her behalf, Legal Aid wrote to the company suggesting it had breached the law in its dealings with Marika and asking for a refund of the premiums she had paid. Let's Insure eventually refunded Marika's premiums, totalling $1890, and agreed to cancel her policies. In a letter to Legal Aid, the company said it had refunded the policy as a gesture of goodwill but disputed the allegations and insisted that 'at all times we have acted properly and in accordance with the law'.

And as if that wasn't enough, the commission revealed that staff working at the Let's Insure call centre were offered incentives – including 'a paid holiday to buzzing Las Vegas, Nevada, USA', three-day cruises to the Sunshine Coast from Sydney and a Vespa scooter – for selling the most policies. The company stopped selling funeral insurance in March 2018, and admitted to mis-selling hundreds of policies to Indigenous consumers.

It seemed that since Allan Fels had uncovered dodgy sales practices targeting Aboriginal people in the early 1990s, little had changed.

Chapter 20

Round 5: Superannuation

Kept in the dark

THE COMMISSION RETURNED TO Melbourne's Owen Dixon building for round five, which was to blast sunlight on the country's $2.7 trillion superannuation sector – a sector built on the backs of millions of disengaged members.

In his opening speech, senior counsel assisting, Michael Hodge QC, used dark metaphors and imagery to create a sense of foreboding. 'Consumers are unable to do anything more than peer dimly through the darkness of their superannuation trustees,' he said, adding, 'There is no dedicated and active regulator shining a spotlight on the trustees and searching out bad behaviour … [so] what happens when we leave these trustees alone in the dark with our money? Can they [the trustees] be trusted to do the right thing with our hard-earned money?

'Trustees are surrounded by temptation,' Hodge warned. These temptations included giving preference to their sponsoring organisation 'to act in the interests of other parts of the corporate group, to choose profit over the interests of members, to establish structures that consign to others the responsibility for the fund, and thereby relieve the trustee of visibility of anything that might be troubling. Their duties oblige them to resist all of these temptations.'

Most people don't know what a trustee is – never mind that they are the guardians of our retirement savings. Trustees are the people appointed to manage a superannuation fund and decide on its investment strategy. Under the *Superannuation Industry Supervision Act*, trustees must oversee their fund with the sole objective of providing *retirement* benefits to members or their dependants. Indeed, they are supposed to apply what's known as 'the sole purpose test' to everything they do: each time they make a decision, they have to ask themselves, 'Will this benefit our members in their retirement?'

At the royal commission, trustees were about to be put on trial, and Hodge's indication that many trustees were conflicted and that the regulators, ASIC and APRA, had been missing in action was a clarion call for any Australian with super to dig out their annual statements and become engaged.

'At the end of your working life, you know how much you have. You do not know how much you might have had but for certain decisions made by your trustee, of which you were not aware or of which you were only notified in an obscure way, if at all,' Hodge said.

*

After making his opening speech Hodge asked for a twenty-minute break to clear his head and prepare for the hard slog ahead. He wanted to return to the fees-for-no-service scandal but look at it in relation to those super trustees who had allowed the practice to go on.

Superannuation is complex and filled with jargon, which made this a challenging yet important round for observers.

Unfortunately, no victims were to be called to explain the human impact of the superannuation gravy train.

One of the major trustee bodies presiding over NAB's super funds, NULIS Nominees, had been caught up in the fees-for-no-service scandal. NULIS offered super through financial planners or sold it to companies. In a submission to the royal commission, it admitted that between September 2012 and January 2017 it had 'incorrectly charged' approximately $35 million in plan service fees (PSFs) to 220,460 members who didn't even have a plan adviser linked to their account. NAB also acknowledged that correspondence sent to members was potentially misleading because it didn't tell them they would be charged a PSF or that members could opt out of PSFs. In other words, members were paying for a planner who didn't exist, they didn't know they were paying for it, and they weren't given the option not to pay for it.

Hodge's first witness, Paul Carter, was a former executive general manager in NAB's wealth division, from March 2013 until February 2017 when he moved to New Zealand to work in NAB's Bank of New Zealand. He was polite and defensive, but his replies to questions from Hodge went round in circles. He had trouble remembering things: he couldn't recall a presentation he'd given to his boss Andrew Hagger, various conversations he'd had with Hagger, or documents he'd 'sponsored' or approved. Nor could he recall certain critical emails.

It made the atmosphere in courtroom 4A surreal, with Hodge becoming frustrated with Carter's obfuscations and the gallery becoming increasingly restless. Some of the interchanges between Hodge and Carter were like skits from Shaun Micallef's *Mad as Hell*. In one exchange, Hodge was trying to find out from Carter whether it was clear to members that they weren't getting advice despite paying for it. Carter said he didn't recall, which led to the following exchange.

> Hodge: Do you recall the specific idea that members who were in Five Star products were not getting advice?
> Carter: I don't recall.
> Hayne: Well, is it, therefore, a matter to which you simply did not turn your mind?
> Carter: In the context of this, I – that would be – I'm not in a position to say, Commissioner.
> Hayne: Is it the position that you did not turn your mind to whether these people were or were not getting advice?
> Carter: I don't know the context in which I would have turned my mind to that question.

The point Hodge and Hayne were trying to get to was the conflict going on inside NAB's retail super fund division. It dated back to 2012, when NAB had believed a PSF could be charged to members without a linked adviser, and that providing online tools and telephone-based advice services would justify the fee. Then in 2016 NAB decided to simplify the structure of its super business to streamline the number of trustees from three to one and use NULIS as its new mega trustee.

The restructure resulted in an internal debate on whether NAB could continue to charge PSFs in light of the Future of Financial Advice (FoFA) reforms, which had banned commissions but allowed grandfathered commissions – the continued collection of trailing commissions on products sold before June 2013. NAB decided it could continue to charge the fees. It did so by relying on legal advice that the removal of the fee would trigger a breach of contract with its advisers, who would take their business – and clients – elsewhere, to a competitior, which would not be in the best interests of fund members.

It was tedious stuff, but Hodge wanted to show that the bank's motivation was to protect the profits of the NAB advisers and the NAB group rather than its members. It also set the scene for the appearance of Nicole Smith, the former chairman of NULIS Nominees, who had been linked with NAB since 2006, become chairman of NULIS in 2013 and resigned a few weeks before giving testimony.

Smith entered the witness box just as the air-conditioner stopped working, causing the room to get hotter and hotter, and frustrations to rise. To make matters worse, Smith spoke so softly it was almost impossible to hear her. When Hayne asked her to speak up, she whispered, 'Sorry. I'm generally quiet by nature.'

Hodge had established with Carter that fees were charged to protect the business. He now had the former chair of the trustee in front of him, whose sole duty was to look after members, and he wanted her to explain how continuing to charge grandfathered commissions could be fair to members.

'You recognise, don't you, that it is not in the best interests of members to be paying commissions?' he asked.

Smith's response was, 'I'm not going to comment on when and how an adviser acts in a member's best interest. We thought the risks called out were real … On balance the trustee believed that grandfathering commissions was in the best interests of members.'

'You agree that management of the administrator [the bank] is in a hopelessly conflicted position?' Hodge asked Smith.

'I believe that they are in a conflicted position. I do not believe it's hopelessly conflicted,' she replied.

Not surprisingly, remediation for the theft of $35 million from hundreds of thousands of clients had been slow: it had taken

NAB ten months to decide whether to compensate customers, as Hodge pointed out: 'Do you think that the trustee acted in the best interests of members by waiting until 26 October 2016 to finally decide to fully compensate … members?'

'At the time and on reflection, my view was that management needed to work through the facts of the matter,' Smith replied, 'and that the administrator came to the right decision for members without using the board as a blunt instrument to do so.'

Exasperated, Hodge asked her, 'Can you see that the problem with the approach that you've outlined is that the board of directors has only one duty, and that is to act in the best interests of members, and that the administrator is conflicted because the administrator is the one who will have to give back the profits?'

Smith replied, 'I think that the issue is timing.'

It turned out that Smith had also had a hand in negotiating with ASIC about a breach notice slapped on NULIS. She had conducted a review that found NAB had been charging fees to dead people. It filed a list of 110 breach reports with ASIC, but submitted them later than the ten-business-day requirement specified in the *Corporations Act*. Despite this, in a letter co-signed in July 2016 with Andrew Hagger, Smith had argued vigorously with the regulator about why it shouldn't slap a court-approved enforceable undertaking on NULIS.

Kenneth Hayne then asked her a killer question: 'Did you think, yourself, that taking money to which there was no entitlement raised a question for criminal law?'

'I didn't,' Smith replied.

*

Hodge's grilling of NAB and its superannuation subsidiaries laid bare some of the dirty tricks it had been using, including pressuring the regulators, breaches, fee gouging and slack remediation payments, and it attracted a lot of publicity – no part more so than Hayne's question to Smith about whether she'd thought taking money to which there was no entitlement raised a question for criminal law. It received top billing on TV, newspapers and social media and prompted NAB's Thorburn to tweet, 'This week we've been confronted at the Royal Commission with examples of where we have failed to serve our customers with honour. I'm sorry ...'[1]

On 10 August, I wrote a column titled, 'Is this company really just a pathological liar? That's the question when it comes to National Australia Bank'. It didn't go down well at NAB. That morning, Thorburn addressed staff to answer any concerns and to say I was wrong. He also called me and told me the same thing.

For all the mea culpas and promises that it had a good risk culture, what NAB said and what it did were worlds apart. While its staff were being grilled about superannuation in the royal commission, NAB quietly instructed its lawyers to lodge an appeal in the Federal Court on a separate but similar matter relating to a landmark ruling from the Superannuation Complaints Tribunal (SCT). The ruling required the trustee of the NAB super fund, MLC Nominees, to pay almost $8500 in compensation to a member who had lodged a complaint about fees for no service. Significantly, it requested that the trustee write to all other current and former fund members of the fund – as far back as 2008 – to inform them about the tribunal's decision. It also required the trustee to inform ASIC of its ruling.

A copy of the SCT ruling had been one of a number of documents ASIC submitted to the commission a week before the round of superannuation hearings. NAB's decision to appeal the SCT ruling ensured it would never be raised at the royal commission because the commission's terms of reference prevented it discussing issues that were before the courts.

I was sent a copy of the SCT decision. It involved a fifty-five-year-old woman who'd lodged a complaint with the SCT in 2015 after discovering she'd been paying a fee of 5 per cent, referred to as an 'administration' fee, for a financial adviser she didn't know she had and who had never contacted her or provided her with services. She was seeking a refund of the fee.

The SCT reported that the NAB trustee had decided in 2008 that members of the MLC Nominees fund no longer had to pay a regular fee for a financial adviser, but had then failed to inform members of its decision. So members continued to be charged for the fee. NAB then began describing it as an 'administration fee', even though the entire fee was paid as commission to an adviser. The SCT said this practice 'could be regarded as being misleading'.

In its notice of appeal to the Federal Court, NAB's MLC Nominees said, 'The trustee is aggrieved by the [SCT] decision.' It asked whether the SCT had erred by proceeding on the basis that it was part of its statutory task to determine whether members were entitled to be told of the 2008 decision and/or that there was a duty on the trustee to notify the members of the 2008 decision.

It made me wonder how many other cases like this never saw the light of day at the royal commission, either because the institution failed to include them on its misconduct list (as with the CBA Dollarmites scandal) or took legal action to prevent them being examined, or the commission simply didn't have the time to investigate them.

*

Act three of the royal commission into superannuation began on Monday 13 August and starred NAB's Andrew Hagger in his second appearance. The theme was the lack of transparency of financial institutions in their dealings with ASIC.

Michael Hodge had a bee in his bonnet. Given the fact that he had already spent an inordinate amount of time with the two other NAB witnesses, calling back Hagger suggested something big was about to go down. Media and the financial community were transfixed.

The normally chilled-out Hagger looked tense, flushed and tired. He'd been served with the summons to appear again on the previous Friday and he hadn't had much sleep while he'd reviewed documents, talked to lawyers to figure out the line of questioning and tried to get his story straight. He knew what documents would appear, so he had a pretty good idea of what was coming. Perhaps he hoped his charm would win the day. However, Hodge was in no mood to allow Hagger to wriggle off the hook.

Hodge referred back to ASIC's October 2016 report on how the big four banks and AMP had charged around 176,000 customers an estimated $178 million in fees for advice they'd never received.[2] Prior to the release of the report, the regulator had sent the various institutions a draft copy containing the banks' and AMP's estimates of how much remediation they owed customers. CBA had provided an estimate of $105 million, ANZ's estimate was $49 million, NAB's was $16.9 million and AMP's was $4.6 million. Westpac hadn't provided ASIC with an estimate.

At issue was a conversation between Hagger and ASIC's Greg Tanzer, which Hagger had described in a file note as a 'proactive communication that was open and transparent'. As Hodge was cross-examining Hagger, extracts from relevant papers flashed up on the courtroom screens. They included a series of board-meeting minutes and other documents that showed the meeting with Tanzer had been anything but transparent.

On the morning of Hagger's meeting with Tanzer, Hagger had attended a NAB executives' meeting where a resolution had been passed to more than double the estimation of compensation NAB had provided ASIC, from $16.9 million to $34 million.

'And you didn't tell Mr Tanzer that?' Hodge asked.

'No, I don't think I did tell him that,' Hagger replied, adding that he'd opened the door 'very wide' to questions from ASIC if it wanted to know more.

'I want to be absolutely clear on this,' Hodge said. 'You regard the way that you dealt with ASIC as being open and transparent?'

'Yes, I do,' Hagger responded.

Commissioner Hayne piped in, saying, 'So being open and transparent was accomplished by saying, "Ask us what you like, but we won't tell you what to ask?"'

Hodge summed up what everyone was thinking: 'Mr Hagger's evidence that he "left the door open" for ASIC to ask the question reveals both a disrespect for the role of the regulator and a disregard for the gravity of the events in question.' Onlookers didn't know whether to laugh or cry.

The reason Hagger and NAB had made the decision not to provide ASIC with its revised compensation figure of $34 million was that the release of ASIC's final report on 27 October 2016 would coincide with the release of the bank's all-important full-year results to shareholders. NAB didn't want bad publicity about its revised compensation figure to mar its annual presentation. The royal commission was shown an email Hagger had received saying, 'The chief [Andrew Thorburn] is keen to ensure Thursday [results day] goes as smoothly as possible.'

On 17 September 2018, Hagger resigned from NAB as a result of what the royal commission had revealed. Hodge had got his scalp.

*

Unfortunately, the amount of time spent on NAB crunched the time spent on other institutions. But the royal commission did manage to highlight some disturbing conduct and a poor culture at IOOF, the financial services company whose frontrunning and insider trading I had investigated back in 2015.

Letters released to the royal commission showed that APRA had written to IOOF at various times over the years outlining serious issues. One letter in September 2015 referred to ASIC's 'difficulty in obtaining accurate and current information in relation to issues such as ... culture, identification of responsible persons and the information flow and relationship between the board and management and the Fairfax Media matter'.[3] 'The Fairfax Media matter' referred to the stories Sarah Danckert and I had written (see Chapter 11).

In mid-2017 an internal APRA memo stated, 'Since December 2015, APRA has identified a number of instances where 'IOOF has failed to adequately identify conflicts of interest'.[4] IOOF's contempt for APRA and an apparent lack of regard for governance and processes were exposed when a board meeting – held one week before Chris Kelaher gave testimony at the banking royal commission – resulted in the production of handwritten minutes on scraps of paper, many of which were illegible.

Chris Kelaher, the CEO of IOOF, came to testify wearing a red tie, with a bright white handkerchief poking out of his jacket. The public gallery was mesmerised by his body language, sarcasm and indifference. He made it obvious he didn't want to be at the commission. He deflected allegations with comments such as 'That's your construction' or by saying something was 'a long time ago'. When Hodge asked him if he understood what was on the handwritten minutes, he retorted that he wasn't a handwriting expert.

Hodge grilled Kelaher over the company's decision to dip into reserves of a super fund to compensate its members for losses suffered following a $6.1 million payment error. This was akin to them getting customers to use their nest eggs to compensate themselves, yet Kelaher told Hodge he believed it passed the 'pub test'. The $6.1 million payment error had been detected in 2010 and become the subject of a breach report to ASIC in 2012 and an internal whistleblower report in 2013.

The commission also heard during Kelaher's testimony that IOOF had decided not to move customers from a super fund that was paying trailing commissions to a new lower-fee product after working out that it would cost the company about $8 million a year to do so. In addition, it was revealed that APRA had been trying to get IOOF to unwind a dual structure whereby IOOF Investment Management was both trustee and responsible entity. Kelaher said it was a matter of indifference to him if the trustee and manager roles were split.

'You don't share the view of APRA that there are legitimate concerns about these structures?' Hodge asked.

Kelaher was unmoved. Trying to get a response, Hodge asked, 'And when you reflect on those events, does that cause you to think that there might be some issues with the structure?'

To which Kelaher replied, 'No, I don't.'

Towards the end of the grilling, Hodge said in exasperation, 'Even now you don't see any problem with the events that occurred.'

The irony of all this scrutiny was neatly summed up in one internal IOOF document, dated 22 March 2018, that was displayed on the screen in the courtroom. It set out how IOOF could justify to APRA their offering different prices to existing and new members: 'I think we could expect APRA to scrutinise this decision and criticise it as another example of us not managing our conflicts accordingly.' It went on to say, 'These days we should have regard not only to the "How would this look on the front page of *The Age* test?" but also to the test of "Would we like to see this decision dissected at the royal commission?"'[5]

At least it got that right.

*

By the time APRA's deputy chairman, Helen Rowell, appeared in the witness box on 17 August 2018 there was little goodwill towards the regulator. Rowell had worked at APRA for sixteen years. She had been appointed deputy chair in November 2015 then reappointed to the position for a further five-year term from 1 July 2018, ahead of her appearance at the royal commission.

Half an hour into Michael Hodge's cross-examination of Rowell, I received a text message from a senior public servant asking, 'Are you watching it? Think train wreck, followed by Chernobyl, followed by tsunami.'

It was a reasonable summation of the interrogation, which provided an extraordinary insight into the mindset of APRA – which, according to Rowell, preferred to be 'collaborative' instead of adversarial. This collaborative approach involved regular engagement with the boards of financial institutions, reviews of these same institutions and – if there were problems – experts being appointed to conduct further reviews. When that didn't work, APRA would write the institution a stern letter.

When Hodge asked Rowell about APRA's use of penalties and sanctions for misconduct, her responses were embarrassing. In the previous decade APRA had only disqualified one super fund trustee – a director of the collapsed Trio Capital – and it hadn't taken any action against likely breaches of the sole-purpose test that might have occurred in the fees-for-no-service scandal.

Everything at APRA was conducted behind closed doors, except enforceable undertakings, but it hadn't made any of those either. To double-check that he was hearing correctly, Hodge asked, 'So enforceable undertakings, if they were to occur, they would be public?'

Rowell: 'Yes.'

Hodge: 'But they [enforceable undertakings] don't occur. So what other public conduct does APRA engage in which would identify specific trustees and specific conduct of those trustees?'

Rowell: 'None.'

For years APRA had shunned the media with a stock standard 'no comment' when asked about anything relating to the banks or super funds. This enabled the regulator to escape the glare of criticism, unlike ASIC, which was more public and transparent.

APRA's collaborative approach to dealing with institutions had resulted in a litany of misconduct that had escaped public scrutiny. One of the standouts was CBA, which had made at least 15,000 criminal breaches in relation to its not moving customers who hadn't selected a specific super product to a default no-frills, low-fee 'My Super' fund, as federal laws introduced in January

2014 obliged the bank to do. Yet APRA imposed no enforceable undertakings or fines.

When Hodge asked Rowell if APRA had contemplated taking action on fees for no service, she said no, and that APRA was waiting for ASIC's conclusions. Rowell even tried to defend the payment of ongoing trailing commissions by superannuation fund members on the basis that she couldn't be sure it wasn't in members' best interests. This was the same regulator that had taken until August 2017 to order an inquiry into CBA's culture and governance after watching a string of scandals, including the financial planning, life insurance and fees-for-no-service scandals, as well as alleged bank bill swap rate rigging and the AUSTRAC money-laundering scandal.

APRA's failure to take effective action in any of these cases was a damning indictment of the regulator.

*

Strapped for time, the royal commission did a light once-over of industry super funds, much to the disappointment of the Coalition. Industry funds are non-profit and therefore escape the myriad conflicts of interest and quagmire of unreasonable fees that characterise retail funds. When it comes to performance, most of them outperform their retail counterparts, mainly because they aren't clipping the fee ticket.

As with other institutions, the royal commission had written to industry super funds asking for a list of inappropriate behaviour during the previous ten years. Most of the misconduct they revealed was minor.

Ian Silk, CEO of AustralianSuper, a not-for-profit industry fund and the country's biggest super fund provider, was called as a witness. The royal commission wanted to question him about AustralianSuper's $2 million investment in online newspaper *The New Daily* and its contribution of $500,000 towards the controversial 'Fox in the Henhouse' ad campaign that portrayed banks as the foxes trying to get their teeth into people's retirement savings. Hodge wanted to know whether spending that money was in members' best interests.

Silk's explanation was that the advertising campaign and newspaper investments had been carefully considered by the board and had been signed off with the best intentions to educate, retain and protect members. AustralianSuper had since written off its investment in *The New Daily* and the ads had involved only a one-off payment.

For those who might have thought both these expenditures an inappropriate use of members' money, Silk noted that $2.5 million was chickenfeed compared with the fund's $140 billion assets, or the antics of retail funds. 'The difference between the best funds and the poorest funds is literally life-changing for people,' Silk told the commission.

It was hard to disagree. However, after only such a cursory look at the numerous industry funds at the royal commission, we still can't be sure that all of them are squeaky clean.

*

Over twenty days of gruelling hearings, the royal commission had demonstrated how trustees in superannuation retail funds had sat in conflicted silence around boardroom tables, earning tidy sums as they rubber stamped a myriad of schemes designed to squeeze as many fees out of members as possible.

Hodge's concluding address to Hayne regarding the hearings was damning. He said, 'Members of superannuation funds, like most beneficiaries, are vulnerable, and in respect of superannuation, many are disengaged and disadvantaged by a lack of financial literacy. They are readily able to be taken advantage of.

'And the evidence, you may conclude, commissioner, suggests that this has occurred in some cases. In most industries, the forces of competition can be relied upon to minimise improper conduct and effective regulation can be expected to address breaches of the law when breaches occur; however, for superannuation, the disengagement of members, amongst other things, may limit the effectiveness of competition.'

For all the complexity of the hearings into superannuation, the scandals exposed resonated with Australians. Official figures from APRA show that industry funds grew by $80 billion or 13 per cent to $677 billion in the twelve months to March 2019, compared with 3.4 per cent growth in retail funds to $623 billion. For the first time, the industry funds were bigger than the retail funds. AustralianSuper was the biggest beneficiary, with Ian Silk estimating net inflows would rise more than $15 billion in the year to 30 June 2019, an increase of more than 60 per cent over the previous year. Silk told the media that more than one-third of AustralianSuper's inflows were coming from members switching out of AMP and funds run by the big four banks. 'Since the start of the royal commission there has been a sharp rise in member contributions,' he said.[6]

This switch to industry funds was also likely influenced by finance expert Scott Pape, aka the Barefoot Investor, who has long banged the drum for low-fee-charging super funds and advised his huge following that he invests his super with industry fund HostPlus.[7] Its membership jumped 350 per cent in 2018.[8]

Low fees, better performance and no apparent systemic misconduct all played a part in the public's rush to park their retirement savings in industry funds. Debbie Blakey, CEO of industry fund HESTA, told *The New Daily*, 'It's about trust. The royal commission has probably made us all realise just how valuable trust is.'[9]

Chapter 21

Round 6: Insurance

Bleeding them dry

WHEN COMMINSURE'S BOSS, HELEN Troup, entered court 4A on 12 September 2018 for the first session of round six of the hearings, on the scandal-ridden life insurance division she had been managing director of since April 2014, it was hard to find anyone in the room who wasn't a CBA lawyer or member of staff.

I sat in the back row of the courtroom waiting for counsel assisting, Rowena Orr QC, to begin the demolition. Lawyers, politicians, staff and victims were also tuning in to watch Troup's testimony via live stream. One of those victims was CommInsure whistleblower Dr Ben Koh, whom Troup had personally sacked.

Life insurance is big business, but it falls through regulatory cracks. The industry has only recently devised a code of conduct, which is still weak and lacking in substance. It has been granted exemptions from laws banning unfair terms in contracts, and insurance companies have been given the power to legally discriminate; for instance, they can discriminate against people with mental illness, even if the illness is episodic.

In her introduction to the hearing two days before Troup's appearance, Orr had told the commission, 'It is important to note that the handling and settling of insurance claims is specifically excluded from the definition of a financial service.' That meant, she said, that the obligation for an insurance company to do all things necessary to ensure that it provides financial services 'efficiently, honestly and fairly', didn't apply to making a decision about a claim, the investigation of that claim and the interpretation of policy provisions. Nor did it apply to negotiations of settlement amounts, to estimates of loss or damage, value or repair costs, or recommendations on mitigation of loss. 'This limits ASIC's ability to take action against insurance companies where, for example, there are unnecessary or extensive delays in handling claims.'

Insurance falls within the *Insurance Contracts Act 1984*, which contains 'a duty of utmost good faith'. If an insurer fails to comply with the duty of utmost good faith in relation to its handling or settlement of a claim, it is deemed a breach, but a breach doesn't attract a penalty or fine. That in turn means ASIC doesn't have the power to bring proceedings against an insurer to recover a penalty where it believes the insurer has breached this duty.

Orr started her questioning of Troup with a bang, describing a mistreated policyholder whose life insurance claim had been rejected on the basis of an outdated medical definition. Orr then provided evidence that CommInsure had misled the Financial Ombudsman Service (FOS) to avoid the $100,000 payout. Even worse, the insurer's misconduct had happened *after* my joint *Age* and *Herald* media investigation with *Four Corners*, 'Money for Nothing', which had revealed issues with outdated medical definitions, including heart attacks, at CommInsure. Following the program, CBA's Ian Narev had 'unreservedly' apologised to CommInsure customers for its poor behaviour and promised to update those decade-old definitions and backdate its new heart attack definition to May 2014.[1]

The CommInsure policyholder had suffered a severe heart attack in January 2014. After watching 'Money for Nothing' he had decided to re-lodge a claim the bank had previously rejected. The bank rejected it again.

The man's heart attack had occurred in January 2014 and the bank had only backdated its definition of a heart attack to May 2014. This was despite knowing the definition was a decade out of date and most other insurers had backdated their definition to 2012. In disgust, he took the complaint to FOS to get it re-assessed by an independent third party. But the bank continued to push back when the FOS requested it hand over documents and a justification for rejecting the claim. Documents submitted to the commission revealed that CBA misled FOS by redacting a medical opinion that said the man met the definition of a heart attack so that it could avoid paying the claim.

'This email to FOS was misleading, was it not?' asked Orr.

'Unfortunately, yes,' Troup replied, looking singularly unimpressed to be there at all.

The heart attack survivor was eventually paid an ex gratia payment of $90,000, but it still cast CBA in a bad light, demonstrating that despite its public apologies after the media exposé, its culture hadn't changed.

The royal commission heard other cases where CommInsure knocked back claims using outdated definitions. One was the shocking case of a woman with breast cancer whose life insurance claim for $169,300, lodged in August 2016, had been repeatedly rejected. The woman, who'd been a CommInsure policyholder for twenty years, had had part of her breast removed and received radiotherapy. As she battled her cancer, she also had to fight CommInsure, which knocked back her insurance claim on the basis it didn't meet CommInsure's threshold of 'radical surgery'.

What CommInsure never explained was that its interpretation of radical surgery was a full mastectomy. But that interpretation was based on a definition that was eighteen years old, and modern medicine had advanced considerably in the meantime.

In February 2017, the policyholder wrote to CommInsure and attached a series of documents from her doctor and surgeon. One was a letter written to her surgeon that said: 'It is my understanding that in performing the surgery, the ample nature of my breasts meant that I did not require a mastectomy. I believe that you mentioned that had this not been the case and my breasts had been small, I would have required a mastectomy. I would appreciate it if you could confirm this by indicating below if this is the case.' The surgeon did so, noting also: 'The treatment received is radical because radiotherapy was required as an alternative to mastectomy.'

His letter was sent to CBA and a new case manager was assigned to the claim. Orr explained how the case manager referred the case to the medical consultant who had previously considered the claim. She asked Troup: 'And the medical consultant again said that radical breast surgery had not been performed, having considered this additional material. Is that right?'

Troup responded, 'That is right.'

On 17 March, the claim was again denied. Orr continued to unpick the bank's shabby treatment of the policyholder, but the more she questioned Troup, the more it became apparent that Troup thought it was an isolated case.

'I do feel that the opinion of what radical breast surgery was initially was reasonable and genuine,' she said. 'But the outcome … did result in us not fulfilling utmost good faith.'

CBA updated the 1988 definition in May 2017 but didn't backdate it, which meant the old definition still applied to anyone who had taken out insurance before that date.

'Why did CommInsure not backdate that definition?' Orr asked.

'So ... the approach is that applies for new claimable events,' was Troup's response.

Orr referred to the heart attack definition which had been backdated and asked why CommInsure hadn't done the same with this one.

'That's because that definition was out of date,' Troup said.

'And you didn't accept that this definition was out of date?' asked Orr.

'No'.

The breast cancer survivor complained to FOS in April and was eventually paid out in September 2017 after FOS reviewed her case and recommended that CommInsure should pay her claim. But the saga didn't end there. On 23 July 2018, FOS wrote to CommInsure saying it found there was a 'definite systemic issue in relation to CommInsure's interpretation of "radical breast surgery" as being limited to a mastectomy'.

Orr asked Troup, 'Do you disagree that it's a systemic issue?'

Troup replied, 'I feel like it was just an isolated event, yes.'

Orr then asked whether CommInsure planned to review its past claims.

'Not at this stage,' said Troup.

'Should there be a decision made to do that, Ms Troup?'

'As I said, I think I would like to discuss that with the business ...'

'But you're not prepared to make a commitment that that will happen?'

'Not today, no.'

*

Next it was time to scrutinise CBA's relationship with ASIC regarding CommInsure's misdeeds. Getting a rare glimpse into the bank's confidential dealings with ASIC was profoundly insightful.

As the basis of her examination, Orr used an investigation that ASIC had undertaken in 2017 into marketing material for CommInsure's life and trauma insurance. The investigation had been triggered by my joint *Four Corners* exposé of CommInsure.

To ensure viewers fully understood what she was talking about, Orr posted CommInsure ads on screens around the courtroom. They showed slick, glossy brochures with photos of babies and toddlers, as well as older people, which were clearly designed to tap into the human fear of getting sick or dying.

Orr read out the wording of one ad which said, 'This cover can pay a lump sum to help with medical costs if you suffer any one of our specified trauma conditions, such as cancer, heart attack or stroke. It's part of our tailored insurance range.' Orr pointed out that nowhere in the material did it mention that 'heart attack' meant only some heart attacks – which was one of the things that had concerned ASIC.

As Troup was shown the various ads, she didn't flinch. Her defence was that the details of the types of heart attacks covered were in the product disclosure statement for the policy. But as Orr pointed out, this was an entirely separate document – one that most people would struggle to find and, if they did, understand.

Orr then showed Troup emails from ASIC relating to how the regulator dealt with the misleading ads. In late 2017, ASIC's senior executive leader of financial services enforcement, Tim Mullaly, sent CBA the wording ASIC proposed to use in its media release regarding the issue and the penalty CBA would incur: 'To resolve ASIC's concerns, CommInsure has agreed to make a voluntary community benefit payment of $300,000.' Quite a bargain if you considered that when the ads were placed, the maximum penalty for misleading and deceptive conduct was 10,000 penalty units, or almost $2 million, for each of the four highlighted contraventions.[2]

ASIC's email to CBA continued: 'We will, of course, need to agree with CommInsure the timing of a number of steps, the community benefit payment recipient and the nature and details of the review.' Mullaly asked CommInsure to get back to him to let him know if 'this is sufficient for CommInsure to resolve the matter' and whether it was happy with making a community donation rather than receiving an infringement notice and a fine (which of course would have been far more serious and embarrassing for CBA).

At this point a silence fell across the room. It was extraordinary to witness so vividly the extent to which ASIC had kowtowed to CBA. Even Hayne couldn't hide his shock, quizzing Troup: 'The regulator asking the regulated whether the proposal was sufficient in the eyes of the party alleged to have broken the law. Is that right?'

Troup's response was deadpan: 'I guess … we could have taken an approach of continuing to defend our position, and so this [coming to an agreement with the regulator] was the alternative.' In light of the misleading ads, it didn't seem that the bank had a position to defend.

If ASIC's obsequious behaviour seemed incredible to the courtroom, Orr had more revelations. On 17 October 2017, CBA replied to Mullaly, saying it would consider the ASIC letter and respond as soon as possible. However, by 2 November Mullaly still hadn't heard from the bank and wrote a follow-up email asking if CBA had considered his proposition. The following day CBA responded with a revised version of the media release (initialled by

Helen Troup). To highlight the number of changes CBA made, the two versions were shown side by side on the screens in the courtroom. They looked like different documents. Among the most significant changes was the deletion of a sentence saying that CommInsure had been deceptive and misleading in its advertising.

ASIC had finally posted the media release on 18 December 2017, a week out from Christmas, when many people are on holidays, including journalists.[3] Not surprisingly, it didn't get much publicity. As Orr read it out, it became obvious that ASIC had accepted key changes suggested by CBA, which had altered the tone of the document and played down the gravity of CommInsure's misconduct. The published press release watered down ASIC's strongly held concerns that the ads were deceptive and misleading. Instead, it said the ads were 'likely to have been' misleading and 'may have led' a policyholder to believe they were entitled to a payout. As Orr noted, 'The media release contained no acknowledgement by CommInsure of any form of wrongdoing in connection with these advertisements?'

Troup replied, 'That's right.'

Hayne asked, 'At the end of the day, Ms Troup, did CommInsure come out of this process thinking it had been punished or brought to book?'

'Yes we did, sir,' Troup defiantly replied.

It beggared belief firstly that ASIC would be party to this, and secondly that a senior executive of a bank generating profits of $10 billion a year would think that such a soft, edited press release and a $300,000 donation was punishment.

It prompted Rowena Orr to ask how the figure of $300,000 had been arrived at, to which Troup said she didn't know. Orr reminded Troup of the maximum penalty under the *ASIC Act 2001*: $2 million per contravention.

To bring home not only the lightness of the punishment but also the entrenched adversarial bias CBA had towards its clients, Hayne pushed Troup: '$300,000 is three times the claim of the particular insured person who forms the foundation of this case study, is that right?'

'Yes, that's correct,' she responded.

Hayne probed further: 'Leave aside whether you count each publication as a separate contravention, if we take the type of alleged contravention, being singular for each advertisement, the maximum punishment was the order of $8 million, was it not?'

Troup looked into the distance. Facing so much evidence and Hayne's disapproval, she finally, begrudgingly conceded that the ads had been misleading – something the bank had never previously admitted, neither to itself nor to ASIC. 'I think at that time we were still defending our position and believed that there were other circumstances around, but sitting here now looking at the way it was positioned, I can see how ASIC's concerns were legitimate,' she said.

Listening to Helen Troup concede this, whistleblower Dr Ben Koh took some comfort. When he'd raised issues of unethical goings-on to Troup, she had been dismissive of his concerns. 'She made me feel that my concerns were misplaced ... like I was the one in the wrong for raising the concerns. It was a bizarro world. Instead of focussing on the wrongdoings, the focus was on the person who brought attention to the wrongdoings,' he said.

The handling of the draft CommInsure media release reflected badly on ASIC: it spoke of capitulation and regulatory capture. It also suggested CommInsure was guilty of bad practice, bad faith and hubris – something, of course, not restricted to CBA. It also reminded me of a statement made by ASIC to parliament in 2015 that it would change its practices on press releases and only offer them to regulated entities twenty-four hours before publication. ASIC had restated that policy in parliament on 31 May 2017, when ASIC's deputy chairman, Peter Kell, told senators including Wacka Williams, 'With large entities, in particular, if there is the prospect at times that the action we are taking may have a material impact for negotiated outcomes, we allow a short window of up to twenty-four hours for checking the accuracy.' The case illustrated by the royal commission suggested this message hadn't been understood at lower levels of the regulator.

In September 2017, CBA had announced the sale of its scandal-ridden life insurance business, booking $300 million less on the sale and slashing $1.4 billion off its goodwill. Troup and many others in the bank mightn't have thought CBA had done much wrong, but the write-down no doubt reflected the reputational damage caused by treating customers poorly. The new owner, Hong Kong–based AIA, didn't continue with the CommInsure trading name.

*

There was widespread concern that the currency of medical definitions and the general practices of insurers were significant issues among other companies too. The royal commission had therefore asked ten life insurers – CommInsure, TAL, Zurich, MetLife, NAB's MLC, Suncorp, AMP, Westpac, ANZ's OnePath and AIA – about their procedures for reviewing and updating medical definitions. The response was illuminating.

CommInsure told the commission it didn't have any deficiencies in its processes and procedures for updating medical definitions. It said its failure to update its heart attack definition was a commercial misjudgement.

TAL told the commission it didn't have a formal process in place to annually review the currency of its medical definitions until 2016. Zurich and MetLife said until 2016 they didn't have a formal process in place to review definitions. MetLife said in 2016 it reviewed and changed twenty-one definitions. It took NAB's MLC until 2017 to document the process for reviewing definitions.

AMP didn't conduct a formal and regular review of medical definitions until 2017. Suncorp didn't have a framework in place and relied on informal processes and 'ad hoc' medical definition updates but, it told the commission, it intended to conduct medical definition reviews every three years.

The royal commission also wrote to the insurance companies asking them about the procedures they used when assessing claims. This yielded admissions of spying on policyholders, including using hidden cameras and stalking. In one case recounted to the royal commission, a nurse diagnosed with an anxiety disorder had lodged an income protection claim with the country's biggest insurer, TAL, in January 2010. TAL had then hired a private investigator as part of a campaign to block her claim. A TAL claims manager told the investigator to 'do a pretext' at the hospital she used to work at to see what information could be found and talk to the local police to see if they had anything on her. The investigator spied on the mentally ill nurse, filmed her undressing before she went for a swim and took photos of her bushwalking and kissing her partner. When the claims manager found out she had once written a book, he sent the investigator an email saying, 'OMG here is another one for you … I want results.'

TAL tracked the nurse's social media and obtained her medical records, Medicare documents and tax and other financial records. At the time TAL was paying the nurse $2750 a month in income protection insurance. As Orr put it to witness Loraine van Eeden, TAL's general manager of claims, who had joined the company in January 2018, rather than just pay up, 'TAL elected to pay $20,000 to a private investigator to try and stop these payments'.

In 2014 TAL rejected the claim and ceased payments, falsely accusing the nurse of fraud. It then threatened her with legal action if she didn't repay almost $70,000 to the insurer. Orr read out letters from the nurse's psychiatrist, who had initially said her condition was improving but in a report six years later found that she had deteriorated and was by then suffering from an 'insidious and malignant psychiatric illness'. The psychiatrist said the condition had originally been triggered by workplace stress but now had 'a life of its own', with the nurse demonstrating 'suspiciousness, lack of trust, social withdrawal and isolation ... panic attacks, anxiety and difficulties with memory and concentration'.

Van Eeden said, 'I can agree to us causing her stress but I cannot comment on the exacerbation of her medical condition as there could be many other factors as well.' She admitted, however, that TAL had breached the former nurse's privacy over a lengthy period. After being contacted by the claimant, the FOS found against TAL. After seeking further ways to reject the judgement, the company finally agreed to pay out $89,000 to the nurse, followed by $35,000. But the insurer had put her through hell.

The statistics provided by insurers to the royal commission showed that most of them engaged spies to monitor policyholders who'd lodged mental illness claims. Suncorp admitted to spying on 17 per cent of policyholders who'd lodged a mental health claim between 2014 and 2015. Westpac's life insurance arm had spied on 9.3 per cent of mental health claimants between 2013 and 2016, while CommInsure, between 2013 and 2016, had spied on 7 per cent of mental health claimants and 1.3 per cent of physical health claimants. Surveillance activity declined after 1 July 2017, when the life insurance industry introduced its code of conduct, which included restrictions on such activity.

TAL's behaviour was symptomatic of an organisation with deep systemic issues, but van Eeden would not concede this. Like most of the other insurance company witnesses, she passed off the bad behaviour as either an isolated incident or as merely inappropriate or below community standards. But it was so much worse than that.

*

After hearing a series of horrifying case studies from TAL and CommInsure, the royal commission turned its attention to direct insurers. ClearView and Freedom Insurance were selected to give evidence about the high-pressure sales tactics they used to sell products such as funeral insurance and life insurance. It was jawdropping stuff.

ClearView's chief risk officer, Greg Martin, admitted that ClearView had clocked up 303,000 criminal breaches of the law after failing to comply with anti-hawking laws laid down by the *Corporations Act*. Under the law, a person must not try to sell financial products during an unsolicited telephone call or an unsolicited meeting.

At ClearView, as emails presented to the royal commission showed, sales executives were awarded with gift cards if they reached particular sales targets, and during so-called incentive days staff were sent messages such as 'Let's rip it up' and 'I want this joint pumping with belling, clapping and SALESSSS.' The name of the game was to sell as many policies as possible, and there was even a plan to target poorer Australians.

Seeing the writing on the wall, ClearView had stopped selling direct life insurance before the royal commission.

It was grubby stuff, but nothing prepared me for an audio recording of a 2016 phone call made by a salesman at Freedom to a twenty-six-year-old man with Down syndrome. The agent was trying to sell funeral, accidental death and injury insurance. It was obvious the young man was having difficulty understanding the conversation, but the agent signed him up anyway.

The young man's father, Grant Stewart, a Baptist minister, told the royal commission that his son remembered speaking to someone on the phone and providing that person with his debit card details, but couldn't explain why he'd done so. When Stewart learned that his son, whose only source of income was the disability support pension, had been signed up for insurance he didn't want, need or understand, he tried to cancel the policies. But Freedom dragged its heels. The commission viewed one internal message in which a sales staff member who had reviewed the sales agent's initial call claimed it wasn't clear Stewart's son was disabled. 'I've had a listen to the call,' the message said. 'Not once does the policy owner mention anything about being disabled, or not being able to make decisions for himself, etc. So it would have been hard for the sales agent to assume that the policy owner had a disability.'

At one point, Stewart called Freedom's retention department and the person he spoke to refused to cancel the policy unless he put his son on the phone and had him say the words, 'I wish to terminate the policy.' He did so, but Stewart said his son was 'quite distressed' by the experience. Furthermore, it took many subsequent letters and calls before Freedom kept its side of the bargain.

Freedom's disgrace didn't end there. Orr read out an internal message in which the retention officer told one of the staff that Stewart was a 'bloody whinger … I don't know what he expects to get out of it LOL.'

Commissioner Hayne said he believed the community might be 'particularly struck' by the phone call Stewart's son had to make, and that it was 'a particularly affecting record'. That was an understatement: the media and twitter went into overdrive.

Freedom operated a classic boiler-room culture. Sales agents were offered incentives, such as gift vouchers and trips to Bali, and retention officers, whose job it was to convince customers not to cancel their policies, earned bonuses for each customer they 'saved'. 'We've got $150 to give away in today's incentives,' one internal sales campaign told staff in an email shown to the royal commission. 'Target is 400 lives by lunchtime. Everyone aiming for seven over the first two sessions. 3.5 lives per session (Easy Peasy) and we'll smash 400 lives to lock in the incentive money for the last part of the day.' In another email dated July 2018, agents were told 'anyone that gets eight funeral lives or more will go into a draw on Monday morning. Newbies, anyone who gets six funeral lives or more will go into a draw … Every life over your target will get a bonus entry. $100 to give away. Get selling.' It was particularly troubling that the emails had been handled by the firm's quality assurance division, which is meant to monitor agents' behaviour and compliance.

When Freedom's chief operating officer, Craig Orton, appeared in the witness box on 11–12 September, he repeatedly stated that he'd only recently joined Freedom, while acknowledging that the behaviour was scandalous. At one stage, he said Freedom 'is a bit of a young company' and on a 'journey'. It was so much worse than that.

The royal commission heard that Freedom had received 37,584 calls to cancel policies in about twelve months. Three-quarters of the calls came from customers who said they either couldn't afford the cover or didn't want it. Of those, only 8118 calls (21.59 per cent) resulted in a cancelled policy.

'Why does Freedom make it so difficult for customers to cancel their policies?' Orr asked Orton.

'The key problem I heard was not taking "no" for an answer on certain calls,' Orton replied.

On the eve of Orton's appearance, Freedom had made a clearly rushed decision and flagged to the royal commission that it would cease selling accidental death, accidental injury, trauma and life insurance over the phone, which represented 15 per cent of its business; it also announced it would stop offering staff non-monetary incentives such as holidays. However, its main business of selling funeral insurance and loan protection insurance via telephone calls would continue.

When Freedom was asked to hand over any documentation relating to how it came to such momentous decisions, it couldn't – which was an indication of how quickly the decision had been made. Orton told Orr that Freedom sales agents felt they could make such a decision 'without creating unnecessary paperwork'. I was sitting in the media room and all the journalists laughed aloud at this explanation. In light of the antics that go on in the life insurance sector, it was definitely a case of gallows humour.

*

Round six of the commission had revealed rampant misconduct across the insurance industry. But one serious issue it didn't have time to tackle was the management of insurance by superannuation funds. About 12 million Australians are passively funnelled into life insurance through their superannuation policies (so-called group insurance), paying a total of $9 billion a year in premiums. Many don't even know that their super fund is deducting these premiums.

Insurance included with a superannuation policy usually provides a death benefit and a lump-sum payment in the case of total and permanent disability (TPD); it may also offer income protection insurance. The policies and the insurer are chosen by the super fund's trustees. As a rule, retail fund trustees, such as those with the big four banks and AMP, recommend their own life insurers.

In 2017, an investigation I worked on with my colleague Ruth Williams revealed that life insurers had been quietly amending aspects of their insurance policies to include additional exclusions and tighter definitions. For example, instead of accepting the standard definition of TPD – that the person can no longer do the work they did previously – some insurers had adopted more stringent conditions requiring claimants to prove that they could not accomplish at least two or three basic tasks, such as showering, dressing, eating, toileting or walking without assistance. Our investigation showed that some, but not all, super fund trustees had accepted these exclusions and restrictive definitions without informing their members, partly to keep a lid on rising costs and premiums.

The revelations prompted one of the country's leading life insurance lawyers, John Berrill, to describe some of the policies trustees had accepted as 'junk insurance' due to the 'hidden nasties' buried in them. In other words, such policies are making it almost impossible for policyholders to make successful claims, even where they are genuinely unable to work. Of course, the more claims that are rejected, the bigger the profit for the insurer. Given the number of Australians potentially affected by these sly moves, it was disappointing that the royal commission hadn't made more effort to step in and protect them.

Chapter 22

The interim report

A taste of things to come?

ANTICIPATION GREW DAILY IN late September in the lead-up to the release of Commissioner Kenneth Hayne's interim report. Under the royal commission's terms of reference Hayne was required to produce this document to indicate his line of thinking. It was also designed to pose the questions 'Why?' and 'What now?', with a view to provoking informed debate in preparation for the last round of hearings and the final report.

Speculation was rife that the interim report would make referrals for criminal breaches, recommend changes to responsible lending laws, ban commissions and overhaul the mortgage-broking industry. There was even talk that Hayne might call for the dismantling of vertical integration to remove inherent conflicts of interest.

The AFL Grand Final was coming up on 29 September and it seemed unlikely Hayne would choose to release his report at that point, with footy fever dominating the news cycle. But on 28 September, as football fans and marching bands accompanied a cavalcade of Toyota Hiluxes carrying the West Coast Eagles and Collingwood teams in the annual AFL Grand Final Parade, word suddenly spread that the interim report was about to drop.

Three volumes totalling more than a thousand pages covered, in gory detail, the first four rounds of hearings into what had gone on in our banking system. In his opening paragraphs, Hayne explained why he thought the systemic misconduct had happened. 'Too often, the answer seems to be greed – the pursuit of short-term profit at the expense of basic standards of honesty,' he wrote. 'How else is charging continuing advice fees to the dead to be explained?'

His executive summary noted: 'Too often, selling products and services became the sole focus of attention ... Products and services multiplied. Banks searched for their "share of the customer's wallet". From the executive suite to the front line, staff were measured and rewarded by reference to profit and sales.'

Hayne's report blamed poor culture and lax compliance on the failure of institutions to mete out meaningful punishment when wrongdoers were caught. But his biggest rebuke was aimed at the regulators, largely ASIC, which had failed to do its job and enforce the law. 'ASIC, rarely went to court to seek public denunciation of and punishment for misconduct,' he said. 'The prudential regulator, APRA, never went to court.' He emphasised the importance of going to court in order to set a binding precedent in law.

ASIC was excoriated for doing little beyond extracting apologies, slowly. Usually that entailed 'a drawn out remediation program and protracted negotiation with ASIC of a media release, an infringement notice, or an enforceable undertaking that acknowledged no more than that ASIC had reasonable "concerns" about the entity's conduct'. More specifically, Hayne criticised ASIC for its handling of contraventions of the law, which he noted were commonly resolved by agreement. He advised that when contraventions of the law occurred, ASIC's starting point should be to first ask whether it can make a case and, if so, 'why it would not be in the public interest to bring proceedings to penalise the breach'.

He stopped short of criticising the law, believing it was more a case of the regulators not applying the powers they had. 'Too often, entities have been treated in ways that would allow them to think that they, not ASIC, not the Parliament, not the courts, will decide when and how the law will be obeyed or the consequences of breach remedied,' he wrote. How else could ASIC explain the infringement notices issued to the major banks over the decade to 30 June 2018, which totalled less than $1.3 million. To drive home this point, Hayne outlined two cases relating to infringement notices. In one, CBA had been fined a mere $180,000 over breaches of responsible lending obligations that continued for four years and affected more than 11,000 customers, who were entitled to remediation. In the other case, ANZ had paid just $212,500 for failing to make 'reasonable inquiries about the credit limit a customer requires when it sent out offers to customers for overdrafts'. In both cases, the ASIC media release included the disclaimer that 'the payment of an infringement notice is not an admission of guilt in respect of the alleged contravention'. In conclusion, Hayne said that if penalties were intended to have a deterrent effect 'then it must be plainly said that the amounts imposed in these cases do not'.

On the issue of remediation, Hayne again blamed ASIC, this time for taking too long to negotiate outcomes. 'There have been too many cases where remediation programs have taken months, even years, to formulate and implement,' he said.

Hayne acknowledged that a lack of competition in financial services didn't help. Competition in the banking sector was weak, barriers to entry were high and to participate in the economy and everyday life, Australians needed a bank account. 'But they are reluctant to change banks,' he said. He didn't elaborate, but it was easy to understand what he meant. Despite all the scandals, there had been little switching from the big four banks, partly because customers think all banks are as bad as each other and partly because Australians tend to sign up to bundles of products, which makes it difficult to move a mortgage, credit card, savings account or insurance policy somewhere else.

Overall, though, bank misconduct was largely the result of greed, plain and simple. 'There being little competitive pressure, pursuit of profit has trumped consideration of how the profit is made. The banks have gone to the edge of what is permitted, and too often beyond that limit, in pursuit of profit.' Hayne found that such conduct occurred in all the major financial institutions, which suggested it wasn't just 'a few bad apples', as the banks so often claimed in their defence.

In addition to these observations, Hayne posed more than six hundred questions and asked businesses to act honestly and fairly and obey the law. He also requested that the regulators do their job. But he stopped short of making recommendations or referrals for criminal or civil breaches. Such judgements would be saved for the final report, due in February 2019.

*

The financial institutions had been given a stay of execution. Within hours of the report's release, the banks and regulators had their statements ready, which included pledging immediate improvement in their behaviour. The Australian Banking Association's chief executive, Anna Bligh, said at a speedily organised media conference: 'Having lost the trust of the

Australian people, we must now do whatever it takes to earn that trust back. To move from a selling culture to a service culture, there is much more work to be done in every bank. But every bank is determined to find the problems, to fix them and to pay back every penny.'[1]

ASIC's chairman, James Shipton, issued a media statement acknowledging Hayne's 'serious and important observations of ASIC's role as a regulator' and promising to 'carefully consider' the criticisms in a full submission due within a month.[2] APRA's chairman, Wayne Byres, took some time to respond; when he did, he said 'the royal commission has suggested, among other things, that regulators can and should do more to actively enforce standards of behaviour within the financial sector, and punish those who breach them. Based on what has been revealed, that is a quite reasonable conclusion.'[3]

Former AMP chair Catherine Brenner issued a statement saying she was 'pleased that the royal commission's interim report has made no finding against her of any personal wrongdoing in relation to AMP's "fees for no service" practices' and that she remained confident that further investigations would completely clear her of any misconduct. In his report, Hayne had been scathing of AMP, saying that 'there were senior persons within AMP (I make no finding more precisely than that) who knew of the charging of fees for no service', that AMP had 'provided ASIC with information that was false or misleading', and that 'senior management and executives who contributed to the misleading of ASIC over a two-year period had knowledge of the true extent and nature of the conduct, and, in at least some cases, were warned by junior staff about it being a breach, but continued with a misleading narrative to ASIC'. He said these matters were now being followed up by the regulator. 'I need not consider whether it is appropriate to refer the matters to ASIC for consideration. Having not heard evidence from Ms Brenner … or from any partner of Clayton Utz, I make no findings about their conduct.'

On the first day of trading after the release of the interim report, the share prices of the banks and AMP rallied 3 per cent. Among the whistleblowers and victims who had waited years for a royal commission, the feeling was that Hayne had so far failed to take action that would really mollify them.

*

In the following weeks, Hayne's musings were pored over by financial institutions looking for hints as to what he might recommend in his final report. For instance, his comments on conflicted remuneration and mortgage broking created an expectation that he would ban grandfathered commissions, restructure mortgage broking and kill off vertical integration.

After reading his comments about greed and incentives, I was confident he would do something radical to tackle the banks' profits-at-all-costs culture. 'Why do staff (whether customer-facing or not) need incentives to do their job unless the incentive is directed towards maximising revenue and profit?' Hayne asked. 'Experience (too often, hard and bitter experience) shows that conflicts cannot be "managed" by saying, "Be good. Do the right thing." People rapidly persuade themselves that what suits them is what is right. And people can and will do that even when doing so harms the person for whom they are acting.'

Hayne asked whether structural change was necessary. 'Should an intermediary be permitted to recommend to a consumer, provide personal financial advice to a consumer or sell to a consumer any financial product manufactured by an entity (or a related party of the entity) of which the intermediary is an employee or authorised representative?' In other words, should the inherently conflicted model of vertical integration be unwound? Many bank executives believed Hayne would bring this about.

Hayne's questions about responsible lending – 'What steps should a lender take to verify a borrower's expenses? Do lenders need to go further than the *National Consumer Credit Protection Act* which only stipulates the contract is "not unsuitable" for the consumer?' – had created a widespread fear among the banks that he might call for a crackdown on the way banks assess the suitability of borrowers for loans.

Debates raged and speculation mounted, but for now everyone had to be content with the inconclusive interim report. In the meantime, we prepared for what promised to be a fascinating and momentous final round of hearings: a showdown with the chief executives of the major banks.

Chapter 23

Round 7: CBA

'Temper your sense of justice'

ON 19 NOVEMBER, THE courtroom in Sydney's Lionel Bowen building was buzzing with excitement as Commissioner Kenneth Hayne walked in briskly, bowed, sat down and nodded to Rowena Orr to open the seventh and final round of the royal commission. This round would delve into the causes of misconduct by financial institutions, and a succession of chief executives would have to leave the comfort of their opulent offices to front up to 'one of the most consequential royal commissions ever conducted in Australia'.[1]

Before round seven had even begun, at least seventeen executives and directors of financial institutions had lost their jobs, or retired early, as a direct result of the royal commission. One remained on stress leave. Wealth divisions of banks and other institutions had been put up for sale, and Freedom Insurance was in turmoil, losing its chief executive and chair, and facing liquidity issues.

First up was CBA boss Matt Comyn, followed by CBA chair Catherine 'the great' Livingstone – 'the great' being her sobriquet until her performance at the royal commission eroded some of that reputation – who had managed to survive the 2017 AUSTRAC scandal, thanks to the main focus then being on former CEO Ian Narev. Others to appear included NAB boss Andrew Thorburn and NAB chairman Dr Ken Henry, a former Treasury secretary, as well as ANZ's Shayne Elliott and Westpac's Brian Hartzer. Due to the tight two-week time frame, the chairs of Westpac and ANZ weren't called to take the stand.

It was a nerve-wracking affair to front up to Hayne, perched on his elevated podium, jotting the odd note as he prepared for the financial institutions' day of reckoning, his final report. As at other rounds, there to observe were whistleblowers, victims and media. Jeff Morris sat in the front row, wearing a bow tie. Others had rocked up in black t-shirts bearing the slogan 'Bank reform NOW!'. The victims included Craig Caulfield, who had formed a support group called the Bank Warriors, as well as others who hoped for five minutes with Matt Comyn to tell him their stories. As Merilyn Swan rushed to the courtroom she almost collided with Comyn and his entourage of lawyers and staff. She took the opportunity to introduce herself, telling a nervous Comyn, 'My parents, Robyn and Merv Blanch, were victims of CBA's financial planner Dodgy Don Nguyen, and are one of the reasons you are here to attend this royal commission hearing today.'

Fittingly attired in black, Rowena Orr QC opened proceedings. She made it clear this final round would be different from the other six. This round was to help clarify whether bank culture, remuneration structures, regulators and the laws dealing with financial institutions needed to change. It would also examine whether there were barriers or obstructions that were preventing financial services companies and regulators from improving their own practices – and, if so, how could they be removed.

Orr got the ball rolling with Comyn's views on where CBA had gone wrong. Comyn boiled it down to a culture of too often putting profits before people, slow remediation, little or no consequences when scandals emerged, and CBA being too 'legalistic and defensive' in its dealings with regulators. He blamed governance failures on remuneration and incentive structures, which 'in some instances, are not aligned to good customer outcomes'. Lax operational risk and compliance also played a role.

Orr then turned to the controversial CBA Prudential Inquiry Final Report, which had been released on 1 May 2018. Commissioned by APRA after the AUSTRAC scandal and prepared by former ACCC chairman Graeme Samuel, company director Jillian Broadbent and former APRA chairman John Laker, it had found that the CBA board had been largely invisible and had failed in its duties to provide oversight and to challenge management.

Orr took Comyn through the report's findings, which supported everything the royal commission had heard about the bank. She wanted to examine the bank's culture, and how Comyn had dealt with the report after its release. More specifically, she wanted to take him through some written responses to the report from 500 bank executives who had been asked by Comyn to discuss the report with their teams and supply a one-page reflection on that discussion. Their responses had been submitted to the royal commission.

Orr read out the response of Marianne Perkovic, who'd been accused of 'dissembling' in an earlier round of the royal commission, and had written: 'I know I have let some of our clients, people and the community down by not speaking up loud enough to stand up to behaviours that I knew were not right.' Larissa Shafir, a compliance manager in retail banking, wrote that the bank's compliance department – which is tasked with ensuring that laws, policies, rules and procedures are adhered to – was lacking authority and widely seen as an impediment or 'blocker' to business. As Orr put it, the voice of finance subordinated the voice of risk.

Orr summed up her comments: 'Mr Comyn, Ms Shafir's comments are an indictment of the culture within CBA in relation to treatment of compliance risk, and operational risk, more generally. Do you agree?'

Comyn replied, 'Yes, I do.'

Orr then questioned Comyn about remuneration. 'Why can't banks pay staff a fixed salary?' she asked.

Comyn responded by saying he believed financial incentives motivated staff to work harder. He even gave an example of what had happened to a bank in the United Kingdom which had removed its short-term variable rewards. He said he asked one of the bank's home lenders whether the removal of rewards impacted her work. 'Her answer was simply, "I probably work 30 per cent less." And it's not just about hours of work. It's also just an alignment between, in her view, "I was going to get paid – I'm basically getting paid the same as I was previously." She was one of their best performing lenders. "I'm now getting paid the same. And I'm doing 30 per cent less work,"' he said to Orr.

At this point, Merilyn Swan whispered to Morris, 'I can't imagine refusing to dispense a script or a doctor refusing to diagnose a patient without a bonus in the offering. What strange moral compasses these people must possess.'

The banks had become so used to targets and bonuses they couldn't imagine a world without them.

*

On the second day of Comyn's testimony, Orr brought up a meeting between Comyn and Narev on 28 May 2015, a month after CBA had discovered rampant mis-selling of consumer credit insurance (CCI). This type of insurance product is designed to help customers with mortgages, credit cards and other kinds of loans meet their repayments if they get sick, have an accident or lose their job. Comyn, who was running the retail bank at the time, told Narev at that meeting that CCI was being sold to more than one hundred thousand customers under false pretences. The customers were students or people in part-time work who would not be eligible to make a claim, as the policy required them to be working a minimum number of hours a week. In a handwritten note Comyn acknowledged, 'We have not met standards we've set for ourselves and we should suspend sales.' The industry had long been aware of such issues with this kind of insurance. Back in 2011, UK banks, including NAB's UK subsidiaries had been caught mis-selling similar products and had had to pay out more than £40 billion in compensation.

Orr asked Comyn when he had first become aware of the problem at CBA. He told her it was in 2014. She then took him to an October 2012 audit report prepared by CBA into problems with its direct life insurance policies, which included CCI products. Comyn, despite being CEO of retail banking at that time, and therefore havng direct responsibility for such products, denied having received a copy of the report.

'That's a significant failing within your organisation,' Orr responded. 'I want to put to you that a report that dealt with sales practices of the product was not provided to the business unit responsible for selling the product?'

'Yes, I agree,' said Comyn.

Orr then took Comyn to another document from May 2013, prepared by the retail banking services risk committee, which reviewed CCI products and reported negatively on what it had found. Comyn admitted he had seen this one.

'But you only developed your concerns about the products in 2014?' Orr remarked. She then referred to a trip Comyn had made in 2014 to the United Kingdom. There he had been warned about the risks associated with CCI products by his former colleague Ross McEwan, who was then running the Royal Bank of Scotland, which was knee-deep in cleaning up a similar mis-selling scandal. She also highlighted an April 2015 internal CBA audit of credit cards, which had flagged issues with the bank's CCI product and revealed that 64,000 CBA customers had been sold the product but would never be able to make a claim.

Orr then returned to Comyn's meeting with Narev on 28 May. In preparation for the meeting, he wrote a list of topics he wanted to discuss, including ceasing to offer CCI products. 'My recommendation to suspend the sales was not agreed with,' Comyn told Orr. 'I suspect we had quite a long conversation about that particular product. And I think we agreed to disagree at that point in time.'

Orr wanted to press him more. 'What did you think of that outcome, Mr Comyn? You were the head of retail banking services at CBA. This was a product that you were responsible for. How did you feel about agreeing to disagree with the CEO about your recommendation that CBA cease sales of the product?'

Comyn's mouth seemed to be drying up as he tried to frame suitable answers.

Then Orr returned to the notes Comyn had made prior to his meeting with Narev, and asked him about a handwritten scrawl that appeared to have been added during or after the meeting and recorded a comment the CEO had made to him then: 'Temper your sense of justice.' There was an air of shocked disbelief in the courtroom as everyone digested what it meant.

'What does that mean, "temper your sense of justice", Mr Comyn?' Orr asked.

'That is what Mr Narev said to me,' Comyn replied.

'And what did you understand him to be conveying to you when he said to you "Temper your sense of justice"?'

Comyn shifted in his chair and told Orr he believed it related to some career development feedback he had received months earlier, 'that I needed to focus more on my personal conviction. And to better manage competing agendas. And to pick which battles. So I believe it was consistent with that reference.' In other words, he was being told to drop his request to ban the product.

Comyn tempered his sense of justice and took the matter no further. Yet the useless CCI insurance continued to be sold until 7 March 2018, when Comyn was still running the retail bank and was also CEO designate (he would become CEO on 9 April 2018). The decision to stop selling CCI was made only a week before the first round of public hearings of the royal commission was set to discuss a case study on CBA's problems with this kind of insurance.

It was another shocking example of a bank product that was both duping customers out of their money and giving them a false sense of security that if something went wrong in their lives, the product would cover them. CBA sold the product knowing it would let those customers down, but the bank wouldn't do anything about it or tell them because that would mean losing profits.

*

Wearing her signature pearls and glasses and her Order of Australia pin, CBA chair Catherine Livingstone sat down in the witness box with a pained, uncomfortable expression on her face, clearly feeling out of her comfort zone. Before the royal commission, Livingstone had rarely been criticised by her peers or those below her: after chairing Telstra and other influential organisations, in 2014 she had gone on to be president of corporate Australia's peak lobby group, the Business Council of Australia. But the royal commission was a leveller, with the top echelons of banking put on trial and assessed on their decision-making abilities, handling of misconduct and the tone they set from the top of the organisation.

Orr opened with a long list of wrongdoings at CBA since Livingstone's appointment to the board on 1 March 2016. The list included the life insurance scandal covered by *Four Corners* in March 2016; the fees-for-no-service scandal exposed by ASIC in October 2016; an enforceable undertaking in relation to misconduct in CBA's foreign exchange business in December 2016; and a May 2017 PricewaterhouseCoopers (PwC) review into CBA's home lending practices that identified concerns with its processes. Then the big one: in August 2017, seven months after Livingstone had become chair of CBA, AUSTRAC's legal action that alleged breaches of the anti-money-laundering and counter-terrorism financing (AML/CTF) laws – resulting in a fine to the tune of $700 million. That same month, ASIC sent out a media release flagging a $10 million refund by CBA to 65,000 customers who'd been sold unsuitable CCI as part of its CreditCard Plus insurance product.

In January 2018, ASIC lodged proceedings against CBA alleging unconscionable conduct and market manipulation in relation to bank bill swap rates, and in May 2018 CBA had entered an enforceable undertaking with APRA after the release of the scathing Prudential Inquiry Final Report into the bank's governance and culture. In July 2018 CBA had entered another enforceable undertaking with ASIC in relation to the way it was distributing certain superannuation products, and as a result of that, APRA stipulated that CBA had to set aside an extra $1 billion in liquid capital.

'Having heard me lay out that chronology of events since your time joining the board of CBA, are there any observations that you would like to make about that chronology of events?' Orr asked.

Livingstone's deadpan response was that she thought it was 'a fairly damning chronology of – in some instances the bank's behaviour, in other instances, the bank's control over its non-financial risks'.

'Fairly damning' had to be the understatement of the year.

Orr then took Livingstone through the shortcomings highlighted in the CBA Prudential Inquiry Final Report.

'Now, the prudential inquiry said that those findings related largely to the operation of the board prior to your appointment as chair,' Orr said.

Livingstone momentarily relaxed, hoping she would get an easy ride.

Then the evisceration began. 'But you were a member of CBA's board for ten months before you were chair?'

'That's correct, ten months, but probably five meetings – five or six meetings,' Livingstone responded.

'Over the course of that ten months?' Orr asked.

'That's correct, because I had leave of absence for the June meeting.'

Orr proceeded to examine the way the CBA board had dealt with the highly contentious AML/CTF laws breaches. She uploaded a series of reports and board minutes to build a case that the board was ineffectual and therefore complicit in the scandal.

The first report confirmed that CBA's internal audit department had identified issues with money laundering and terrorism back in 2013, then 2015 and 2016, giving them an overall red rating. The most serious rating that could be given in an audit report, a red rating meant controls were failing.

Orr noted that these audit reports with red ratings had been reported to the board audit committee, and she reminded the commission that Livingstone had been on the board audit committee in 2016 when a third red rating was identified. Orr pointed out that Livingstone was also on the committee when it received three regulatory reports of CBA's interactions with AUSTRAC, including three statutory notices from AUSTRAC requiring it to provide information about its AML/CTF laws compliance.

It was an embarrassing moment, and one that Livingstone tried to salvage by saying she had asked questions and expressed concerns but had been given assurances by management, including the bank's then chief financial officer, David Craig, that the statutory notices were being dealt with. 'I have to say, I was concerned about the fact of the [statutory] notices and I had had experience with AUSTRAC in a previous role,' she said to Orr. 'So it didn't feel quite right to me that AUSTRAC would be comfortable with where we were, but management provided assurances.' She told the commission she had raised the issues at one of the board meetings.

However, as subsequent documents were uploaded and presented to the commission, it became clear that the board hadn't done its job. Orr reminded Livingstone and the commission that 'CBA admitted ... that it had failed to report millions of dollars of suspected money laundering and that money was laundered through CBA accounts ... [and] that included the proceeds of drugs and firearms importation, and distribution syndicates.' And on 5 December 2016, the audit committee had been handed another audit report with a red rating, relating to the same issue.

It was difficult to digest all this. Even harder to swallow was the fact that, as Orr made clear, CBA's board audit committee allocated a total of thirty minutes to three big items, and had spent no more than a few minutes on the AUSTRAC audit with the red rating. But the biggest shock was what the committee did about the information presented to it. The committee was shown a report including a table that highlighted a number of high-risk areas that had overall red ratings including compliance with AML/ CTF laws, and the Commonwealth Financial Planning fees-for-no-service matter. Under the table in the report highlighting the risk areas was a line saying, 'Copies of all audit reports are available upon request.'

'And having received this document with the one-line summary of the red audit reports, did you request a copy of any of the audit reports?' Orr asked Livingstone.

Livingstone, whose face and neck were now blood red, replied, 'No I did not.' Nor had Livingstone asked for previous audit reports, despite the seriousness of the issue.

Nevertheless, Livingstone was adamant she had raised concerns at board level and been given assurances by management at previous board meetings that everything was under control. Orr challenged this by pulling up board minutes from previous monthly meetings and pointed out that no comments had been recorded about the AML/CTF laws audit issues. Nor were there any records of minutes to prove that Livingstone had noted her concerns in a discussion with management. By law, board minutes are supposed to reflect discussions and any dissenting voices. If these aren't included, the assumption is they didn't take place. If the discussions did take place and they weren't recorded, it's a breach of the law. It was a bad look for Livingstone.

Livingstone left the commission and reflected overnight on her testimony. She returned the following day, wanting to put the record straight about her role on the board audit committee. She now said she recalled having directly challenged management, led by Ian Narev, about her concerns with the bank's anti-money-laundering controls at the October 2016 board meeting. Orr took her to the minutes, where there was no record of any such challenge. It was another embarrassing slap-down for Livingstone.

Orr then moved on to the matter of remuneration at CBA, which provided another insight into the science – or otherwise – behind executive stipends. On 8 August 2016, at a time CBA was drowning in the CommInsure and fees-for-no-service scandals, and had received a series of red alerts on its anti-money-laundering audit controls, the board remuneration committee allocated ten minutes to discussing the remuneration of top executives. Based on a series of papers prepared by the bank's staff, David Cohen, the chief risk officer, recommended that all senior executives should receive their bonuses.

Executives were rated against a scorecard, which included reputation. It meant if an executive ran a business that had a problem that damaged the bank's public credibility, their score would be affected. Cohen assured the board there were no big risks in the near term that would prevent his colleagues being awarded their bonuses: 'In summary, for the financial year ended 30 June 2016, I do not believe there to be any risk issues or risk behaviours that would suggest STI [short-term incentive] awards should be modified from that recommended based on other achievements or results.'

Narev agreed his colleagues should receive their full bonus. That year Narev himself was awarded 108 per cent of his short-term bonus. With a lack of consequence for scandals, it was little wonder the bank had been described as the gold medallist for misconduct.

Though Livingstone wasn't on the remuneration committee, she was on the board, which ultimately approved decisions about remuneration for executives. Presented with the misconduct, Livingstone was forced to take another bite of humble pie: 'As I've indicated, we have all reflected on these outcomes, and would regard them as inappropriate.' ('Inappropriate' had become a much-used euphemism in the corporate world.)

One executive who did receive a reduced bonus was Annabel Spring. Spring was running the wealth management arm of CBA when it was exposed to reputational damage from CommInsure in March 2016, when *The Age*, *Sydney Morning Herald* and *Four Corners* exposed wrongdoing. She was ultimately docked 5 per cent of her $1.05 million 'target'.

At that time, CBA was already aware of the issues relating to the AUSTRAC inquiry, fees for no service and mis-selling consumer credit insurance. 'But those failings weren't yet known to the public at the time that the remuneration report was released in August 2016?' Orr asked.

Livingstone gave a monosyllabic response: 'Yes.'

Orr then presented a remuneration report, which included a reference to 'concerns raised in the media about CommInsure'. But the report didn't mention any of the other issues identified by the bank. 'Was it CBA's approach at this time to wait until a risk had eventuated publicly before imposing any sort of consequence for failing to manage that risk?' Orr asked.

'I don't believe that was the intention, but it might be the impression created,' Livingstone replied.

When Orr asked Livingstone what message Spring's reduced bonus sent, Livingstone responded, 'There will only be consequence if there is a public event, a media event.'

It wasn't until shareholders took a stand and voted against CBA's remuneration report at the November 2016 annual general meeting that Livingstone, who became chair in January 2017, was forced to rethink the bank's policy. In the 2017 financial year, in the wake of the AUSTRAC scandal, Livingstone requested executives and directors – some of whom had left – to take a 20 per cent fee cut. All agreed, except for former chairman David Turner, who was asked to give back 40 per cent of his fee. He declined and Livingstone never bothered to chase him for the refund.

The questioning of Livingstone continued as Orr turned to the decision to promote Matt Comyn as CEO. 'I want to ask you,' she said, 'about the sort of message that you think it sent to others within CBA and to the broader community to promote the person who was in charge of the division in which all of those issues occurred?'

Livingstone replied, 'The easy answer for us would have been to appoint an external person. To find an external person globally at that level who hasn't been involved in some regulatory event is almost impossible.' This provoked an outbreak of laughter in the courtroom, to which she snapped back, in a school-marm voice, 'And I don't mean that as a joke.'

Livingstone's appearance in the witness box demonstrated that a warped and self-serving culture reigned at CBA and in the financial sector more widely. Orr had exposed serious flaws in the board, the committees and the follow-up to serious risk and compliance issues at CBA. Yet it was clear that Livingstone and other CBA board members had felt no compunction or responsibility to look into the bank's operations and the well-founded claims of endemic and systemic malpractice.

In a parting query, Orr asked Livingstone what she hoped to achieve five years from now.

'Well, [that] the CBA – and hopefully in less than five years – is one that customers trust and the community trusts,' she replied, 'and that we're delivering the products that really fit our purpose, which is for the financial wellbeing of – of our customers.'

On that note Livingstone took her battered pride and walked out into a windy day in Sydney to return to the safe sinecure of her office.

*

After Livingstone left, the courtroom emptied and crowds gathered in the foyer, gossiping about her performance. I headed to a pub down the street with Natasha (Tasha) Keys, a single mother who'd been battling CBA for seven years. We had organised to meet days earlier when she'd sent me a series of documents.

Keys' troubles had begun in 2009 after she divorced her partner and applied to CBA for a loan to buy a picturesque tea tree farm called Tanglewood, in the Northern Rivers area of New South Wales. A trained scientist with a passion for the land, Keys believed she could turn the tea-tree farm into a thriving commercial enterprise on the back of a rising demand for organic oils worldwide.

CBA had known of Keys' financial situation when she took the loan, yet the bank had agreed to sign off on a credit card to help pay the bills. But shortly after she bought the farm the area was hit with a severe flood, which damaged the property and virtually wiped out the harvest.

As her financial situation worsened, Keys applied for hardship assistance but was knocked back by CBA. 'If I wasn't able to harvest due to flooding, that was my problem and I had to deal with it,' she said.

By 2010 she was working three jobs to stay afloat. 'I would end up crying from exhaustion ... [I'd go] from one job to the next, rush back, pick up my daughter, cook dinner then drive to the farm to try and do some work there,' she recalls.

In February 2010, CBA got serious and filed a statement of claim against Keys in relation to the credit card debt. CBA told her if she didn't pay $110 per week it would take her to court. CBA also put pressure on her regarding the repayments on her other loan.

Keys didn't realise it at the time, but the bank had misclassified her loan. She should have been given a farm loan, tailored to farmers, with payment moratoriums and interest rate reductions, debt relief and provision of specialist agricultural business banking support. It also hadn't offered her farm debt mediation, which was mandatory in NSW.

In August 2011, without notice, CBA took possession of Keys' farm. Keys then lodged a complaint with the FOS asking for help on the basis that she was a single mother, had no credit rating left, no car, the bank had seized her property and she was living in her mother's garage with her daughter.

Keys also wrote to CBA, saying, 'I am writing to you as a matter of urgency ... Since the bank has locked my property I have been unable to access the property. The house is situated over 1km to the rear of a 100-acre property. The property must be maintained to reduce the chance of major issues ... I am pleading with the bank to hand back my property ... to reduce further financial pressure on me whilst the matter is being resolved by the FOS ...'

It took CBA two years before it listed the property for sale. During that time, it went from being a well-maintained, attractive tea-tree farm to a run-down, ramshackle property that had been broken into and was dank from the elements. It sold for $165,000, less than half its valuation before it was left to rot.

Keys decided to take legal action, alleging the bank had breached its duty of care by failing to obtain two independent valuations. She also alleged CBA should have offered mediation before seizing her property.

In May 2018, Jeff Morris heard about Keys' case and decided to help. He could see she was out of her depth against CBA's battalion of barristers and lawyers. Morris mentioned the case to Matt Comyn – who was familiar with it, as Keys had written to him.

At the time Keys and I had our beer, she was hoping to reach a settlement. (Weeks later an offer appeared, which she accepted.) After our chat, we strolled up the road to have dinner at a cheap Italian restaurant. When we arrived, Morris was sitting with at least ten bank victims. It felt surreal as, one by one, they asked if they could tell me their story. During the course of the evening I heard a lot of heart-wrenching tales. Some of these people had been fighting the banks for years. Some had been suicidal, others had suffered divorce, lost their businesses or their homes.

These were the human faces of bad banking. They were the collateral damage of a system that had allowed banks to bully customers in the shadows. They were the forgotten people who had lodged submissions in the hope they would get to tell their stories to the royal commission. They didn't stand a chance. Only twenty-seven out of more than ten thousand were given that opportunity.

Chapter 24

Round 7: Westpac

Agreeing to disagree

WHEN WESTPAC BOSS BRIAN Hartzer arrived in the witness box just before 2 pm on 21 November, he had an air of confidence lacking in the other chief executives who had so far appeared at the royal commission. Hartzer had been running Westpac since 2015, after being promoted from its financial services division, home to its problematic financial planning business.

Michael Hodge QC had been assigned to the cross-examination. His aim was to highlight misconduct, examine how the bank had dealt with it, and look at what it was doing to change. Although Westpac had emerged relatively unscathed from the early rounds of the royal commission, Hodge was about to show it was no cleanskin.

Hodge opened with Westpac's response to a request by ASIC in 2012 for all banks to start properly assessing the financial capabilities of customers before offering credit card limit increases. In 2014, it became clear to ASIC that Westpac, unlike the other banks, had failed to amend its processes. It would take Westpac until March 2015 to comply with ASIC, and led to a penalty of $1 million.

Hodge asked Hartzer to comment on why ASIC was ignored.

'It's kind of moot because credit limit increase offers have ceased altogether,' he said to Hodge. 'I haven't spent a lot of time thinking about it, because we stopped doing it.' He did, however, concede that Westpac should have been more pro-active about resolving those issues: 'I think there was clearly a deficiency in understanding the seriousness with which regulatory disagreements needed to be dealt with.' Hartzer insisted that a serious disagreement with the regulator would now be pushed to the top levels of management.

Having failed to land a glove on Hartzer, Hodge moved on to a more sensitive topic: why Westpac was retaining its financial advice business when the other banks were selling theirs off after accepting that they resulted in conflicts of interest. Hodge cited two issues that appeared to be endemic across the large financial advice businesses: poor or non-compliant advice and the charging of fees for no service.

Westpac has a significant wealth-advice business, BT Financial Group, which directly employs financial advisers and operates two authorised representatives, Securitor Financial and Magnitude, which operate under the BT licence. Their advisers aren't directly employed by BT, but if things go wrong, BT is responsible for remediating customers. It's a similar arrangement to the one between CBA and Financial Wisdom.

Hodge referred to an audit in late 2017 which showed that only six out of ten Westpac financial advice files passed a compliance audit. 'Outcomes from recent file audits … are showing results at a level that does not indicate a sufficiently robust control environment to comply with ASIC's expectations,' the audit said.

Fees for no service had been identified as an issue at Westpac in January 2016, but it took the bank until December 2017 to commence remediation payments to victims of this malpractice. The commission heard that Westpac had set aside $117 million for compensation, but the bank's records were so poor that Hartzer still couldn't give an estimate of its total exposure. He admitted that some of the fees went back eleven years and that Westpac had not yet calculated the remediation payments that needed to be paid on behalf of its authorised representatives – financial advisers who aren't directly employed by Westpac but operate under its licence. He estimated those representatives had received $991 million in ongoing advice fees over the previous decade, but he didn't know how much of that represented fees for no service.

In other words, Westpac's advice business was much like that of the other banks. Systems were old, record-keeping poor, compliance processes questionable and remediation too slow. Nevertheless, Hartzer wanted to maintain the status quo. This was made abundantly clear when Hodge read out some of Westpac's objections to industry reforms that had been proposed in the royal commission's interim report. As an example, he asked if Westpac was against 'requiring annual as opposed to biennial opt-in notices for ongoing fee arrangements'?

Hartzer agreed that it was.

'It opposes structural separation between product manufacturers and advisers?'

Hartzer agreed.

'It opposes a ban on trail commissions for intermediaries?'

Hartzer agreed.

'It opposes a ban on introducer programs?'

Hartzer agreed.

'It opposes industry codes being given legal or further legal effect?'

Hartzer agreed.

To provoke a different response, Hodge asked, 'And do you think that one of the reasons that Westpac opposes each of those changes is because there will be an effect on the profitability of Westpac's business?'

'That's a component of it,' Hartzer conceded, 'but that's not the main driver. The way you described that sounds like we're completely opposed to change, which we're not.'

But it was too late. Hartzer's responses had made it clear that Westpac would only modify its procedures if it was forced to.

*

As at other bank AGMs held in late 2018, the company's investors registered a massive protest vote, with 64 per cent of shareholders rejecting Westpac's remuneration report – one of the highest votes recorded against a Top 50 company on record. There was also a big vote against the granting of shares to Hartzer and the re-election of a former AMP boss, Craig Dunn, to the Westpac board. Investors were unimpressed that executives had only been docked an average of 25 per cent of their bonuses. Hartzer's total remuneration in 2018 dropped almost 10 per cent to $4.9 million.

Due to time constraints, Westpac chairman Lindsay Maxsted wasn't called as a witness. However, he gave an insight into his thinking in his December 2018 address to shareholders, saying that Hayne's summation of banks being greedy didn't apply to Westpac. 'We are not an organisation based on greed or short-term profit,' he claimed, adding that much of the conduct aired during the royal commission had been 'historical, has been previously reported to regulators, and in many cases, had been resolved or is being addressed'.

Despite all that had been said at the royal commission, Westpac still didn't get it.

Chapter 25

Round 7: ASIC and APRA

Regulatory twin peaks

ASIC's CHAIRMAN, JAMES SHIPTON, had put a lot of thought into his appearance at round seven of the royal commission. He had taken on the role of chairman just ten months earlier and was under no illusion that the corporate regulator was seen as anything but a toothless tiger. The interim report had made it clear that the royal commission held a bleak view of ASIC's weakness as an enforcement agency and believed it was too close to the companies it was supposed to be regulating. 'When misconduct was revealed, it either went unpunished [by the regulators] or the consequences [imposed by the regulators] did not meet the seriousness of what had been done,' Hayne had written.

It was a damning indictment. Likewise Hayne's comments that ASIC's negotiated outcomes with entities had 'taken far too long', including many cases where remediation programs had taken 'months, even years, to formulate and implement'. Hayne also expressed the view that the way ASIC had dealt with financial institutions would have allowed the institutions to think that 'they, not ASIC, not the Parliament, not the courts' could decide when and how the law would be obeyed or how the consequences of breaches would be remedied. 'A regulator "speaking softly" will rarely be effective unless the regulator also carries a big stick,' Hayne wrote.

The clear implication was that Shipton needed to find a big stick and make some tough choices, including distancing himself from ASIC's sins of the past by shifting the blame to his predecessor Greg Medcraft and castigating staff caught brokering cosy deals with regulated entities, such as letting the banks vet draft media releases.

By the time Shipton sat down in the witness box on 22 November, the courtroom had filled with bank victims, whistleblowers, academics and his ASIC entourage. Shipton was nervous. Treasury, politicians, ASIC staff and other decision makers would be watching. The royal commission was the ideal place for him to set a new tone.

Rowena Orr wanted to explore why ASIC was a reluctant regulator. She began by asking about ASIC's budget and its remit, which was wider than most of its regulatory counterparts overseas. Orr wanted to find out whether a restrictive budget was impeding its performance. Shipton confidently made it clear it was: 'It means … we are constrained in probably every aspect of our regulatory work. Certainly in investigations, certainly in other matters relating to enforcement, but I would also make the case that we are constrained in our surveillance, our supervision, our important work on financial capability, and – and other work that we undertake.' Over the years ASIC's responsibilities had expanded and its budget had been cut by the government in some years, but these weren't the only reasons for its disappointing track record.

Orr then turned to ASIC's stakeholder engagement strategy, which listed regulator meetings with boards and senior executives

details of pending client orders, and then using the information to enter prices into the trading platforms to set currency exchanges. In response, ASIC said it was concerned NAB wasn't ensuring that its systems, controls and supervision were adequate to prevent, detect and respond to such conduct, and it issued an enforceable undertaking with the bank.

Orr produced an email written by ASIC commissioner Cathie Armour, then chair of ASIC's enforcement committee, and circulated to her colleagues in August 2016, before the enforceable undertaking had been announced. The email discussed a settlement deal with NAB's then chief risk officer David Gall. Armour, who had joined ASIC in 2013 after working as Macquarie Group's general legal counsel for more than a decade, wrote in the email, 'I did say to [Gall] that, given the relatively early stage of the investigation, we would be willing to consider a proposal that did not involve a court outcome if [the proposal] otherwise met our key regulatory outcomes.' She had also told Gall that 'the longer investigations go, the more prospect of us developing case theories … which would limit our flexibility on outcomes'.

Orr said to Shipton, 'Can I ask you to reflect on whether anything about that response by Ms Armour, a commissioner of ASIC, to Mr Gall, is problematic beyond a lack of professionalism?'

Shipton defended his commissioner: 'I just want to be absolutely clear that I firmly believe in Ms Armour's professionalism at all times and that shouldn't be in any doubt in this case study.'

Commissioner Hayne told him to answer the question. His response was 'No.'

Orr suggested that a more appropriate way for a regulator to have handled this situation would have been to complete the investigation, form its views, then negotiate armed with information on how serious the misconduct was and how many civil or criminal breaches had occurred. Instead, ASIC had preferred to take the softer, less combative option, and do deals before they had all the facts to hand. Orr felt that automatically reduced the regulator's bargaining power because it didn't have the full picture of what had gone on. She was of the view that a regulator should start by asking, 'Why not litigate?', then work backwards, instead of the other way around. Until it did that, it would never be an effective regulator.

The royal commission then heard that by the end of March 2018 – more than fifteen months after ASIC had initiated the enforceable undertaking against NAB – the bank still hadn't developed a remediation program. In other words, it had failed to comply with its enforceable undertaking. Instead of penalising NAB, ASIC gave the bank a three-month extension.

Shipton's response to that was that he didn't think it had been unreasonable to vary the enforceable undertaking. 'This was a difficult regulatory choice. Our resources are not limitless.' But the message was clear: ASIC needed to grow a spine, and Shipton would need to come down harder on staff agreeing to soft options before investigations were completed.

Orr cited numerous other cases where ASIC had been too accommodating when it came to negotiated settlements. She presented a September 2017 email from ASIC's Tim Mullaly, a senior executive leader of financial services enforcement, to colleague Michael Saadat, saying, 'We either resolve by way of an enforceable agreement with a community benefit payment of $250,000 or we push for … $300,000.' Saadat replies that they should start with $300,000. Mullaly then responds: 'As you will recall, James Myerscough [CBA's risk officer] was concerned that by just paying a community benefit payment and not having any regulatory outcome, it looks like they [CBA] are paying off ASIC to avoid action.' The community benefit payment Mullaly was referring to was the penalty ASIC wanted to impose on CBA in relation to the series of misleading and deceptive life insurance ads covering heart attacks and cancer, which Helen Troup had been quizzed about in the royal commission back in September. CBA was worried that a donation of $300,000, instead of a fine in the vicinity of $8 million, might attract unwanted attention.

Mullaly's email continued, 'He [Myerscough] was hoping to see something from us about how this would be messaged.'

Orr asked Shipton, 'How do you respond to a concern expressed by one of your regulated population [CBA] that by making a community benefit payment, CBA would look as though it was paying off ASIC to avoid action?'

Shipton said it was 'extremely concerning'.

But it was much worse than that. It showed how choreographed the entire process of ASIC negotiating penalties with the banks had become. In late 2017 – two weeks after the royal commission had been called – CBA was weighing up the appearance of the suggested donation.

It went to the heart of what was wrong with ASIC. Since its inception as the Australian Securities Commission, it had been a light-touch regulator. It had also been accused of being captive to the organisations it regulated, not least because of the constant movement of staff between ASIC and the banks. ASIC media advisers had moved to banks, commissioners had moved from banks to ASIC, and lawyers had moved between the two.

Over decades, millions of Australians had been ripped off by the banks. Instead of being the tough cop on the beat and taking legal action on their behalf, ASIC preferred negotiated outcomes with the offenders. Remediation had been slow – if it had occurred at all.

As noted, ASIC had even shied away from naming and shaming wrongdoers. In a series of industry reports over many years listing a litany of sins on the part of institutions generally, it had failed to name the ones involved. It was, as Orr pointed out, a practice that had continued under Shipton.

Shipton conceded it was a good point and promised that in future ASIC would be a tougher regulator: it would be 'more adventurous in pushing points of law', take more risks and use the courts more, including taking criminal actions against financial institutions for misconduct. To prove this, Shipton told the commission that ASIC had launched an investigation into CBA's mis-selling of consumer credit insurance (CCI) products to more than 156,000 people.

But this failed to impress Orr, given ASIC had only decided to launch the investigation two weeks earlier, despite having known about CBA's mis-selling of CCI for two and a half years. And in any case, as Orr pointed out, ASIC was only investigating whether it should pursue enforcement.

Orr asked, 'Do you agree that the matters that you referred to, the fact that this was an industry-wide challenge, the fact that 156,000 customers were out of pocket, the fact that this was a systemic issue, were all matters that reinforced the need for you to take strong action and commence an investigation?'

Shipton replied, 'You should have confidence that it's different today, because we now have issued guidance that would mean that a decision like the one in CCI … would have a very different starting point … The starting point today would be to ask the question and turn our minds to why not litigate this demonstrable breach.'

'And that's as of a few weeks ago?' Orr asked.

'That is of two or three weeks ago, yes,' Shipton replied.

It all seemed ad hoc and panicked. Shipton had squandered an ideal opportunity to paint ASIC in a new light.

*

Peter Kell, the former deputy chairman of ASIC who had overseen the regulator's investigation into fees for no service and a number of other investigations, later told me that in the wash-up of the royal commission it was clear the finance sector couldn't fix itself. Kell was in a good position to make some observations after leaving the corporate regulator in December 2018.

'This isn't an issue with just one bank or insurer, it's a market-wide problem,' he said. 'And you're dreaming if you think that the fundamental problems with competition in the finance sector will disappear in the short to medium term.'

Kell believes a greater level of intervention is required from government. Having said this, he pointed out that the key issues were not new and had been talked about for a long time. He thinks it is more a matter of commitment, and that if a few key reform areas were seriously and promptly addressed it would make a very big difference. They include:

- the removal of structural conflicts of interest in remuneration and product manufacture and distribution;
- the introduction of laws and powers enabling individual financial-sector managers and executives to be held accountable more readily for conduct and consumer protection failures;
- increasing the powers, penalties and resources available to regulators, which would in turn have a positive

impact on regulator culture and facilitate more
impactful enforcement;

- meaningful and sustained government support for
organisations that represent and assist consumers, such
as financial counsellors, consumer legal centres and even
new advice services.

Kell also believes whistleblowers need greater protection and
support, and that there needs to be an increase in public reporting
on bank 'outcomes' or 'performance' that impacts consumers, for
example public cross-industry comparative data on the numbers
and causes of complaints, disciplinary and enforcement actions, or
insurance claims outcomes. The big question for Kell is whether
governments have the will and capacity to get these reforms over
the line. 'When it comes to consumer protection,' he pointed out,
'the history of finance sector reform is not a happy one. Industry
lobbying has too often won out over consumer interests. The
response to this lobbying in the future will determine whether we
do see meaningful change.'

*

The chairman of APRA, Wayne Byres, was visibly uncomfortable
when he entered the witness box later in the hearings. His half-
hearted smile and awkwardness were a dead giveaway for those
who knew him well. Ahead of his appearance, the Morrison
government had decided to renew Byres' term as chairman of
APRA for another five years, which at least gave him some
confidence that his appearance wouldn't cost him his job.

Until the royal commission, most of the criticism of poor
regulation had been aimed at ASIC, while APRA had been given

a relatively easy time. And unlike ASIC, APRA had never been subject to a capability review into its structure and performance. But during the various royal commission hearings, the failure of APRA to hold institutions to account had been revealed time and time again. In particular, while overseeing Australia's $2.7 trillion superannuation system, APRA had allowed companies to operate with little transparency and accountability, to the detriment of the retirement savings of millions of Australians.

Now APRA would be placed under the spotlight. Byres would be taken through various scandals and how APRA had reacted to them. For example, APRA had allowed CBA to get away with scandal after scandal for years before finally bowing to pressure to conduct its prudential inquiry into the bank in August 2017. The final report, released on 1 May 2018 and discussed during round seven of the commission, had been damning of CBA's culture, compliance, systems, management and board, showing that CBA had made at least 15,000 criminal breaches in relation to not moving some customers to MySuper products.[1] Yet APRA had failed to take any action or impose any fines.

In his interim report, Hayne noted that banks have a special position in the economy and that it is APRA's job to regulate the banks to ensure the proper functioning of the banking system and to avoid failure of individual entities. 'If competitive pressures are absent, if there is little or no threat of enterprise failure, and if banks can and do mitigate the consequences of customers failing to meet obligations, only the regulator can mark and enforce those bounds,' he said. 'But neither ASIC nor APRA has done that in a way that has prevented the conduct described in this report.'

As the prudential regulator, APRA's key focus is governance and risk culture. The legislation that governs APRA says the regulator must promote financial system stability in performing its duties. Or, as Hayne put it, 'APRA is obliged to look at issues of governance and risk culture through the lens of financial system stability.'

Where APRA had failed was in not paying enough attention to governance and risk culture, fearing it would upset the stability of the financial system. This 'hear no evil, see no evil' type of regulation allowed insurers to behave badly, banks to run rampant with irresponsible lending, and super funds to operate in the dark. Remuneration was another issue that concerned APRA, and Michael Hodge used dealings with CBA to illustrate its shortcomings. The rules for remuneration are set out in APRA's Prudential Standard CPS 510 Governance, which covers a number of issues including that performance-linked remuneration, including targets and bonuses, don't undermine the long-term financial soundness of the institution. Referring to APRA's notes of a meeting with the CBA board in December 2016, which Byres had attended, Hodge commented, 'There doesn't seem to have been a discussion or an issue raised as to what exactly had happened with CBA's 2016 executive remuneration.'

Byres nodded sheepishly. By August 2016 CBA had been drowning in scandals – which APRA had been aware of – and CBA's operational risk management framework was not identifying, escalating or addressing significant operational risks. Despite this, Ian Narev had been granted a 108 per cent bonus on his short-term performance. Hodge wanted to know why APRA hadn't discussed CBA's 2016 remuneration at the December meeting, given that it was required to do so under CPS 510. Byres said the discussion had been dominated by the results of a historic shareholder protest vote against the remuneration package at the AGM and how the bank planned to respond.

Hodge turned to a report prepared by an internal staffer at APRA which said, 'APRA could and should have called out inadequate remuneration practices earlier (at least by late 2016).' The point was that remuneration was in APRA's remit and CBA was battling scandals, but APRA had failed to challenge the bank. It hadn't even worked out what constituted a desirable remuneration framework, which was an alarming revelation.

Hodge asked Byres if APRA had ever taken action against a financial institution for not complying with the remuneration rules under Prudential Standard CPS 510. Byres responded with another sheepish no, but said that in 2019 APRA would release a new model for executive remuneration and rewrite its prudential standards.

Hodge then quoted an internal APRA board paper dated 19 June 2018, which had been prepared in response to the APRA-commissioned report into CBA. He drew attention to the heading 'Supervision Mongrel', the name for a new attitude – 'to get tough' – that APRA wanted to promote, which entailed, among other things, 'stronger support of supervisory gut feel, together with strengthened supervisor tenacity'.

As the paper noted, 'Senior leadership in APRA would need to set the tone on how this supervision mongrel would operate in practice.' People who knew Byres were sceptical he could 'ratchet up the mongrel' at APRA. He was perceived as a nice person whose natural disposition was not to offend people. Academic Pat McConnell wrote, 'It is hard to believe that after many years of being rolled over and tickled on the tummy by the banks, APRA will turn from a sycophantic shiatzu to a regulatory rottweiler any time soon.'[2]

The next interchange epitomised the problem of a light-touch, trusting and forgiving regulator. Hodge asked Byres, 'Do you have any view as to what the extent of the problem tells you about the adequacy of APRA's supervision?'

Byres responded, 'It says that there are limits to supervision … We don't audit accounts. To some extent, we are dependent on institutions bringing issues to our attention when we're talking about those sorts of matters of detail.' The best Byres would concede was that APRA didn't go deep enough on some of the issues: 'My general lesson … is [APRA has] to think more about how do we get deeper, potentially doing more transaction testing or other things, or asking other people to do it on our behalf [to] help us more readily identify these issues earlier.'

In other words, APRA still hadn't figured out what to do.

It was a sad indictment of the regulator. Its cosy, behind-closed-doors supervision hadn't worked. If Byres had hoped to instil confidence that APRA was doing a good job, he'd failed dismally.

Chapter 26
Round 7: NAB

'Hubris wrapped in arrogance'

WHEN THE HIGHLY ENERGETIC Andrew Thorburn walked into courtroom 4A of Melbourne's Commonwealth Law Courts on 26 November 2018, wearing a dark plaid suit and pink dotted tie, he looked every bit the stereotypical banker. The courtroom for part two of the seventh round, which had resumed in Melbourne, was packed. Thorburn had brought along lawyers and staff to fill the seats. There were also some familiar faces. The Bank Warriors, who'd become a common fixture at the hearings, were there dressed in their usual bow ties – both to symbolise the importance of the royal commission and to pay respect to whistleblower Jeff Morris who had worn a bow tie to the royal commission a week earlier.

Thorburn's colleagues hoped their boss would be able to keep the focus on how NAB had changed its practices, rather than on the adverse publicity it had received weeks earlier in the commission's closing submission at the superannuation hearing, which had lambasted NAB for its 'total disregard' for the law and regulators and concluded that NAB's behaviour in the fees-for-no-service scandal was in part due to 'culture and governance practices within the NAB group'.

When senior counsel assisting, Michael Hodge QC, started cross-examining Thorburn, the NAB boss treated each question as if it were a landmine, to be avoided at all costs. Like his peers, he had been rehearsing for weeks how to steer the conversation to safe ground. A few jokes and some personal stories about his love of fishing would create the right tone – or so he hoped. But Hodge wasn't going to be diverted by Thorburn's spin. He'd heard it all before from other witnesses and wanted to drill down into NAB's culture, board and management accountability.

Thorburn tried to ingratiate himself by admitting he had been wrong to oppose a royal commission; he said he'd been defending the system because he 'thought it was right'. He claimed that what had come out in the hearings had 'provoked critical self-examination and driven change for customers' and said, 'When you read the case studies you say this is, like, so upsetting and so damning, what went wrong?' He went on to proudly outline his new management strategy, EPIC, standing for 'Empathy, Perform, Imagine, Connect'.

Hodge pointed out that the malpractice revealed during the royal commission shouldn't have been a shock because Thorburn must have been very familiar with the case studies that had been highlighted, including fees for no service, the widespread false witnessing of customer documents by staff, and the bank's introducer program, which paid members of the public a kickback for referring customers for home loans but resulted in illegal activity as well as the sale of loans that were unsuitable, resulting in severe financial stress for many customers.

Commissioner Hayne didn't buy Thorburn's spin either. 'You spoke of the commission raising real cases, in effect, publicly. Is that right?' Hayne asked.

'That's right,' Thorburn replied.

'The real cases it raised publicly were cases within your organisation,' Hayne reminded him before asking: 'What does that say about the need for different supervision and governance within the bank to recognise the reality and importance of the kinds of cases that have been the object of public scrutiny and publicity?'

Governance and culture were just the start. Hodge moved on to highlight dishonest practices, including accepting fees for no service and attempting to avoid paying customer remediation. He referred to one situation when customers were transferred from one fund to MLC Direct, which didn't provide personal advice, and were still charged fees for advice by NAB Financial Planning, which never paid them back.

In June 2015, ASIC had asked NAB to review all its licensees and NAB Financial Planning for ongoing service-fee issues. The review made it clear that NAB had been charging fees for no service and requested it remediate its customers. NAB put forward three proposals in 2016 and July 2017 which ASIC found unacceptable. Then in October 2017 ASIC sent NAB a report titled *Outlined Suspected Offending by NAB Group*. The report referred to a series of complaints from super fund members who had been wrongly charged fees from 2011, and outlined a number of breaches that indicated the bank had engaged in misleading and deceptive conduct and failed to fulfil its regulatory reporting duties.

NAB's response to ASIC's report, according to the royal commission, was to deny it had a systemic issue. On 13 April 2018, NAB sent ASIC a new remediation proposal, signed by the bank's chief legal and commercial officer, Sharon Cook. The proposal suggested using an interpretation of the law to divide affected customers into two categories: those who had signed up before the 2013 implementation of the Future of Financial Advice (FoFA) laws, and those who had signed up after that. NAB offered to review all post-FoFA cases, but said it would not reassess the cases of pre-FoFA clients unless they came to NAB and attested that they hadn't received any service in return for the fees they had paid. It was a discriminatory policy and clearly aimed at reducing NAB's exposure to remediation. What made it worse was that the other major banks were already remediating their customers for fees for no service in ways acceptable to ASIC.

Hodge turned to a meeting Thorburn had had with ASIC's chairman, James Shipton, on 26 April 2018. He asked Thorburn to summarise the meeting.

'He made it very clear to me that ... they had been very disappointed with the legal technical way that we had been dealing with this matter. I walked out thinking we've got to do something to change the course here because that's not the reputation we want,' Thorburn recalled.

Hodge then brought up a 30 April board risk-committee meeting attended by Thorburn and the chief risk officer, David Gall, which included a presentation by Sharon Cook on the status of ASIC's investigation into the fees-for-no-service scandal and the bank's remediation proposal.

Hodge asked: 'And as I understand it nobody said then, "This is not doing the right thing"?'

Thorburn, squirming in his chair, said no.

'And it didn't strike you at the time that the position was unacceptable?' marvelled Hodge.

Just over a week later, on 9 May, ASIC formally rejected NAB's proposal for remediation.

'Do you think, Mr Thorburn, reflecting on that letter of 13 April 2018 that that was an ethical approach for NAB to take?'

Thorburn gave a convoluted answer that tried to deflect blame while at the same time appearing to be supportive of his staff: 'I believe it was Andrew Hagger's and others' intent that we would solve this ... But I don't think we were intending to create this issue and to be, in your words, unethical ... To the people – the people I deal with, I have dealt with on this, Mr Hodge, I believe are ethical people and bring ethical principles to work.'

Thorburn had mentioned Hagger's name too many times for Hodge's liking. He responded: 'Somebody looking at your statement and listening to the evidence that you've given today might think that you are, to the maximum extent possible, passing responsibility for this to Mr Hagger, the senior executive who has been made redundant and left the bank. Is that what you are doing?'

Thorburn said no.

Hodge continued, 'You don't seem to have asked yourself the question, "Why couldn't we three see that we were not doing the right thing?"' Hodge was referring to the executives who had attended the risk meeting – Sharon Cook, David Gall and Thorburn himself, who were all still at the bank.

Again, Thorburn tried to offer excuses. 'I just don't think we saw it with the clarity we do now,' he said. 'You know, it wasn't an agenda item on a busy board schedule. It was a matter that had been going for two years ... It has been a challenging exercise for me to really look at it and find out where our failings have been, and I think this has been one of them.'

As Thorburn exited the royal commission, stage left, EPIC, the new NAB management strategy he'd so proudly outlined during his evidence, had already been renamed 'Earnings, Profit, Incentivised, Conflicted'.

*

The moment Dr Ken Henry started speaking at the hearing on 26 November, Twitter went into a frenzy. By the time he had finished the following day, NAB was battling yet another crisis, this time about its chairman.

Each time Henry answered a question posed by Rowena Orr QC he gave a greater insight into the arrogance of bank boards. Instead of answering simply and directly, he philosophised, responded with rhetorical answers, and sometimes answered his own questions. It greatly frustrated Orr.

Early in the proceedings, Orr tried to delve into the culture at NAB. She asked Henry about an initiative he had developed with Thorburn two years earlier, called 'Back the Bold', which involved 'taking a stand for customers' and 'winning together' and training staff to back exceptional people 'who move this country forward'. Essentially Orr wanted to know whether there was any substance to the catchy 'Back the Bold' slogan.

Orr asked Henry, 'In what way do you want your staff to be bold? In what way do you want them to be exceptional?'

Henry replied that he wanted them to put a high value on excellence, on always getting it right. 'I want them not to feel intimidated by those who are above them, to feel that if they think there's something going wrong in the organisation, that they can speak to people above them in the organisation and get their message through to the highest levels of the organisation, and, if necessary, to the board.'

'What about "win together"?' asked Orr. 'What is it that you want won?'

'That's about corporate collegiality,' Henry replied. 'It's more about the together than the winning although the winning is intended to be motivating, that we come to work energised and motivated, but, importantly, that we do it together. But also, and it's in that second behaviour under "win together", that we understand that we're not going to be successful as a team unless we make it simpler and faster.'

'Is it winning business, for customers? What are they winning?'

'We want our people to be – to know that they are part of a business which stands out among its peers. That's what it's about. That they feel proud of working for National Australia Bank, because they see it as Australia's leading bank.'

Henry might have meant it, but it sounded like management-speak: empty but well-rehearsed slogans.

Orr drilled down further, wanting to find out how Henry had arrived at Back the Bold. She told him that Thorburn had explained that the purpose of the initiative was to back those who move Australia forward. 'What does that mean, Dr Henry?'

'I thought he explained it rather well. We didn't come to this purpose quickly. You know, we didn't just go into a dark room and have a quick chat about what might look good as a – as a slogan for the organisation,' Henry said defensively. But the more he talked, the more it sounded like gibberish. And when Orr asked how long it was going to take to embed the right culture, Henry responded, 'It could be ten years. It could be. I hope not. But I wouldn't be at all surprised. That would not be unusual for organisations that seek to embed challenge in cultures.' Investors listening in, many of whom see things from a more short-term perspective, were horrified by this response.

Orr then used NAB's handling of charging customers fees for no service to show how the board and the risk committee had failed in its duties, asking Henry why they didn't take the issue more seriously. Orr pointed out that when a report from the chief risk officer was sent to the board's risk committee, it failed to point out that this was a serious issue, explain its causes or identify which laws had been contravened.

'That's, perhaps, not so unusual, but that is true,' Henry responded.

Dissatisfied with his response, Orr asked him why a breach wasn't discussed. Henry's response, that it was up to the chief risk officer to say whether there may or may not have been a breach, resulted in more frustration from Orr.

'Isn't that something the risk committee should know: "This might contravene the law and these are the provisions that at the moment we're concerned might have been breached?"'

Henry responded with another 'perhaps'.

'Why only perhaps, Dr Henry?' Orr asked, to which Henry replied that it wasn't clear cut about breaches and there were many differing views about whether breaches may or may not have occurred.

Orr pressed on: 'Surely someone within your business at that point was thinking about whether this conduct contravened the law, and, if so, how it contravened the law?'

'Yes,' was Henry's abrupt reply.

'Surely those were matters that the chief risk officer should have reported to the risk committee?'

'Perhaps,' Henry responded.

'Back to where we started, "perhaps", Dr Henry?'

'Yes, perhaps,' Henry answered.

'And I'm afraid I still don't understand the reason for your hesitation,' said Orr.

'I probably can't explain it to you,' he replied.

It was just one of many excruciating exchanges. At one point Henry likened working with the regulators to dealing with children. He was speaking of the tussle with ASIC over the various remediation proposals put forward by NAB in the fees-for-no-service scandal and the delays in remediating customers. He blamed ASIC, saying it didn't give clear indications of what it wanted from the bank. 'It's almost like that game that children play: you're getting colder, you're getting warmer,' he said.

Orr was having none of it and fired back, 'I want to suggest to you, from the documents that I will take you to, that ASIC was very clear in relation to adviser service fees, that the proposals that were being put by NAB were not adequate to address customer detriment.'

Reprising the curly topic of board accountability and executive accountability, which had left CBA's Matt Comyn and Catherine Livingstone floundering, Orr referred to the NAB board's handling of remuneration. She uploaded an email Thorburn had written in 2016 saying executives, including himself, should be entitled to 100 per cent of the funds that had been set aside for bonuses. His proposal had the support of the chief risk officer, David Gall. Yet at the time of the email, NAB was engulfed in regulatory breaches and scandals, including taking fees for no service, manipulating the benchmark interest rate, and misconduct on its foreign exchange trading desk. Thorburn neglected to mention any of these issues in his email, though the board knew about them anyway. The board backed Thorburn and Gall's proposal.

However, the board remuneration and risk committees, which advises the board on these issues, challenged Gall and Thorburn on the poor risk outcomes and expressed unease at paying out the full bonuses. Before making a recommendation to the board about the bonuses, the two committees asked Thorburn to consider two options: one, that the bonus pool should be paid out in full but that a strongly worded statement should be issued by senior management echoing the board's request that there be further improvements in risk management; or two, that five per cent should be deducted from bonus payments to underline the board's concerns.

The risk and remuneration committees left it to Henry and NAB director and chairman of the remuneration committee Danny Gilbert, co-founder of law firm Gilbert + Tobin, who had held the remuneration role at NAB for ten years, to make the final decision. Henry and Gilbert then asked Thorburn for his recommendation. Not surprisingly, he chose option one. Asking the recipient of the proposed bonus for his recommendation was akin to ASIC asking the banks how they'd like to be punished. It was a red flag of poor governance and gave an insight into the company's lack of good judgement as well as the power of the CEO over the board. Thorburn's argument for retaining the full bonus was that the business had met its financial targets in 2016 and the bonus pool had previously been reduced in 2014.

'That was because of the mis-selling of payment protection insurance [PPI] by your businesses in the UK?'

Henry couldn't remember the details, except that it was UK-related.

Orr read out Thorburn's explanation: 'The reason incentives were reduced in that year was not because of the poor management of risk, but because the remediation of those issues meant that cash earnings hadn't been achieved.'

She summed up the breaches and asked Henry, 'Given the very significant compliance breaches and other breaches in [2016], do you think that you made the right decision in deciding that there should be no risk-related reduction to the bonus pool?'

'Yes,' said Henry.

The exchange harked back to Hayne's comments in his interim report about the banks being motivated by greed, and it underlined the fact that no matter how big the scandal or how serious the risk management concerns, bank boards seldom reduced executive bonuses.

Orr continued to press the point about remuneration with Henry: 'You said earlier, Dr Henry, that you weren't sure what the board could have done differently or when it could have done something differently. I want to suggest to you squarely that this was a point at which the board could have conducted itself differently. It could have sent a strong message by reducing the [bonus] pool in response to these very significant compliance issues?'

'Of course, we could have, and we decided not to. For very good reasons,' Henry responded. 'And I'm still happy with those reasons.'

The more Orr highlighted how wrong it was of the board to approve full bonus payments in such circumstances, the worse Henry's mood became.

'What better way to demonstrate intolerance of practices which are not in the customer's interest than to reduce the bonus pool as a result of risk?' Orr proposed.

'Well, we could have fired everybody, I suppose,' was Henry's flippant response.

It was a watershed moment in the royal commission. Andrew Hagger had already been scalped as a result of his testimony, Thorburn's reputation had been tarnished by his responses to questioning, and now Henry's pompous and at times elitist tone was about to go viral, leading to calls for his head.

A NAB board member since 2011 and board chairman since December 2015, Henry had presided over numerous scandals and was therefore in no position to take the high ground. This was amply illustrated when Orr asked him whether NAB's board should have stepped in earlier after customers were charged fees for no service and the bank dragged its feet on remuneration.

Henry replied, 'I have answered the question how I could answer the question.'

'I'm sorry, is that a yes or a no, Dr Henry?'

'I've answered the question the way I choose to answer the question,' Henry reiterated.

'Well, I'd like you to answer my question, Dr Henry,' Orr insisted. 'Do you accept that the board should have stepped in earlier?'

'I wish we had,' responded Henry.

'I'm going to take that as a yes, Dr Henry,' Orr said.

Henry replied, 'Well, you take that as a yes. All right.'

As chairman, Henry was supposed to set the tone for the culture, governance and image of the bank. In a few short hours he had shattered any perception that it was admirable and provoked a storm of condemnation. One customer tweeted: 'Question for @AndrewThorburn, is Ken Henry's indifferent and flippant attitude a real window into the culture at @NAB? My wife still has transaction accounts with NAB (after I pulled my super from MLC), she is now adamant they are closing this week #bankingRC.'

ABC journalist Dan Ziffer also took to Twitter to comment: 'The wild performance of Ken Henry – scoffing at counsel's questions, talking under his breath, grunting responses – could be how he responds to tough discussions, but it has come across as lacking any respect for #BankingRC or the issues it's tackling. Very surprising.'

In an interview with me, Dr Andy Schmulow, a senior lecturer in law at the University of Wollongong in NSW, described Henry's performance as 'hubris wrapped in arrogance surrounded by conceit'. It was a damning indictment of the chairman of one of the biggest companies in Australia, and formerly one of the country's most powerful public servants.

Despite all the talk about culture, being bold, putting customers first, and adopting the trite 'EPIC' slogan, both Thorburn and Henry had demonstrated a yawning disconnect with customers and regulators in relation to executive remuneration and other issues. It was another case of too much focus on profits. If profits were up, then the apparent conclusion among executives and the NAB board was that rewards should come aplenty, no matter how those profits had been obtained.

Hard-working NAB staff were horrified by what they'd heard. Following Thorburn's and Henry's revelations of the bank's profit-focussed culture, some were abused on buses and trams. Shareholders also made their anger clear, notably at NAB's annual general meeting on 19 December 2018. Those investors had already held meetings with Henry and others about the bank's high levels of remuneration, but Henry and the rest of the NAB board clearly had tin ears. This time, the shareholders made themselves heard, 88 per cent of them voting against NAB's latest remuneration decision – the biggest investor protest against a remuneration report in ASX history.

As the chairman of NAB's board, Henry had given Australians a glimpse into the ugly face of elitism. His performance, and Thorburn's, would have extremely serious consequences – for the bank and for the executives' future careers.

Chapter 27

Round 7: ANZ

Slow to respond, loath to change

TIME WAS NOT ON the Commission's side. Hayne had given himself just two weeks to hear from the big four banks, AMP, Macquarie and the regulators. If he expected more than motherhood statements and apologies, he must have been disappointed.

Shayne Elliott, the boss of ANZ since January 2016, appeared on 28 November. It was obvious that he had listened to the testimony of CBA's Matt Comyn and Catherine Livingstone and NAB's Andrew Thorburn and Ken Henry, and learned from their mistakes. Elliott spoke clearly and directly and kept to the topic of the seventh round of hearings – why misconduct had occurred and what could be done to prevent it in the future – without being asked.

Rowena Orr asked Elliott to explain what he meant by a statement in his submission to the royal commission that misconduct had occurred at ANZ largely due to a culture that had become overly focussed on revenue and sales.

He replied, 'People who drove good revenue outcomes were seen to be doing a good job, and we paid less attention to how they achieved those outcomes.'

Orr then listed a series of other causes that Elliott had identified in his submission including poorly calibrated performance and remuneration plans. 'You accept that that has been a contributing cause?'

Elliott replied, 'Yes, I do'.

'Failures to quickly recognise systemic issues and to elevate them to senior management for action?'

'Yes,' said Elliott.

'Insufficiently clear lines of responsibility and accountability?'

'Yes.'

'And inadequate investment in things such as customer remediation programs?'

'Yes'.

Orr then asked, 'Has ANZ's technology and its oversight of technology also been a contributing cause, in your view?'

'Yes.'

Admitting everything, he then tried to put what went wrong into its context. The industry, he said, had had the good fortune to be profitable and fast growing at the same time. But that had encouraged it to get bigger and it created complex organisations that were difficult to manage. The only clear measures of success were profit and revenue.

At this stage of the hearings, though, after the testimonies of so many board chairs and senior executives, it was impossible not to be cynical. 'Margin Call', a business column in *The Australian*, didn't buy Elliott's spin: 'It was hard to believe this self-flagellating man was the same banker who once ran ANZ's infamously fast-and-loose institutional bank back in the Mike Smith-era. The same banker who as ANZ's CFO sat on the board of Malaysia's scandalous AmBank. The same banker currently fighting a criminal cartel case launched by Rod Sims' ACCC [Australian

Competition and Consumer Commission] over ANZ's August 2015 capital raising.'[1] There was also a reference to the revelation that around two million ANZ customers had been overcharged on their credit card and home loan accounts or hadn't received discounts the bank had offered in relation to their home loans. It amounted to hundreds of millions of dollars falling into the pockets of ANZ and its staff. According to Elliott, the discrepancies were 'processing errors' due to the legacy systems in use at ANZ.

Despite the mea culpas, it was clear that when it came to identifying problems, reporting them to ASIC and remediating customers, ANZ had performed poorly. Orr turned to a September 2018 ASIC investigation into the breach reporting practices of twelve entities, including ANZ, over a three-year period from 2014 to 2017. ANZ had provided ASIC with data on eighty-seven significant breaches that it had reported in that three-year period. ASIC found that the twelve entities took, on average, 1517 days to identify an incident that was later determined to be a significant breach. ASIC hadn't been any more specific, but Orr was. She revealed that on average it had taken ANZ more than four years to identify problems linked to customer detriment, another seven months to file a breach report with ASIC, and another six months after that to make the first repayment to customers.

'How did it get to the point, Mr Elliott, in ANZ where it took more than four years for you to identify incidents that involved significant breaches?' Orr asked.

Elliott blamed it on ineffective systems and processes which didn't proactively identify issues. He said staff weren't always encouraged by senior management to identify and report compliance issues, and the bank's compliance and operational risk database was complex and difficult to navigate. He claimed that in the past year ANZ had been trying to fix its systems, but when

Orr asked him to commit to a shorter time frame for identifying incidents, Elliott started to duck and weave.

'What average would you like to see, as opposed to the 1517-day average?' Orr asked.

'I'm not – I'm not sure it's the type of statistic that lends itself to a target ... I don't know that I can put a number on that. But I would say it's significantly lower than 1500 days,' Elliott replied.

Orr then returned to the ASIC document which had referred to one institution where 'there was less focus on customer remediation. It was seen as a distraction, at the expense of earning revenue, and therefore not always given the highest priority.' She outed the institution as ANZ. In fact, the ASIC assessment was based on an internal ANZ document entitled 'The changing focus of customer remediation', which concluded that remediation was 'delivered in an ad hoc and inconsistent way'.

Orr asked Elliott, 'What happened at ANZ that led to it treating remediation of its customers, for errors that ANZ had made, as a distraction?'

Elliott tried to distance himself from the document. He said it had been pulled together by a team of mid-ranked executives and was not 'an official analysis', so therefore it didn't reflect a widespread attitude. In other words, it was another case of 'nothing to see here'.

Bank victims sitting in the courtroom shook their heads in disgust. Susan Henry, a former trauma counsellor and victim of the collapsed managed investment scheme Timbercorp, which had been bankrolled by ANZ, sent me a message which expressed the mood: 'Noble assurances, claims of shame, contrition, learning and commitment to change are hollow spin ... It's about so much more than cataclysmic loss of money for victims and their families. Abuse of power and betrayal of trust [have] wide-ranging detrimental impacts extending to society as a whole.'

It wasn't a good look for Elliott or the bank. Nor was Orr's revelation that ANZ had missed several ASIC deadlines, including a refund of trailing commissions to about six thousand customers and the repayment of adviser services fees to about three thousand customers. Elliott responded: 'Our limitations to date relate to the complexity we've built into our business over time. Again, [it was] our fault, [and] shouldn't have happened, but it did ... We are getting better at this. In the future, with better processes and a simpler bank, the time scales will come down dramatically.'

The bank had changed its attitude to remediation, he said. 'There has been a significant uplift in ANZ's understanding of the importance of remediation. And the reason I know that is it is talked about more at our board. The facts are that we are now beginning to get first payments to customers faster than we were before. That we are learning from mistakes and being able to apply learnings from one set of remediations to another. So I do believe there has been an impact of those but there's clearly more to ... more to do.'

Orr moved on to the subject of executive remuneration and suggested there should be more transparency around payments and bonuses, and that executives should be held accountable when things go wrong.

Elliott rejected this, arguing that publishing more details about bonuses would amount to little more than 'ritualistic public shaming' which would be of little value 'in fact, potentially a significantly negative consequence in terms of attracting, retaining, motivating the very best people for the future'.

'Can I suggest to you that it's not so much about a public shaming; it's just a part of holding them accountable?' Orr said.

Elliott vehemently disagreed. 'I have forty thousand people who come to work every day at ANZ in thirty-three countries. They have all sorts of backgrounds ... For me to be able to confidently assess that I can nail that communication and it not to be misunderstood, that it not create a culture of fear, I think would be extraordinarily difficult.'

Unperturbed, Orr asked why Elliott was prepared to inform the public that his variable remuneration had been reduced. 'You tell us in your statement that it has been reduced on account of conduct issues raised in the Royal Commission and consequent reputational damage?'

'Yes,' said Elliott.

'I just want to ask you to reflect on what the difference is between publication of the consequences for you and publication of the consequences for your senior executives?'

Elliott said it was because he was the CEO. 'I have a higher degree of responsibility and accountability than anybody else in the company,' he said.

Orr turned to the email where Elliott had requested his own pay be deducted in line with the senior executives. 'It's about unity, accountability and frankly credibility, externally but even more importantly internally,' he had written to ANZ's chairman, David Gonski. 'I can't ask my people to be down 22 per cent unless my own rem reflects a similar number. I want you to reassess your recommended CEO rem as a result and have time to consider.' Elliott said he made the decision after announcing on 8 October that the bank would set aside $374 million to remediate customers who had received inappropriate advice or been charged fees for no service.

All very well, but Orr was trying to understand why Elliott considered the perception created internally was more important than the perception of the public. One of the problems with bank misconduct and poor culture was executives had managed to avoid the public glare and avoid public accountability. ANZ was no different.

Orr pointed out that it was the first time in a decade bonuses had been cut and asked, 'Why is it that it has taken until the last financial year for ANZ to exercise this important power of withholding deferred remuneration?'

Elliott said he believed it was a failing on ANZ's part.

Yet while Elliott received a reduced short-term bonus, his overall package in 2018 was still $5.25 million, down from $6.2 million in 2017. To many observers, the fact that he and his executives had received a bonus of any kind during the royal commission, with all the dirty laundry it had aired, beggared belief. Investors reacted accordingly. At the bank's annual general meeting in December, 34 per cent of shareholders protested against the remuneration report. It was a first strike against the board.

Before finishing with Elliott, Orr asked him about the results of an internal culture survey which showed that only 67 per cent of staff felt they could raise issues and concerns at ANZ without fear of reprisal or negative consequences. It was a 3 per cent decrease on the last survey in 2016.

Elliott understood the significance. 'If we don't have a culture where people feel free to speak, we will fail,' he replied. 'We will fail in terms of our responsibilities of being well managed and ultimately we will fail our customers.'

Clearly, ANZ still had a long way to go to rebuild trust and change its culture.

Chapter 28

Too close for comfort

Banks and their auditors

THE CURTAIN FELL ON the royal commission on 30 November 2018. The final round of hearings had been full of promises of a bright future, with executives of financial institutions saying they'd learned their lessons and regulators promising to be tougher. But the whole thing had a hollow ring to it.

There had been more than 10,000 submissions to the royal commission, but fewer than thirty victims had been called. Moreover, many guilty former executives had not been summoned to the dock to account for their misconduct. Some were still in their jobs; others had moved on to different institutions, spreading poor behaviour further.

It seemed to me that too many stories had been left untold, and I wasn't the only one feeling that way. Not long after the hearings finished, a whistleblower emailed me, expressing fury at ongoing bad behaviour at NAB and concern that the inquiry had only brushed the surface. 'After working for many years in the financial services industry, I'm tired of turning a blind eye to the lies and unethical behaviour so executives can keep their bonuses,' the whistleblower wrote. 'I've decided to take a big risk in disclosing a cache of highly sensitive NAB documents after losing patience with APRA, ASIC and the royal commission in exposing the true extent of failures in NAB's risk management practices ... a symptom of cultural decadence and operational incompetence.'

The cache was shocking both in what it revealed and in how little of it had been canvassed in the royal commission. For connoisseurs of scandals and misconduct in the financial sector, it made for fascinating and compelling reading.

One incident that concerned the whistleblower was the alleged fraud perpetrated by Rosemary Rogers, former chief of staff under Andrew Thorburn and his predecessor, Cameron Clyne. During 2018 Rogers was investigated by NSW police over allegations that she had received kickbacks from events management company the Human Group to secure inflated bank contracts – kickbacks potentially amounting to $110 million worth of corporate travel. (Police subsequently froze nearly $8 million in assets owned by Rogers, including a $1 million NAB bank cheque.) At the time of writing, the case had still to come to trial.

Thorburn had done nothing illegal, but why, the whistleblower asked, had the alleged fraud been discovered only when a staff member came forward with concerns? That certainly raised questions about NAB's risk controls and auditing, and Thorburn's judgement, given it had gone on under his nose, and it spoke of a systemic blind spot in risk management.

In addition, the whistleblower was disappointed that APRA and ASIC and the royal commission had not investigated NAB's failure to fix issues with its regulatory, operational and compliance processes, which, as the leaked documents showed, had attracted 'amber' and 'red' ratings on an internal traffic-light rating system in 2018. Persistent red ratings were indicative of a breakdown in the capability of people, processes and technology inside the bank, and, based on a report dated March 2018, some of NAB's ratings had been red for at least twenty months, while others had been amber for thirty-five months.

One of the leaked documents, prepared in April 2018, revealed that NAB had made an 'error' – which it described as an 'emerging issue' – with regard to the prudential rules requiring it to report quarterly on how much capital it is holding as a measure of its financial health. (All Australian banks are legally required to put aside capital to protect themselves if things go wrong.) The 'error', made in March 2018, involved understating its risk-weighted assets by $2.8 billion, which made it look like it was in a stronger capital position than it really was. The report said that the issue would be discussed at a 'significant event review' to be held on 26 April, and then a fix would be implemented to correct the results in time for the 31 March 2018 half-year results. That 'significant event review' was just two days after NAB executive Andrew Hagger's grilling at the royal commission over why NAB staff were unlawfully falsely witnessing the documents of thousands of customers. Hagger wrote it off as 'sloppy and unprofessional' and a practice that had got out of hand inside the bank; the documents supplied by the whistleblower suggested it was due to poor systems controls and a culture that made excuses for poor behaviour.

Ongoing issues regarding NAB's compliance with anti-money-laundering and counter-terrorism finance (AML/CTF) laws were also exposed by the leaked documents. In March 2018 NAB had uncovered and reported a fresh breach of AML/CTF laws after finding a 'subset of customers' in its financial planning businesses – Antares Capital Partners and MLC Investments – had not been screened or risk rated. It said it had so far identified one thousand impacted customers and remedial actions were still under discussion. I found that astonishing in light of CBA's AUSTRAC scandal and statements NAB had previously made about AUSTRAC. A few months after the CBA scandal erupted in August 2017, a senior executive at NAB had told the media, 'The main point is that we are very confident we've got the monitoring, the oversight, the supervision we need. All our dealings with AUSTRAC are professional and open and transparent, and we're meeting all our obligations.'[1]

A separate internal document prepared in April 2018 revealed that NAB had breached its AML/CTF 'know your customer' obligations, which require banks to collect and verify certain information about their customers' identities to deter terrorists and criminals. The breaches dated back as far as 2016, and the bank still hadn't fixed them. The document deemed NAB's practices in this regard 'ineffective' in business and private banking, in consumer banking and in its wealth business.

There were also still problems in NAB Wealth's risk and controls systems relating to the detection of financial advice breaches – problems that had been identified as far back as October 2014 – including forgery, fraud and misconduct among financial planners. 'NAB had always cut close to the bone when it came to investing in systems and culling risk staff,' the whistleblower said. 'They're obsessed with keeping as many full-time staff off the balance sheet as possible in order to keep the banking analysts happy and the share price buoyant at the expense of its risk profile and control posture. Exit stage left: full-time employees. Enter stage right: consultants.'

Keeping a lid on costs was at the heart of one of Andrew Thorburn's signature strategies: in November 2017, six thousand jobs were cut – one in every five members of NAB's workforce – to reduce costs by $1 billion, boost profits and replace staff with automated systems. Sadly, the impact of cost-cutting hadn't featured prominently during the royal commission.

Ironically, the leaked documents showed that as Thorburn was publicly spruiking technology as the answer, the bank had serious issues in that area. As an example, a letter from APRA to Thorburn on 4 October 2017 summarised an IT risk review, outlining four broad areas of 'fundamental weaknesses': systems health, systems recovery, information security, and board and executive oversight.

In other words, just about everything.

*

Reading the many internal reports, it appeared that virtually no part of the bank was functioning properly. Even a core area like conduct risk was rated internally as 'unsatisfactory' — and poor conduct risk can result in regulatory fines, remediation costs, reputational damage and litigation costs. It became clear to me that many of these serious inefficiencies were the result not just of the negligence of senior executives but of the failure of the supposedly independent review processes NAB is obliged to set up, including regular financial audits conducted to show customers and shareholders that the company's accounts are in order, and APRA-supervised reviews of risk management to ensure they have effective systems in place to monitor misconduct. And at the heart of it all was a disturbingly close relationship between the bank and its theoretically impartial auditors, Ernst & Young.

Conflicts of interest in the roles of external auditors was something that especially troubled the whistleblower. At the same time as they carry out audits, so-called independent consultants — including the big four global accounting firms, KPMG, Deloitte, Ernst & Young and PwC — are often pitching for high-fee-paying consulting and advisory services to the same financial institutions. The whistleblower felt this issue of conflicts hadn't been properly investigated by the royal commission. It had emerged briefly when AMP's senior management and board were shown to have directed law firm Clayton Utz to revise numerous drafts of a report to ASIC on its behalf, but the commission hadn't dug any deeper to examine other organisations to find out if this was common practice. None of the major accounting firms had been called to give evidence at the royal commission, as they were not included in its terms of reference. That was despite the fact that the practice of combining auditing and consulting services was of widespread concern. Weeks before stepping down from his role in November 2017, ASIC's chairman, Greg Medcraft, had warned that 'declining audit quality was a sleeper' issue in Australia and could lead to an Enron-style corporate collapse.[2] In April 2019, similar concerns were raised by the UK Competition and Markets Authority, which recommended that the audit and consulting arms of the big four global accounting firms be split into separate operating units to reduce the influence of the consulting practices upon the smaller auditing divisions and avoid conflicts of interest.[3]

NAB's latest annual report showed that it had paid Ernst & Young more than $21 million for audit and non-audit work in 2018, plus another $3.9 million for its work on non-consolidated trusts. It also revealed that Ernst & Young had been allowed to carry out NAB's vital risk assessment review.

Every three years APRA requires all banks to organise a review of their risk management framework (RMF). The requirement is known as Prudential Standard CPS 220, and it states that the review must be conducted by 'operationally independent, appropriately trained and competent' people.[4] In a letter to NAB pitching to win the job, Ernst & Young spruiked the fact that it had been the bank's auditor for thirteen years and therefore had a deep understanding and knowledge of the company. While that should have rung alarm bells, APRA decided Ernst & Young was sufficiently independent.

Ernst & Young's proposal for the review, sent to NAB in 2018, outlined the rules of engagement, including that both NAB and Ernst & Young would together identify or agree on key people to interview and discuss interim findings, and that Ernst & Young would prepare a draft report with recommendations and send it to NAB management for review. Ernst & Young also offered to provide proactive end-to-end stakeholder management and early communication of findings based on a 'no surprises approach'.

Once NAB had reviewed the draft report, the letter said, Ernst & Young would 'socialise with key management'. A revised report would then be presented (along with the draft report) to NAB's board risk committee and/or the board audit committee. Finally, a working group of NAB and Ernst & Young staff would amend the document, which would then be presented to NAB's group chief risk officer.

The proposal letter was co-signed by one of the executives who signed off NAB's accounts after Ernst & Young had audited them. Another document listed the Ernst & Young staff assigned to work on the project; it included a partner who played a role in the external auditing of NAB's accounts.

Even more intriguing and alarming were the documents generated during the review, notably the draft report prepared for APRA, collections of minutes containing comments from dozens of NAB executives and directors, including Andrew Thorburn, Ken Henry and Phil Chronican, and a log of confidential notes compiled by Ernst & Young. In particular, the contrast between the language of Ernst & Young's draft report and that of its 'telling it how it is' confidential notes was stark and shocking.

Whereas the report to APRA was written in a neutral, passive style, laden with jargon which had the effect of downplaying some of the challenges NAB faced, the private observations were much more frank. For example, the draft report rated NAB's RMF design as 'adequate and appropriate', assessed its application of the RMF as 'partially effective', concluded that overall NAB 'largely' met APRA's regulatory requirements, and noted approvingly that 'NAB has made significant improvements'. In contrast, the confidential notes stated that when issues were identified internally by NAB or raised by the regulator there seemed 'to be inadequate analysis [by NAB] of the root cause of these identified weaknesses', despite the fact that proper analysis would have allowed NAB to put in 'place a suitable long-term plan that would help close these issues'. Even more damningly, the notes concluded: 'The bank focuses only on addressing the issues through Band-Aid fixes rather than investing in long-term solutions.'

Likewise, the draft report praised the introduction of 'divisional-value chain-risk management committees', which were set up to break down divisional silos, provide oversight of risk management and improve customer experience, saying, 'The benefits and intents of these committees are clear, and we consider NAB more advanced than [its] peers in the design of these arrangements.' But the Ernst & Young internal notes observed more pessimistically, 'Feedback has been mixed around the effectiveness of these committees … the mapping causes some ambiguity in terms of tracing information through to its source and may risk some information being lost,' and the committees 'seem to be causing more confusion than clarity'.

Similarly illuminating were the minutes from the interviews with senior NAB officials. NAB's general manager of consumer risk admitted that there were inconsistencies in the risk dashboards, or indicators, being produced by different divisions at NAB. In his interview, the chairman, Ken Henry, said he didn't feel exposed around credit risk but said he did feel exposed around operational risk and compliance, but that was partly because financial institutions were going through an 'unprecedented time'. Essentially, he was blaming the royal commission for making him feel that way.

Henry also confessed in his interview that he wasn't sure if NAB was better or worse in relation to compliance than when he joined the board. He acknowledged too that NAB was selling products that it would 'need to remediate in the future' and gave the example of self-managed super funds that borrowed to invest in managed funds. On risk appetite, he questioned the usefulness of risk limits, saying 'the value is really in the discussion rather than the limits themselves'. The minutes also included a statement from Henry that 'some odd appetites have been given to the board', including an appetite for some level of non-compliance, which he saw as nonsensical. 'When [is it] sometimes okay [to] break the law?' he asked. These were extraordinary statements from the chairman of a big four bank.

In his comments to the consultants, Phil Chronican, a NAB director and chairman of the board's risk committee, expressed concerns about the long delays in addressing the bank's red and amber compliance ratings. He was also frustrated that the money-laundering issues had been allowed to 'get to that point' and that the initial remediation had been insufficient. 'Had they embarked on more comprehensive plans two to three years ago, they would not have spent as much today,' he said. Clearly he understood the depth of NAB's problems.

When I read the interview the consultant had conducted with Andrew Thorburn in June 2018, I didn't know whether to laugh or cry. Thorburn's main concern was 'around risk culture and the bank becoming too risk averse' and [he] saw this as the biggest emerging risk the bank faced going forward. He also saw 'reputation risk as a major emerging risk'. When asked how he would like to see NAB's risk governance structure develop over the next three years, he said he thought the only improvement the various risk committees could make was to set aside more time for reflection. At every fourth committee meeting, he suggested, committee members could allocate one hour, without paperwork, just to 'sit on the couch and think through which risks they had not considered yet'.

Given what we had learned at the royal commission and the sanctimonius promises we'd heard from NAB executives in recent months, these revelations were truly staggering. Clearly the royal commission had left regulators and politicians with a lot of work to do in terms of highlighting negligence and, especially, ongoing conflicts of interest in the banking sector. As the whistleblower told me despairingly, 'The royal commission gave the banks' auditors and consultants a free pass. It was a shortcoming that needs to be addressed. They are the random variable in the equation. Politicians need to shed further light into their opaque world to improve certainty and confidence. If not, little will change.'

Chapter 29

A waiting game

Sweating on the verdict

THE SUMMER OF 2018–19 was heavy with portent for executives and boards of financial institutions. After a long and turbulent year of royal commission scrutiny, the bank chiefs and chairpersons, still bruised by the misconduct revelations, planned their annual Christmas holidays. For most, the break would be overshadowed by the impending release of the final report of the royal commission on 1 February 2019.

As well as the bank CEOs having copped flak in the final round of the royal commission, three of the big four banks – ANZ, Westpac and NAB – had taken a walloping from shareholders at their annual general meetings in December. (CBA's AGM had been held in September.) NAB's chief executive, Andrew Thorburn, was battling the scandal surrounding his former chief of staff, Rosemary Rogers, as well as allegations that he'd taken a luxury holiday to the exclusive Fiji island resort of Laucala that had been arranged through and partly paid for by the Human Group and Rogers, and received gifts from them. But instead of staying around to deal with this latest scandal, Thorburn told the NAB board he needed a break and would return to work for

Hayne's final report, before taking another break until March 2019. It was an inexplicable decision that drew heavy criticism from everyone except NAB's board of directors, who acquiesced.

What Thorburn and NAB's chairman, Ken Henry, didn't realise was that Henry's disdainful attitude during the final round of hearings had profoundly angered the royal commissioner. Hayne set great store by the idea that the tone of an organisation is set at the top, and Henry's and Thorburn's performances during their testimonies had reminded him of the importance of this principle. Henry had received extensive feedback about his performance in front of Hayne and had been advised to apologise publicly, but he blithely ignored the warnings and went off on his break too.

With both men out of the media glare, Hayne was working out the most effective way to deal with Henry and Thorburn, particularly after reading a media report which quoted a leaked internal NAB email urging staff to flog more home loans before 'the Xmas lull to fill our funnel'. The email went on to say, 'The banker that can land 5 apps [applications] first this week with 1 refi app [refinance application] included in that will earn 2500 NAB recognise points.'[1] Hayne was not impressed. He and his senior counsel assisting had spent the last twelve months hammering home the message that this type of bank conduct was unacceptable. It must have seemed to him that NAB and its leadership team were either slow learners or simply unwilling to change.

*

Unlike Thorburn and Henry, senior executives at ASIC didn't want to leave anything to chance before Hayne released his final report. Aware that ASIC needed to be tougher, ASIC's deputy chairman, Daniel Crennan QC – who had joined the regulator in June 2018 – decided to be proactive.

The son of former High Court judge Susan Crennan, Daniel Crennan had accepted his role at ASIC with the aim of making it a feared and respected regulator. He had got to know Hayne during his previous life as a barrister, and wanted to demonstrate to him that concrete changes were taking place at ASIC. So, after a series of discussions with ASIC's chair, James Shipton, he decided to show Hayne a copy of a report on an internal ASIC review he had led into the regulator's enforcement processes.

Crennan met Hayne on 21 December and handed him a 120-page draft containing a set of recommendations and a hefty appendix with links and references. He also briefed him directly on the report's key recommendations including the creation of a separate new 'Office of Enforcement' inside ASIC to investigate contraventions and take enforcement actions against them.

In fact, Hayne had already been made aware that ASIC was in the process of transforming. Alongside Crennan, Karen Chester had been appointed ASIC's second deputy chair. A former Treasury economist and more recently deputy chair of the Productivity Commission, Chester had co-authored the capability review into ASIC in 2015, which had been scathing of the regulator and provided a set of recommendations, many of which had been effectively ignored by ASIC's former chairman, Greg Medcraft. Chester was a force to be reckoned with. She had become well known to the commission after conducting a series of briefings to royal commission staff, including one to Michael Hodge in relation to superannuation, trustees and potential conflicts of interest. Chester was seen as an expert on superannuation, having written a groundbreaking report into the performance of superannuation in May 2018 while she was still at the Productivity Commission.

That report had exposed deep flaws, including poor governance, conflicts and underperformance.

While ASIC had been heeding lessons since the final round of hearings, a number of economists from Treasury were pushing the view in submissions and briefings to the royal commission that any radical changes to vertical integration, small-business lending or responsible lending laws would have unintended consequences and could trigger a credit crunch that would have devastating effects on the country. The banks had already put a brake on lending and it was starting to hurt. On the eve of the final report, Prime Minister Scott Morrison echoed these views in an interview with *The Age* and the *Sydney Morning Herald*, saying, 'It will be a question of what suggestions or measures [the royal commission puts] on the table but I will be very mindful that I want to see the oil that lubricates our financial system – which is access to credit – continues to flow, otherwise the consequences would be quite significant. Any major reduction in lending would hurt the economy and damage small businesses.'[2]

*

On Friday, 1 February 2019, the imperturbable Kenneth Hayne put on a dark grey suit and flew to Canberra to deliver his report to Governor-General Peter Cosgrove. As a matter of courtesy, he had agreed to meet the Treasurer Josh Frydenberg for a private briefing at which he would present him with a copy of the report.

Frydenberg invited the media to attend, and come the meeting he was beaming from ear to ear, thinking he'd got one up on the federal opposition. But Hayne is a stickler for protocol, and Frydenberg's media circus wasn't part of the deal.

'Can we please get a handshake?' a photographer asked Hayne. 'Nope,' he replied.

'Can we maybe get you just shifting [the report] to him?' another photographer asked.

Hayne shook his head vigorously from side to side. This was someone not used to being told what to do, and his silence spoke volumes. As Hayne frowned and Frydenberg's smile froze, the PR stunt became a train wreck, the awkward exchange captured on video and in photos and quickly going viral across all media platforms.

The theatrics added to the growing excitement, and the countdown began for the public release of the report at 4.20 pm on Monday, 4 February. Having got their hands on it early, Frydenberg and Scott Morrison decided to exploit this advantage over the opposition and use the weekend to review its contents and compile a response. With both sides of federal politics in pre-election mode, the government needed every advantage it could gain, especially as it had resisted a royal commission for so long.

A select group of powerful public servants – including representatives of ASIC, APRA and Treasury – were also given special access to Hayne's final report that weekend, under strict embargo. There had been considerable chatter in those circles that the final report would contain no surprises, and this intelligence proved correct. Every recommendation had been accurately anticipated by Treasury, even Hayne's recommendation to end commissions in the mortgage-broking industry.

Hayne's final report included a recommendation for an immediate capability review into APRA. During the weekend, Graeme Samuel received a call from the government asking him to consider heading a root-and-branch review of APRA, similar to the capability review that ASIC's Karen Chester had conducted back in 2015. By the time the media and some other interested parties, including the Australian Banking Association, had assembled at Parliament House to read the final report on Monday afternoon, Samuel had accepted the role, and it had been included in Frydenberg's detailed response to Hayne's recommendations.

Chapter 30

The final report

Day of reckoning

WHEN I FLEW INTO an unusually hot and sticky Canberra for the media lockup to read the final report of the royal commission before its formal release, the corridors of the press gallery were buzzing as journalists speculated one last time what might lie within. There was a general air of expectation that Hayne would recommend some corporate scalps for criminal misconduct. I wasn't so confident that this would be the case.

At 12.45 pm a group of journalists headed into the lockup. Those from the *Sydney Morning Herald*, *The Age* and the *Financial Review* were allocated room 1R3, one of a number of windowless committee rooms located in the House of Representatives. Security was tight. We had to provide photo ID and sign a witness form agreeing to the terms and conditions, including not being allowed to leave before the report was made public. We also had to hand over our mobile phones and smart watches and disable the connectivity of our laptops to ensure nothing was transmitted, broadcast or published until the embargo was lifted. Anyone who needed to go to the bathroom had to be escorted by security.

At 1 pm, we were finally given the report. We had only a little over three hours to read it and consider the government's response, so the atmosphere in our airless room was charged. As we scrutinised the seventy-six recommendations, my heart sank. It was soon clear that Hayne's report had failed to address the systemic issues that had got the banks into trouble in the first place. Despite the royal commission's scathing assessment of a sector that had presided over institutionalised theft of customer money on an industrial scale, it baulked at enforcing major structural reform of the banks or regulators. For the most part, Hayne had decided to keep things as they were. It meant there would be no new financial services regulator, no recommendation for financial services giants to dismantle their vertically integrated models, no radical changes to superannuation, and no changes to responsible lending laws or small-business lending.

Overall, the final outcome was disappointing.

*

In hindsight, Hayne's report was never going to upset the status quo. Hayne was and is a member of the Melbourne establishment. He'd been carefully handpicked by Malcolm Turnbull. The Commonwealth Treasury, a conservative and powerful organ, had also backed Hayne as the best person to lead the inquiry; he had a good reputation, a good brain and was a safe pair of hands. Turnbull and Treasury had just wanted to plug the holes in a leaking boat, nothing more.

Hayne had agreed to the government's strict budget, tight terms of reference and short twelve-month time frame. That was far less time than it took to complete the royal commissions into trade unions, which ran for eighteen months, and Institutional Responses to Child Sexual Abuse, which ran for five years. Over the course of the hearings, there were numerous calls for Hayne to request an extension to the royal commission, but he refused point blank, citing risks to the economy, as he noted in his final report: 'I must execute those tasks conscious of the fact that the banking system is a central artery in the body of the economy. Defects and obstructions in the artery can have very large effects. Likewise, prolonged injections of doubt and uncertainty can affect performance.'

These comments provided a profound insight into Hayne's way of thinking. It showed that he wasn't prepared to do anything that might create doubt or uncertainty in the financial system, even if that meant allowing some important areas to escape scrutiny. It meant he didn't have enough time to call up several executives and directors, such as CBA's former CEO Ian Narev, ex-head of wealth Annabel Spring and former chairman David Turner; AMP's former chair Catherine Brenner and former CEO Craig Meller; and the chairs of Westpac or ANZ. Nor did he have time to investigate the Macquarie Group or call up the former chairman of ASIC Greg Medcraft. Some financial services companies escaped scrutiny altogether. Pay-day lenders were not examined, nor were buy-now-pay-later businesses such as Afterpay. There was no time to discuss bank remediation programs or forensically examine the crucial $2.7 trillion superannuation industry, including the $700 billion self-managed super fund sector, which is opaque and has its own set of challenges.

Hayne's refusal to extend the deadline also meant the royal commission had failed to give the many thousands of victims of banking malpractice who had lodged submissions an opportunity to tell their stories in a legally protected forum. The twenty-seven victims who did get the chance to speak publicly were chosen, according to Hayne, as being 'reasonably illustrative of kinds of conduct and general issues' emerging from the commission, but he conceded in his report that 'the choices that were made will have disappointed those not chosen'.

Partly to save time, Hayne had left it to the industry to provide details of its misconduct, instead of serving subpoenas to key players, which would have demonstrated a tougher stance. His trust in the financial institutions to do the right thing seemed misplaced, given that it was a sector that had grown fat on dishonesty, and it meant some scandals, either by accident or design, were left off the institutions' lists, and remained unexamined.

*

So perhaps it wasn't surprising that the final report focussed on easy targets. Hayne's most controversial recommendation was aimed at the mortgage-broking sector, which arranges more than half of all new home loans. Hayne proposed a ban on all upfront commissions and trailing commissions on new loans and suggested that customers should pay mortgage brokers an upfront fee instead. When I read that recommendation, I was surprised because it was a plan that would penalise mortgage brokers and benefit the banks. Customers would most likely go straight to the banks to obtain their loans in order to avoid paying the fee, and the banks would save an estimated $2.4 billion a year they were currently paying brokers in commissions. It seemed odd that Hayne hadn't recommended that the banks should pay the fee, instead of the customer.

Vertical integration had been a root cause of misconduct, but Hayne decided it was too difficult to tackle. 'Ultimately, whether there should be a separation between the manufacture or sale of financial products and the provision of financial advice will depend on whether the benefits of such a separation would outweigh the costs.' While agreeing that separation would reduce conflicts, Hayne said it would 'involve significant disruption to that industry, and the financial services industry more broadly'. This conclusion ignored the overwhelming evidence that conflicts can't be controlled, and there was no better illustration of this than a report on vertical integration compiled by ASIC in January 2018, which found that 75 per cent of the customer arrangements it reviewed from the big four banks and AMP were not in the best interests of clients.[1]

On many fronts, Hayne's views were consistent with those of Treasury, and he had certainly heeded the warnings Treasury had made in its various submissions, briefings and background papers that anything that might negatively impact credit could harm the economy. For example, he refrained from imposing restrictions on mortgage lending and small-business lending, despite the conflicts in these areas revealed in the royal commission, including introducer programs and staff referral bonuses, and the apparent flaws in establishing realistic benchmarks for assessing household expenses and income, which had helped fuel the property boom.

*

The royal commission had spent a year hearing about the many ways in which government regulators had failed in their duty to regulate the financial services industry. Hayne's solution was to give them more powers and more work in the hope that they would start to do their job more efficiently. Again, that was placing a lot of faith in institutions that had previously let down the public.

He did, however, include one firm caveat: 'Although I do not now recommend the establishment of a specialist civil enforcement agency, ASIC's progress in reforming its enforcement function should be closely monitored. If, over the coming years, it becomes apparent that ASIC is not sufficiently enforcing the laws within its remit, or if the size of its remit comes at the expense of its litigation capability, further consideration should be given to developing a specialist agency.'

In other words, if ASIC continued to play the timid cop, it should be stripped of its enforcement powers. It was a great pity that Hayne hadn't recommended a similar structural remedy for financial institutions who failed to change their ways.

*

In his interim report, Hayne had asked some tough questions about the use of financial incentives, including big salaries, bonuses and targets, to drive business. But despite spending so much time over the previous year discussing greed and the lack of will on the part of boards to cut executive bonuses in the face of scandals, his solution was to leave it to the remuneration committees of those boards to continue to consider misconduct and compliance when setting bonuses, and for APRA to take a more active role in supervising the implementation of remuneration frameworks by the entities it regulates. In other words, little change.

When it came to the use of targets and bonuses to motivate front-line staff, Hayne also went soft, recommending only an annual review of procedures and systems. Although he wrote in his report that 'culture, governance and remuneration march together', he nevertheless left it up to the institutions to address this. 'Making improvements in each area is the responsibility of financial services entities,' he said. It was a common and disappointing refrain of the report.

Hayne tried to appear tough on financial advisers, calling for a ban on grandfathered commissions, but he was preaching to the converted, as the big four banks had already taken steps to reduce or eliminate such payments.

*

Over many decades hundreds of thousands of customers – possibly millions – have been ripped off by shonky financial advisers, dodgy financial and insurance products or the fees-for-no-service rort. Farmers have lost their farms, small businesses have gone belly-up, and individuals have been financially destroyed. Consequently, many observers hoped a royal commission into financial misconduct would address compensation and remediation for these victims.

Leading banking analyst Brett Le Mesurier gave me an estimate of at least $10 billion due to be paid out by the big four banks and AMP in consumer refunds, reviews and litigation. CBA, which has been embroiled in the most scandals in recent years, is expected to have the highest remediation payout at $3 billion, including its $700 million AUSTRAC fine. There is, however, little transparency about how this money will be repaid by the financial institutions, or when.

Though the royal commission was supposed to be for the benefit of the people, the report barely mentioned remediation. Hayne proposed a compensation scheme of last resort, but little else. That meant the various compensation schemes set up by the banks over the previous few years wouldn't be scrutinised to ensure they were assessing people fairly and paying out promptly.

Nor did Hayne look at whether victims of misconduct should also be compensated for their pain and suffering. The royal commission had received numerous submissions from farmers who had been kicked off their land after generations of farming and suffered not just financial devastation but mental anguish, exacerbated by aggressive attempts by the banks to claim repayment.

It was a missed opportunity, another glaring omission.

*

The most startling part of the report was Hayne's dressing-down of NAB executives Ken Henry and Andrew Thorburn. As well as singling them out for a public shaming, Hayne noted that, with regard to the behaviour of its most senior executives, 'NAB stands apart from the other three major banks'. He was 'persuaded that Mr Comyn, CEO of CBA, is well aware of the size and nature of the tasks that lie ahead of CBA'. He was also positive about Shayne Elliott's commitment to the tasks 'that lie ahead of ANZ'. And although Westpac had taken a combative approach to ASIC, Hayne said he did not doubt that Brian Hartzer 'has sought to "reset" [Westpac's] relationship with ASIC'.

NAB was a different story. 'Having heard from the CEO, Mr Thorburn, and the chair, Dr Henry, I am not as confident as I would wish to be that the lessons of the past have been learned … Overall, my fear – that there may be a wide gap between the public face NAB seeks to show and what it does in practice – remains.'

He made his disapproval of Henry obvious: 'I thought it telling that Dr Henry seemed unwilling to accept any criticism of how the [NAB] board had dealt with some issues.' He also condemned Thorburn, writing, 'I thought it telling that Mr Thorburn treated all issues of fees for no service as nothing more than carelessness combined with system deficiencies when the total amount to be repaid by NAB and NULIS on this account is likely to be more than $100 million.'

The commissioner's censure of Thorburn and Henry sealed the fate of both men. At the same time, Hayne was sending an important message to directors and senior management at other institutions that they were on notice and that their words played a fundamental role in setting the culture of their organisations.

Hayne's comments about Henry and Thorburn triggered a frenzy of media speculation about their futures. The day after the report was released, Thorburn decided to cancel his long service leave and try to repair the damage. The bank drafted a joint media statement, to be lodged with the ASX in time for the market's opening on Tuesday, 5 February. In it Thorburn said, 'As the CEO, this is very hard to read, and does not reflect who I am or how I am leading, nor the change that is occurring inside our bank … While we have made mistakes, I believe there is a lot of evidence that we are making sustainable and serious change to once again regain the trust of all our customers.'[2] Like Thorburn, Henry found it difficult to accept Hayne's criticism, saying, 'I am disappointed that the Commissioner formed this view. I know that it is not so. The board and I have reflected deeply on those and other issues and, as I have said previously, we take them very seriously.'

By Thursday, 7 February, as calls for Thorburn's and Henry's heads reached fever pitch, both men were in constant contact with the board about their positions. Eventually a decision was reached, and they agreed it was time to go. At 3.35 pm, NAB's shares were placed in a temporary trading halt pending an announcement. To those of us in the media, it was obvious the halt related to leadership changes. Speculation was rife it would be Thorburn *or* Henry, but not both.

At 5.14 pm a three-page statement was lodged with the ASX confirming that both men had resigned. New Zealand–born NAB director Philip Chronican, a former executive from ANZ and Westpac who'd missed out on the top job at both banks, would step in as chairman of NAB and acting CEO until a replacement was found.

The royal commission had turned Thorburn's and Henry's lives upside down. Thorburn's wallet took a battering too. He was granted a $1.04 million severance pay, but the NAB board cancelled his performance rights, which were estimated to have been worth $22 million.

*

Perhaps the most telling verdict on the report came on the day after its release, when investors added more than $19 billion to the combined market values of the big four banks, AMP and IOOF – the biggest one-day gain in years for these financial giants.

The report clearly pleased executives and boards, including AMP director John Fraser, who until 31 July 2018 had been the head of Treasury. Fraser had joined the ranks of AMP on 8 August 2018 as a key proponent of vertical integration, bringing with him a powerful network of contacts in Treasury and the government.

From the day the final report was publicly released, it became a political football. Labor went out on the hustings, calling for better whistleblower protections and reminding the community how Labor had backed a royal commission long before the Coalition was dragged kicking and screaming into calling one. Shorten wanted some real accountability, saying, 'Banks somehow seem to think that community attitudes don't apply to them ... I think if no one out of the banks goes to jail, if no one gets prosecuted or charged, I think Australians would say there's been a cover-up.'[3]

The two major parties began trying to outdo each other with proposed responses to the report. The Coalition launched a $30 million compensation scheme of last resort to compensate victims with unresolved complaints going back as far as 1 January 2008, to be administered by the industry-funded external-dispute resolution body, the Australian Financial Complaints Authority. It would include compensation of up to $500,000 for consumers, $1 million for small businesses and $2 million for primary producers. Labor upped the ante, pledging a $640 million Fairness Fund to help victims of financial misconduct. It said it would double the number of financial counsellors from five hundred to one thousand; they would offer free help to victims and rely on federal and state grants for funding. It also promised to increase the number of community lawyers by two hundred, again to help victims of financial crimes. 'Labor will make the big banks pay what they owe. We will fight for victims to get what they are owed,' Shorten said.[4] The catch was this would only happen if Labor won the impending federal election.

*

Hayne's report did contain many powerful recommendations that will improve the system if they are properly implemented. Banks and financial institutions have been put on notice. As Reserve Bank Governor Philip Lowe told Federal Parliament on 17 August 2018, 'Sunlight is acting as a very good disinfectant here.'[5] Every financial institution is spending more on compliance costs, and since the release of the final report all banks have announced profit downgrades on the back of increased remediation provisions. Scores of directors and executives have lost their jobs, some organisations are mortally wounded – including Freedom Insurance, which closed – grandfathered commissions are dead and financial advisers are in chaos.

Vertical integration might have survived, but most of the banks have sold their life insurance businesses and flagged that they want to get rid of their wealth management arms. ANZ is in the process of selling its wealth management business to IOOF, CBA and NAB have flagged that they want to spin off their wealth businesses to reduce the risk of more scandals, and even Westpac, after defending it during the royal commission, has decided to offload its financial advice business.

The public shaming of APRA and ASIC at the royal commission has spurred both into action. APRA is finally flexing its muscles. After years of putting up with non-compliance, conflicts and failures to meet regulatory imposed deadlines, in December APRA took legal action in the Federal Court against IOOF's chief executive Chris Kelaher, general counsel Gary Riordan, chairman George Venardos, chief financial officer David Coulter, and general manager of risk and compliance Paul Vine, seeking to disqualify them on the basis they were not fit to run a superannuation fund. It also requested IOOF restructure several entities to meet its obligations under the law – a move that sent shudders through the financial services sector. It was the first legal action of this type APRA had taken in a decade. In April, it also set out a new enforcement approach to hold organisations to account, after an internal review by its new deputy chairman, John Lonsdale, who had joined APRA from a senior role in Treasury in September 2018.

ASIC is also making the right noises. It has appointed a few new gung-ho commissioners who are committed to changing its culture to become more enforcement focussed and announced it has started more than forty investigations and reviews of alleged corporate civil and criminal breaches – some referred by Hayne, some relating to case studies raised during the royal commission. In May 2019, ASIC's deputy chairman, Daniel Crennan, reinforced the regulator's new hardline approach, telling an ASIC annual forum that in the post–royal commission world enforceable undertakings are 'fairly unlikely to be provided' by the regulator because they do not require an admission of liability.[6] ASIC will be keen to throw a few bodies on the funeral pyre and use tough new sanctions introduced for white-collar offences. Executives will now face maximum jail terms of fifteen years for criminal offences and companies will be liable for fines of up to $525 million per civil violation. But if ASIC goes for middle managers, instead of senior executives and directors, it will have little impact.

*

The reset is now upon us. How that will look will depend on many factors, including how successful the lobby groups are in watering down the royal commission's recommendations, and how determined the regulators are to prosecute after the spotlight has gone and further political developments play out.

The six principles outlined in the final report of the royal commission are that institutions and individuals need to:

- obey the law;
- not mislead or deceive;
- act fairly;
- provide services that are fit for purpose;
- deliver services with reasonable care and skill; and
- when acting for another, to do so in the best interests of that other.

These principles will only be effective if the law is applied rigorously, penalties are big enough and the regulators are willing to put executives and directors behind bars. Only then will fear override greed.

As Hayne said in his interim report, 'Too often, the answer seems to be greed – the pursuit of short-term profit at the expense of basic standards of honesty. How else is charging continuing advice fees to the dead to be explained?' Sadly, it seems to be in few people's interests to change bank culture. Greed has become part of the economic fabric. It accounts for a huge part of the economy and the sharemarket, and, as we have seen, there are deep links between the banks, the regulatory authorities, the administrators and the political class. Ex-NSW Premier Mike Baird is now a senior executive of NAB; former Queensland premier Anna Bligh runs the peak lobby group for the banks, the Australian Banking Association; Bob Carr did a stint at Macquarie; and when it comes to ministerial advisers, the list of people who have crossed over to the financial and banking sector is too long to include. The meshing of the political class into the finance sector both reflects the power of the banks and, in turn, contributes to the power of the banks. It is why lobbying by the banks has been so effective and made them so successful: today the big four banks make a combined net profit of $30 billion a year – which places them among the most profitable banks in the world.

Of course, bad behaviour isn't isolated to Australian banks. In Europe and the United States similar misconduct has taken place. A report by Hong Kong consultancy group Quinlan & Associates estimated that since 2009 US and European regulators have slapped the top fifty global banks with fines to the tune of US$342 billion for misconduct, rigging markets, money laundering, mis-selling financial products, misreporting, misleading investors and trading scandals. That figure will rise to US$400 billion by 2020.[7]

For now, though, the Australian banks – and their massive profits – are safe. When the Coalition won the election on 18 May, the big four banks added a combined $27 billion in market value. Days later they had another win when APRA loosened regulations on mortgage credit. Whereas it had previously stipulated minimum requirements for borrowers seeking loans, it was now leaving it up to the banks to set their own minimum assessment rates – a vote of confidence that the banks had learned their lessons on irresponsible lending.

But have the banks learned their lessons? What will happen as memories of the royal commission fade and media and political attention turns elsewhere? Will the banks revert to arrogance and greed? Will the regulators slip back into their old ways of being timid and too trusting? Will peak bodies and industry lobby groups water down the recommendations – as they always have? Will the media be strong enough to report on financial misconduct? And will whistleblowers be able to come forward without facing criminal prosecution?

In the current environment, speaking up is becoming increasingly difficult. In June 2019, a series of Australian Federal Police raids on two media organisations made global news as a serious violation of press freedom in Australia. At the same time, ATO whistleblower Richard Boyle talked publicly about the personal toll of being charged with sixty-six offences that could result in a 161-year prison sentence if he is found guilty – a longer sentence than meted out to some of our worst serial killers – even though he had initially spoken out under the provisions of the *Public Interest Disclosure Act*, which is supposed to protect whistleblowers. It seems truth-telling is being punished in frightening ways.

Epilogue

As Senator John 'Wacka' Williams arrived at Parliament House on the morning of 13 February 2019, it was a day like no other. His wife, Nancy, was sitting next to him in the back seat of the car as he fiddled nervously with his favourite blue silk tie. Wacka was set to disappear from Canberra. At 5 pm sharp, he would stand up in the Senate and give the most important speech of his life, his valedictory speech. It was his goodbye to politics after a stellar eleven-year career, a move hastened by a recent diagnosis of Parkinson's disease.

Sitting in the chamber later that day and staring at his watch, it struck Wacka that the timing of his departure was serendipitous. The royal commission was over, the final report had been released, and the voiceless had, to a degree, been heard. He was disappointed the royal commission hadn't called for structural separation of vertically integrated models, which had been the cause of so many conflicts and problems. But he was thankful the inquiry had gone some way towards addressing the problems of farmers and scrutinised the financial sector's many failings.

As he began to speak, he glanced up at the people he'd invited to witness the moment, all of whom had contributed to his legacy. He smiled up at the front row of the president's gallery, where his wife, three children and grandchildren were seated. I was in the row behind them, along with media friends Janine Perrett from Sky News and the *Daily Telegraph*'s Piers Akerman.

Other invitees included CBA's Matt Comyn, who had visited Wacka at his farm in Inverell shortly after becoming CEO in an attempt to earn the trust of one of the bank's toughest critics; ASIC's Daniel Crennan, who was flying the flag for the regulator; and Sean Hughes, whom Wacka had met in 2013 and had recommended to various financial services ministers for the role of chairman of ASIC; CBA whistleblower Jeff Morris; bank victims; and some of the country's most respected journalists, including the *Financial Review*'s political editor Phillip Coorey, ABC's *AM* presenter, Sabra Lane, and veteran journalist Michelle Grattan. Prime Minister Scott Morrison was also present, as were former Prime Minister Tony Abbott, Deputy Prime Minister Michael McCormack and the former Nationals' leader and Deputy Prime Minister Barnaby Joyce. It was a rare achievement for any backbencher to pull in a current prime minister, never mind a former one as well.

But Wacka was no ordinary backbencher. He'd come into politics with firsthand experience of going up against the Commonwealth Bank, with its deep pockets and ruthless culture. He understood better than most that the necessary foundations of financial organisations – trust, customer service and risk management – were deficient. During his political career he had acted without fear or favour to help other hard-working battlers like himself. Along the way, he'd exposed wrongdoing and never compromised himself or his beliefs. Years before it was popular, he had pushed for a royal commission into banks and the financial sector.

Wacka told the crowd of onlookers he'd had a fortunate life, 'I never had to go to war. Perhaps the only wars I've fought were in this building,' he said. 'Had a few wins, had a few losses.'

He talked about his family, colleagues, the media and collaborations with journalists like myself. 'In this job, you get to meet some great people, and, Piers Akerman, you're one of them,' he said. 'But one of the great things Piers Akerman did was many years ago in Adelaide at *The Advertiser*. He gave a young lady a start in the media. Her name was Adele Ferguson. Adele, we've done a lot of work together and we've achieved a lot together … I will cherish the memories. As Adele said to me, "When the media and politics teams up, it becomes very powerful."

'When I first met with Jeff Morris, the whistleblower from Commonwealth Financial Planning, he asked, "Senator, what should we do?" I said, "I think you should give it to the media." He asked, "Do you know anyone?" I said, "Yes, I do." I handed the story to Adele Ferguson: nine hundred pages for her to read. Out of that came some changes for the betterment of all Australia, and a Gold Walkley Award for Adele Ferguson. Well done! You'll have to extend your house soon, Adele, to fit all the awards in!'

I teared up, feeling a sense of pride at all that we had achieved, but also sad that Australia had lost one of its greatest politicians.

Then, as he signed off, Wacka was given a standing ovation – another rarity in politics.

Endnotes

Unless otherwise indicated, all quotes in the text are from interviews conducted by the author for this book.

Prologue

1   Australian Banking Association press conference, Anna Bligh responds to the release of the banking royal commission's interim report, 28 September 2018.
2   Janine Perrett, 'Opinion: Banking royal commission uncovers more than a few bad apples', *Courier Mail*, 28 April 2018, p.34.

PART 1 – WHAT GOES ON IN THE SHADOWS

Chapter 1: Caught in a trap

1   Bob Hawke, 1983 federal election speech, Sydney, 16 February 1983.
2   Paul Kelly, *The March of Patriots*, University of Melbourne Press, Melbourne, 2009, p.4.
3   Gareth Boreham, 'Borrowers knew the risk, says Westpac', *The Age*, 23 May 1991, p.6.
4   Anne Lampe, 'Farmer thought bank "got" witness', *Sydney Morning Herald*, 21 May 1998, p.29.
5   *Williams & Others v Commonwealth Bank of Australia* [1999] NSWCA 345.
6   Anne Lampe, 'Lender gets a franc reappraisal from Court of Appeal', *Sydney Morning Herald*, 28 September 1999, p.34.
7   John McLennan, *Bankers, Bastards and other Unarmed Bandits*, unpublished memoir, p.14.

8 Ibid., p.4

9 Paul McLean, *Bankers and Bastards*, Hudson, Hawthorn, 1992, p.4.

10 Ibid, pp.37–50.

11 Quentin Dempster, *Whistleblowers*, ABC Books, 1997, p.24.

12 Ibid., p.32.

13 Max Walsh, 'The Westpac Letters: Reasons behind the fight to prevent publication', *Sydney Morning Herald*, 11 March 1991, p.17.

14 Mark Beyer and Sarah Mills, 'Martin cautious on bank attacks', *Financial Review*, 19 March 1991, p.40.

15 Paul Cleary, 'Claims of fraud dismissed', *Sydney Morning Herald*, 19 March 1991, p.25.

16 Ibid., p.viii.

Chapter 2: Diversify or perish

1 Kerry O'Brien, *Keating*, Allen & Unwin, Sydney, 2015, p.322.

2 Ibid, p.323.

3 Simon Lloyd, 'Which bank has a new identity?', *Financial Review*, 2 September 1991, p.39.

4 Roger Hogan, 'Commonwealth result encourages sale plans', *BRW*, 8 September 1993, p.28.

5 Sue Neales, 'Bank facing revolt over country cuts', *The Age*, 7 January 1994, p.3.

6 John Quiggin, 'The "People's Bank": the privatisation of the Commonwealth Bank and the case for a new publicly owned bank', *Australian Options*, 30 March 2001, p.3.

Chapter 3: A soft touch

1 Virginia Trioli, 'ASC lists achievements of its first year's work', *The Age*, 20 December 1991, p.18.

2 Anne Lampe, 'Corporate fighters may clash', *Sydney Morning Herald*, 9 March 1992, p.21.

3 David Walker, 'A slanging match worth watching rouses a laid-back Duffy', *The Age*, 11 September 1992, p.19.

4   Tony Kaye, 'Banks facing revenue, profits crunch: Argus', *Financial Review*, 17 June 1993, p.38.

5   Denise Cullen, 'Are you being served?', *Sydney Morning Herald*, 24 July 2000, p.7.

6   Sean Aylmer, 'Banks try to restore reputation', *The Age*, 3 August 1998, p.21.

7   Alan Kohler, 'The men who would eat each other', *Financial Review*, 12 September 1998, p.12.

Chapter 4: Bigger is better?

1   Anthony Hughes and Kate Askew, 'Tempting the trident', *Sydney Morning Herald*, 11 March 2000, p.1.

2   Mark Westfield, 'Hand over fist', *The Australian*, 11 March 2000, p.31.

3   Tim Boreham, 'The Mega bank "good for the nation": Jobs to go, but chief defends deal', *The Australian*, 11 March 2000, p. 25.

4   'The Cohen Brown Rule', document supplied to author by Marty Cohen.

5   Andrew J. Macey, 'When incentives go wrong', LinkedIn, 7 August, 2017; www.linkedin.com/pulse/when-incentives-go-wrong-andrew-j-macey/.

6   Cohen Brown, Onebankism; see https://web.archive.org/web/20030603194724/http://www.cohenbrown.com:80/promotional.htm.

7   AAP, 'Banker gets five years for $19m theft', *Financial Review*, 30 October 2003, p.20.

8   Anonymous email to author, 24 June 2013.

9   James Kirby, 'Which Bank? Why morale at the Commonwealth Bank is sinking', *BRW*, July 2004.

10 CBA Annual Report, 2005, p.4.

11 O'Brien, p.332.

12 Commonwealth Bank, Ralph Norris profile; www.commbank.com.au/about-us/shareholders/pdfs/2005-asx/140605-Ralph-Norris-bio.pdf.

13 Michael Sainsbury, 'Marty Cohen: the man behind CBA's sales culture unveiled', Michael West.com.au, 11 May 2018.

Chapter 5: Giving with one hand ...

1 Duncan Hughes, 'How CBA stepped up for Storm Financial', *Financial Review*, 11 June 2009, p.1.

2 Adele Ferguson, 'Easy lending raises hard questions', *The Australian*, 31 January 2008, p.1.

3 Adele Ferguson, 'Ex-gang boss takes Opes hunt abroad', *The Australian*, 8 April 2008, p.1.

4 Adele Ferguson, 'Macquarie in the spotlight amid $5bn refinancing fears', *The Australian*, 17 September 2008, p.38.

5 ASIC media release 08-202, 'Enquiries into market manipulation', 17 September 2008.

6 Quoted in Stephen Lunn, 'Crikey, website changes its spots', *The Australian*, 19 September 2008, p.3.

7 Greg Baxter, 'Adele Ferguson deserves an apology: News Ltd', *Crikey*, 19 September 2008.

8 Quoted in Lunn, 'Crikey, website changes its spots'.

9 Stephen Mayne, 'Fur flies over Macquarie analyst coverage', 2 February 2010; www.maynereport.com/articles/2008/09/19-1059-7237.html.

10 Mark Hawthorne, 'ASIC in rumour raids', *The Age*, 14 January 2009, p.24.

11 Senate Debates, Senator John Williams' speech 'Matters of Public Interest: Storm Financial Ltd', 25 November 2009; www.openaustralia.org.au/senate/?id=2009-11-25.33.

12 ASIC media release, 'Directors of Storm Financial penalised for breach of duties', 22 March 2018.

13 Tony Raggatt, 'Storm Financial heading back to court to appeal judgment', *Townsville Bulletin*, 25 April 2018.

Chapter 6: Profit before people

1   ASIC letter to Tim Gunning, General Manager, Wealth Management
    Commonwealth Financial Planning and Financial Wisdom –
    surveillance findings from Darren Williams, director compliance
    financial services at ASIC, 29 February 2008.
2   Adele Ferguson, 'ASIC process in need of change', *The Age*, 11 June
    2013, p.28.
3   Economics Legislation Committee, Senate Estimates, 4 June 2013.

Chapter 7: 'Banking Bad'

1   Adele Ferguson and Sarah Danckert, 'Committee hears of CBA's
    $8.2 billion "fraud"', *The Age*, 13 November 2015, p.23.
2   John Durie, 'Pointless inquiry', *The Australian*, 21 June 2013, p.28.
3   Adele Ferguson, joint ABC/Fairfax investigation, 'Banking Bad', *Four
    Corners*, 5 May 2014, www.abc.net.au/4corners/banking-bad/5433156
    (for replay and transcript).
4   Adele Ferguson and Mario Christodoulou, 'Rollo Sherriff and
    Meridien Wealth: How a rock-solid institution backed impenitent
    maverick', *Sydney Morning Herald*, 3 May 2014, p.1.
5   Adele Ferguson, 'ASIC to feel heat over "star" planner', *The Age*,
    7 May 2014, p.28.
6   Tony Boyd, 'ASIC roasts CommBank execs', *Financial Review*, 6 June
    2014, p.60.

Chapter 8: Reluctant concessions

1   Senate Standing Committees on Economics, *The Performance of
    the Australian Securities and Investment Commission*, 2014, Executive
    Summary.
2   Ibid, p.xix.
3   Ibid, pp.xxi and 179.
4   Senate Economics References Committee hearing, 10 June 2014.
5   Ibid, p.20.

6 Parliamentary Joint Committee on Corporations and Financial Services, *Inquiry into Financial Products and Services in Australia*, November 2009.

7 Ben Butler, 'CBA's Ian Narev on holiday while planning scandal boiled over', *The Age*, 4 July 2014, p.4.

8 Adele Ferguson, 'Narev needs to speak up and soon for CBA's good', *Sydney Morning Herald*, 2 July 2014, p.23.

9 Adele Ferguson and Ben Butler, 'Planners weigh in on royal commission CBA scandal, Kennett joins chorus', *The Age*, 3 July 2014, p.8.

10 Century Private Wealth, 'FPA calls for full compensation of CBA clients', 20 October 2016.

11 Adele Ferguson and Ben Butler, 'Banking scandal compensation scheme open to 400,000 customers CBA sorry "too little, too late"', *The Age*, 4 July 2014, p.1.

Chapter 9: Flawed schemes

1 Adele Ferguson and Ben Butler, 'Down the hole: The silver doughnut that left a big hole', *Sydney Morning Herald*, 2 August 2014, p.4; Adele Ferguson and Ben Butler, 'Macquarie advisers used "cheat" document', *The Age*, 2 August 2014, p.3.

2 Pat McGrath and Michael Janda, 'Senate inquiry demands royal commission into Commonwealth Bank, ASIC', ABC News online, 27 June 2014.

3 Adele Ferguson and Ruth Williams, 'Victims seek olive branch from ANZ over Timbercorp collapse', *The Age*, 8 November 2014, p.1.

4 Adele Ferguson and Ruth Williams, 'Victims seek olive branch from ANZ over Timbercorp collapse', *Sydney Morning Herald*, 8 November 2014, p.6.

5 Georgia Wilkins and Yolanda Redrup, 'ANZ faces financial scandal over Timbercorp', *The Age*, 12 November 2014, p.24.

6 Peter Whish-Wilson, press release, 'Timbercorp and the MIS Senate Inquiry: this is just the beginning', 12 November 2014.

Chapter 10: Trouble on the Death Star

1   APRA, *Report into Irregular Currency Options Trading at the National Australia Bank*, 23 April 2004, p. 6.

2   Andrew Hagger, 'Memorandum for group risk return management Committee', p.111.

3   Adele Ferguson and Ruth Williams, 'NAB compensation takes years after investment nightmare', *Sydney Morning Herald*, 21 February 2015, p.1.

4   Adele Ferguson and Ruth Williams, 'ASIC allowed NAB to check and alter media release into bank's Wealth's Navigator errors', *Sydney Morning Herald*, 20 February 2015.

5   Adele Ferguson, 'NAB's dream-destroying death star', *The Age*, 21 March 2015, p.1.

Chapter 11: Shooting the messenger

1   Adele Ferguson and Sarah Danckert, 'Boiler room throws customers to the wolves: IOOF sacks whistleblower', 20 June 2015, *Sydney Morning Herald*, p.1.

2   Adele Ferguson and Sarah Danckert, 'IOOF scandal sparks calls for royal commission: Finance wrongdoing by staff', *Sydney Morning Herald*, 22 June 2015, p.23.

3   ASIC media release, 'ASIC's inquiry into IOOF', 8 July 2016.

4   Michael Roddan, 'IOOF looks to future as ASIC drops inquiry', *The Australian*, 9 July 2016, p.28.

5   Adele Ferguson, 'Again, ASIC punishes with velvet gloves', *The Age*, 9 July 2016, p.2.

Chapter 12: Claims denied

1   Adele Ferguson, 'Money for Nothing', *Four Corners*, ABC TV, 7 March 2016.

2   Adele Ferguson, 'On protecting whistleblowers', keynote address to the 2016 Press Freedom Australia Dinner, Sydney, 6 May 2016.

Chapter 13: Battle lines

1   Phillip Coorey and Patrick Durkin, 'Turnbull tells banks to clean themselves up', *Financial Review*, 7 April 2016, p.1.

2   Question Time, ABC TV, 18 April 2016; see also 'Turnbull and Morrison's greatest hits on royal commission' at www.chrisbowen.net.

3   Matthew Knott, 'Shorten's banking call a "populist whinge"', *Sydney Morning Herald*, 8 August 2016, p.7.

4   Australian Government, *Fit for the Future: A Capability Review of the Australian Securities and Investments Commission*, December 2015.

5   Doorstop interview with Scott Morrison, Sydney, 11 April 2016, Treasury Transcripts.

6   Michael Bennett and Richard Gluyas, 'Banks respond to PM's censure', *The Australian*, 22 April 2016, p.23.

Chapter 14: Banksters

1   https://twitter.com/AUSTRAC/status/892934753967513600.

2   AUSTRAC media release, 'AUSTRAC seeks civil penalty orders against CBA', 3 August 2017.

3   Concise statement, *CEO of AUSTRAC v CBA*, Federal Court, 3 August 2017, p.6.

4   Michael Evans, 'Police "follow the money" in laundering case and bust cocaine supply ring', *Sydney Morning Herald*, 12 November 2017.

5   Andrew Tillett, James Eyers, Sally Patten and James Frost, 'Morrison warns all options open', *Financial Review*, 9 August 2017, p.1.

6   James Frost, Andrew Tillett, Sally Patten and James Eyers, 'Scott Morrison warns Commonwealth Bank over money laundering scandal', *Financial Review*, 8 August 2017, p.1.

7   Andrew Tillett, James Eyers, Sally Patten and James Frost, 'Morrison warns all options open'.

8   CBA media release, 'Statement by the Chairman of the Commonwealth Bank of Australia, Catherine Livingstone AO, on executive remuneration', 8 August 2017.

9   Adele Ferguson, 'Watchdog rips into banks on trust deficit', *The Age*,
    12 August 2017, p.2.

Chapter 15: About-turn

1   Paul Karp, Michael McGowan and Melissa Davey, 'Australia's PM
    wants marriage equality by Christmas after "overwhelming" vote',
    The Guardian, 15 November 2017.

2   Mark Kenny and Jacqueline Maley, 'Blizzard of changes likely for bill',
    Sydney Morning Herald, 10 November 2017, p.4.

3   Adele Ferguson, 'Banking royal commission nears', *Financial Review*,
    20 November 2017, p.38.

4   Ibid.

5   Sharri Markson, 'Turnbull Cabinet discusses an about-face on
    holding a Royal Commission into Australia's banks', *Daily Telegraph*,
    22 November 2017, p.1.

6   Mark Kenny, James Massola and Clancy Yeates, 'PM dogged by leaks
    and rebellion by the banks', *Sydney Morning Herald*, 24 November 2017,
    p.1.

7   Phillip Coorey, 'Nats go rogue after Qld loss', *Financial Review*,
    27 November 2017, p.1.

8   CBA media release, 'ASX announcement: Major banks unite to call
    for certainty and stability', 30 November 2017.

9   Mark Kenny, 'Banks face commission after Turnbull caves', *Sydney
    Morning Herald*, 1 December 2017, p.1.

10 '"Mistake" not calling royal commission earlier: Turnbull', video,
    Sydney Morning Herald, 22 April 2018.

11 Paul Karp and Gareth Hutchens, 'Malcolm Turnbull orders
    royal commission into banks and financial sector', *The Guardian*,
    30 November 2017.

12 Doorstop interview with Nick Champion, Adelaide, 30 November
    2017, Parliament of Australia transcript.

PART TWO - A BLAST OF SUNLIGHT

All extracts from the public hearings are from the transcripts on the royal commission website, https://financialservices.royalcommission.gov.au.

Chapter 16: Round 1: Consumer lending

1   Shayne Elliott, 'Why ANZ backs the royal commission', letter to ANZ staff, https://bluenotes.anz.com.

2   Kenneth Hayne, *The Interim Report of the Financial Services Royal Commission*, 28 September 2018, vol.1, p.42.

3   Reserve Bank of Australia, Financial Stability Review, April 2017.

4   Jonathan Mott, Rachel Bentvelzen and George Tharenou, 'UBS Evidence Lab – $500 billion in "liar loans"?', UBS, 11 September 2017; Jonathan Mott, Rachel Bentvelzen and George Tharenou, 'Aussie Banks – UBS Evidence Lab: liar loans #2 – Interest only', UBS, 4 October 2017.

5   ASIC media release 15-128MR, 'Sydney man pleads guilty to home loan fraud', 26 May 2015.

6   Stephen Sedgwick AO, Retail Banking Remuneration Review, 19 April 2017.

Chapter 17: Round 2: Financial advice

1   ASIC, *Report 499 Financial advice: Fees for no service*, 27 October 2016.

2   Phillip Coorey and Andrew Tillett, 'Morrison to hit banks even harder', *Financial Review*, 20 April 2018, p.1.

3   Malcolm Farr, 'Malcolm Turnbull admits his mistake as Labor demands an apology', *Daily Telegraph*, 23 April 2018.

4   https://twitter.com/barnaby_joyce/status/ 986566461706547201?lang=en.

5   Malcolm Farr, 'Malcolm Turnbull admits his mistake'.

Chapter 20: Round 5: Superannuation

1   Richard Gluyas, 'Banking royal commission: NAB CEO Andrew Thorburn says sorry for "letting you down"', *The Australian*, 9 August 2018.

2 ASIC, *Report 499 Financial advice: Fees for no service*, 27 October 2016.

3 Adele Ferguson, 'IOOF flunks both the pub test and the front page test', *The Age*, 11 August 2018, p.21.

4 Adele Ferguson, 'Banking royal commission: APRA a "hear no evil, see no evil" regulator', *Financial Review*, 19 August 2019, p.49.

5 Adele Ferguson, 'IOOF flunks both the pub test and the front page test'.

6 Glenda Korporaal, '$80 billion boost for industry super funds', *The Australian*, 29 May 2019, p.23.

7 Scott Pape, 'A super fund with ZERO fees?', Barefoot Investor website, 17 December 2018.

8 Lucy Battersby, 'Billions move from retail funds into industry funds', *The Age*, 14 April 2019, p.22.

9 Rod Myer, 'Industry fund inflows booming in the wake of royal commission', *The New Daily*, 16 November 2018.

Chapter 21: Round 6: Insurance

1 Adele Ferguson, Mario Christodoulou and Klaus Toft, 'Heartless attack', *The Age*, 5 March 2016, p.1.

2 As per section 12DB of the *ASIC Act*.

3 ASIC media release, 'CommInsure pays $300,000 following ASIC concerns over misleading life insurance advertising', 18 December 2018.

Chapter 22: The interim report

1 Australian Banking Association press conference, Anna Bligh responds to the release of the banking royal commission's interim report, 28 September 2018.

2 Michael Roddan and Ben Butler, 'Banks face regulation revolution', *The Australian*, 29 September 2018, p.27.

3 Richard Gluyas, 'In for the long haul: Byres' call to life industry standards of behaviour begins with regulator', *The Australian*, 12 October 2018, p.23.

Chapter 23: Round 7: CBA

1 Justin O'Brien, 'How Kenneth Hayne will change Australia', *Financial Review*, 5 October 2018, p.4.

Chapter 25: Round 7: ASIC and APRA

1 APRA, Prudential Inquiry into the Commonwealth Bank of Australia, April 2018

2 Pat McConnell, 'Out of their depth at the royal commission', RFI Group website.

Chapter 27: Round 7: ANZ

1 'Margin Call', 'Melanie's a chip off the old block', *The Australian*, 29 November, 2018, p.18.

Chapter 28: Too close for comfort

1 Michael Roddan, 'NAB meeting AUSTRAC obligations: Andrew Thorburn', *The Australian*, 15 December 2017.

2 Edmond Tadros, '"Appalling" audit quality could lead to next Enron: ASIC's Greg Medcraft', *Financial Review*, 31 October 2017, p.23.

3 'Big Four vent fury at watchdog's plan to split audit and consulting divisions', *The Telegraph*, 19 April 2019.

4 APRA, Prudential Standard CPS 220: Risk Management, Clause 45, July 2017, p.11.

Chapter 29: A waiting game

1 Elysse Morgan, 'Despite the banking royal commission, NAB pursues high-pressure pre-Christmas sales drive', ABC Online, 29 November 2018.

2 Bevin Shields, 'Scott Morrison warns against rash response to banking royal commission', *Sydney Morning Herald*, 31 January 2019.

Chapter 30: The final report

1 ASIC, *Financial Advice: Vertically Integrated Institutions and Conflicts of Interest*, January 2018.

2 NAB media release, 'NAB CEO and Chairman comment on royal commission final report', 5 February 2019.

3 Clancy Yeates and Elizabeth Knight, 'Bank leadership clearout needed to clean up culture', *Sydney Morning Herald*, 9 February 2019.

4 Phillip Coorey, 'Labor wants new bank levy to boost compensation scheme', *Financial Review*, 21 February 2019, p.1.

5 House of Representatives Standing Committee on Economics, Hansard transcript, 17 August 2018.

6 Misa Han, James Eyers and Edmund Tadros, 'ASIC: Deals unlikely in post-Hayne world', *Financial Review*, 17 May 2019, p.21.

7 Benjamin Quinlan, Yvette Kwan and Hugo Cheng, 'Value at risk: A look at banking's US$850 billion behavioural problem', Quinlan & Associates, September 2017, p.4.

Glossary of terms

ACCC: The Australian Competition and Consumer Commission is the consumer and competition watchdog. It promotes competition and fair trading.

APRA: The Australian Prudential Regulation Authority is the prudential regulator set up to supervise financial institutions, including banks, to ensure financial stability.

ASIC: The Australian Securities and Investments Commission is the corporate regulator set up to enforce and regulate the law to protect Australian consumers, investors and creditors.

ASX: The Australian Securities Exchange is the country's primary securities exchange.

AUSTRAC: The Australian Transaction Reports and Analysis Centre monitors financial transactions to identify and act against money-laundering by organised crime and terror groups.

Bancassurance: The manufacture and sale of insurance and other financial products such as super funds by banking institutions.

Bank credit: Money that banks lend to customers.

Basis points: The percentage change in the value of a financial instrument such as an interest rate. One basis point is equivalent to 0.01 per cent.

Big four banks: Australia's four largest banks: CBA, ANZ, NAB and Westpac.

Breach report: A report filed to the regulator by an institution advising the regulator of a breach of the law, including misconduct, by the institution or its staff.

Capability review: A company-wide review of an organisation's ability to meet future objectives, obligations and challenges.

Continuous disclosure (obligation): Any company listed on the ASX has an obligation to continuously disclose information which may have a material effect on its share price.

Current account deficit: The measurement of a country's trade overseas where goods and services imported exceeds the value of goods and services exported.

Enforceable undertaking: When misconduct occurs, an entity can enter an enforceable undertaking with the relevant regulator to make changes, as an alternative to civil or administrative action.

FoFA: Future of Financial Advice legislation was introduced by the Labor Government in June 2013 to ban the payment of upfront commissions and trailing commissions on all new financial products, excluding life insurance, to remove conflicts of interest.

Foreign currency loans: Loans, often in the form of mortgages, with interest and principal repayments denominated in a currency other than the currency of the country in which the borrower is a resident.

Forex (foreign exchange): The exchange of one currency for another.

Four pillars: A policy introduced by Treasurer Paul Keating in 1990 to stop the big four banks merging.

Frontrunning: The most immediate form of insider trading, frontrunning occurs when an investor steps in front of a large order to gain an advantage in the price.

Grandfathered commissions: Commissions and fees paid on products sold before June 2013.

Hedging: A strategy to reduce the risk of a negative price movement on financial markets.

Industry super fund: A not-for-profit super fund, often affiliated with the relevant industry's union.

Margin call: A request from the provider of a margin loan to the borrower to add funds to the original investment, normally triggered by the value of the investment falling below a certain amount (known as the loan to valuation ratio).

Margin loan: A loan used for the specific purpose of investing in approved shares or managed funds, where the shares or managed funds are used as security for the loan.

Mortgage funds: Funds that invest in mortgages that are secured by properties.

Regulator: One of the agencies responsible for enforcing financial services, corporations, competition and/or anti-money-laundering laws.

Retail super funds: For-profit superannuation funds which are largely managed by financial institutions, including banks and insurance companies.

Return on equity: A key measure used by investors to gauge how effectively management is using a company's assets to create profits.

Securities loan: A loan backed by a listed asset such as a share.

Significant breach: A breach of the law made by a company. By law, the company has to report a breach, or likely breach, to ASIC within ten business days of becoming aware of it.

SoFA The Scrutiny of Financial Advice inquiry set up by the Senate Economics References Committee in September 2014 to inquire and report on the financial advice reforms introduced under FoFA.

Statement of advice: A document given to a customer by a financial planner which sets out the financial products that have been recommended to a customer, and on what basis. It must also include the date the advice was given and any payments the adviser or licensee will receive.

Tailored business loan: A business loan that has an embedded interest rate hedge. When interest rates fell after the Global Financial Crisis, these products – often targeted at small businesses – started to unravel and blew out interest rates.

Vertical integration: The ownership or control of several components of the wealth management chain by a bank or financial institution. For example, the ownership of financial advice, asset management, life insurance and superannuation entities by one company.

Wealth management: Incorporates financial planning, financial advice and related investment products, such as life insurance and superannuation.

Acknowledgements

'Sometimes people don't want to hear the truth because they don't want their illusions destroyed.' Friedrich Nietzsche

In my coverage of the Australian financial services sector, many illusions were destroyed. The blind belief that the banks were ethical and trustworthy was the biggest illusion. When Malcolm Turnbull 'reluctantly' called a royal commission, there was nowhere to hide.

My role in telling this story was made possible by many incredible and brave people. Their sacrifices may have seemed almost futile in the face of the biggest corporations in Australia, but they fought on regardless. They are the whistleblowers, journalists, victims and politicians to whom we should all be hugely grateful.

A special thanks to Jeff Morris, Dr Ben Koh and the many anonymous whistleblowers who had something important in common: a sense of justice that would never be tempered – a quality that led them to reveal unconscionable conduct.

To the many bank victims who fought back and spoke out, I owe you my deepest gratitude: Merilyn Swan, Jan Braund, Veronica Coulston, Teghan Couper, James Kessel, Naomi Halpern and Bob Nissen, to name a few.

Thanks to the politicians who fought for a royal commission before the idea became popular, including Peter Whish-Wilson, Mark Bishop, Sam Dastyari and, especially, Wacka Williams.

Writing a book on a topic as big as this one, with a history spanning almost forty years, meant dealing with sources and events outside my own journalistic experience, and I acknowledge that I have stood on the shoulders of many journalists and mavericks, including Anne Lampe, Judith Hoare, Pamela Williams, John McLennan and Paul McLean.

I would like to thank the journalists I worked with on various bank exposés over the years, including Chris Vedelago, Ben Butler, Ruth Williams, Sarah Danckert, Mario Christodoulou and Klaus Toft.

Thanks also to those talented individuals who reported on the royal commission and who did such a great job unpicking the testimonies and prevarications of the witnesses and keeping the subject on the front pages of newspapers, TV and radio news bulletins, and websites for a year. James Thomson, your commentary was outstanding.

Writing and researching this book was a gigantic project. My heartfelt thanks to my dear friend Ruth Williams, whose meticulous eye, insights and encouragement helped shape this book.

I would also like to pay homage to Malcolm Hughes for his tireless work and belief in the project.

Many thanks to Brett Le Mesurier for his financial expertise – and humour – and to John Berrill for his patience and passion in explaining complex legal issues and life insurance policies.

A special thanks to the staff at the *The Age* and the *Sydney Morning Herald*, especially the business editor, Mat Dunckley, and the group executive editor of Australian metro publishing, James Chessell, for their encouragement and support and their preparedness to back the stories and give me time off to write the book. I couldn't have done this without them. Thanks also to the *Four Corners* team, including Marian Wilkinson, Sue Spencer, Sally Neighbour and Morag Ramsay.

Thanks to Michael Fraser, Maddison Johnstone and Angela Cipri for their contributions and also to my literary agent, Fiona Inglis.

I would also like to thank the HarperCollins team, notably Mary Rennie and Scott Forbes, whose editing, hard work and professionalism have been second to none.

Finally, I would like to thank my wonderful family for encouraging me to write the book and spurring me to keep going – no matter what: my beautiful daughter, Emma, whose star will always shine bright; my incredible husband, Christian Townsend, who is my rock; and my dad, Tom Ferguson, for being my biggest fan.

Banking Bad is living proof of that old adage that evil can only prosper when good people fail to act.